BUILD WITH IMPACT

Fulphil Publishing

979-8-9877411-2-2 (hardcover)
979-8-9877411-0-8 (paperback)
979-8-9877411-1-5 (ebook)
979-8-9877411-3-9 (audiobook)

Library of Congress Catalog Card Number: 0000-0000

Tiffany Yau (Author and Narrator)
Aditya Desai (Author)
Brooke McCormick (Author)
Fulphil Students (Author)
Geethika Koneru (Illustrator)
Yubin Huh (Illustrator)
Kathrina Miranda (Foreword)

Published March 2023

DEDICATION

This book is dedicated to Aja'nae, Freya, Judah, Shia, Indreal, and Tiara, among the first and brightest of our Fulphil students. Thank you for inspiring me and our team in continuing to find purpose in this work.

This book is also dedicated to Kathrina Miranda, Benjamin Pietrzyk, Vanita Lee-Tatum, Rick Charles, and Laura Jagroop, among the most impactful and transformative educators I have met and have had the chance to work with and learn so much from. The good work you do every day is immeasurable. Thank you for educating the minds and hearts of our students—their futures are infinite and bright in your hands, and so is the future of the world.

Empathy is our awareness
of others' emotions
and our attempt to understand how they feel.

Compassion is our emotional response to empathy
and is our desire to help.

CONTENTS

Foreword

By Kathrina Miranda

Compassion is one of the most underrated things we can learn and teach. Migrating from the Philippines and growing up in Oakland, California, I distinctly remember promising myself I would always pay it forward.

While figuring out ways to make a living, I never forgot about the promise I made to myself. I actively find ways to make a difference in my work and give back where I am able.

I founded a boutique marketing agency in 2012: MiMA LLC, a consultancy that has advised hundreds of entrepreneurs and international startups from the San Francisco Bay Area to Poland. I launched MiMA because I wanted to be a supermom and a CEO. It was not done beautifully, but it was done. I was scrappy and it was the best feeling in the world--and still is.

In 2016, a client introduced me to Eden Area Regional Occupational Program (ROP). ROP courses are designed for students to provide quality career technical education and hands-on experience. I found myself teaching entrepreneurship for the next three years at a public high school in Hayward, California.

I remember feeling like I was assigned to mission impossible. Many of the students in my class didn't want to be there. Not having any prior experience as an educator, I dove in head-first, unaware of what I was really getting myself into. Nevertheless, I had signed up for it and would put my best foot forward.

To my surprise, it wasn't even about teaching standard concepts in my classes, but about building relationships and finding ways to empower them.

Education for me is a complex yet beautiful thing our world has to offer. I am thoroughly convinced that teachers have the most important job in the world, but unfortunately, they remain unsung heroes.

Having first-hand experience of being an entrepreneur and teaching students based on what I've learned has been one of the most meaningful experiences—not just because I was able to impart any advice but because I was able to show them the value of what they were learning in the classroom and how they could apply it to the real world.

So much of what we learn in school as students can be difficult and even boring. I really wanted the time I spent with my students to matter. As educators, we have the unique opportunity to be able to help students make sense of a complicated world through what we choose to teach them and how we choose to teach. Teachers are the one of the few people who can make an impact on students external to their usual circle of family and friends, exposing them to concepts they might otherwise never have the chance to learn—philosophies, ways of viewing the world, creativity, and problem-solving.

The youth who walk through our classroom doors have the potential to become the leaders of organizations and their communities. Teachers get the opportunity to be with them at the most developmental stages of their lives—what they experience at a young age is what they often carry with them throughout their lives, whether they know it or not. Throughout my time teaching and interacting with students, I realized that anyone who is able to impact children in a society has the power to change the trajectory of their lives, and even the trajectory of the world.

I have been lucky to have great teachers and role models in my own life, and I wanted to be just as intentional with how I taught in the classroom. I challenged my students with questions like, "How do you make your city a better place to live for your immigrant parents? How do you really help your community thrive, not just survive?"

In my experience starting MiMA, I learned that there is a certain beauty in following your passion and solving the problems that matter to you the most. This is the power of entrepreneurship, or at least having an entrepreneurial experience. I wanted my students to understand that what they learned in the classroom was relevant and applicable to their lives. We live in a society where many of us are required to go to school throughout our childhoods and early adulthoods. But why? Why do we go to school?

It is my belief that one's education is meant to help them understand how to create value and leave it better than they found it.

One's impact and value-creation cannot be simply measured by a dollar amount—it goes beyond that and is determined by the value you create. I've always hoped that my students would bring value to themselves by impacting their communities. I feel fortunate that I have been able to witness firsthand how they've done so:

Joseph landed in the top three of a national entrepreneurship pitch competition in New York City. He beat out 23,000 students with his business idea. Joseph was in the foster system and created an app dedicated to connecting foster youth to a peer network and the tools they need to become successful.

For me, building relationships with my students has been just as important, if not more, than the result itself. This is especially true of my relationship with Tiffany Yau and her endeavors in social impact and entrepreneurship.

I met Tiffany in 2017, not too long after I first began teaching. We met in London at the Hult Prize Foundation summit retreat for their campus directors. Maybe it was because I was teaching entrepreneurship at the time, but I was really coming to terms with just how game-changing it could be, especially when applied to real-world social problems. With entrepreneurship hovering in my mind, I felt an immediate spark when Tiffany and I began to talk.

Tiffany is a bright, curious, optimistic, compassionate, and humble go-getter—perhaps everything you could ever hope a female leader to be. But most of all, Tiffany and I spoke the same language: we were both entrepreneurial-minded, though not only for the sake of making a living but also for the sake of having a positive impact on the world. We were paired together for a group ideation activity, and we came up with the idea of teaching social entrepreneurship to high school students. She understood the importance and the world of impact and education, and shared just as much excitement and enthusiasm for the sector as I had.

After we presented that idea at that retreat in London, we parted ways—I returned to the Bay Area to continue to teach my students and run MiMA. Tiffany headed back to Philadelphia to finish the rest of her semester at Penn. Six months later she reached out to me, mentioning that she had the itch to start something along the lines of what we had worked on in London. Since that call, I've had the chance to work with Tiffany and watch her grow the idea from a napkin sketch to a nationally scaled organization.

She proposed that we find some way to democratize the concepts of social entrepreneurship to youth. Specifically, this meant not just to teach them how to be entrepreneurs but to inspire them to make an impact in the world. This was everything I poured my heart and soul into during my time as a teacher, so she didn't need to convince me—I was already in. Since then, we've been in the weeds together, discovering parts of ourselves, weathering the highs and lows, knowing we would always be there for each other.

It has been one of my greatest joys to be part of Tiffany's journey—mentoring her, witnessing Fulphil evolve over several iterations, watching her grow, and seeing her inspire everyone else around her.

Working with Tiffany and the Fulphil team has made me reflect a lot about my time in the classroom as an educator. I thought I was going in to teach entrepreneurship, but it wasn't just that. When you can relate to students and make them feel heard, you make a meaningful impact on them and have the power to help. The great intention, thoughtfulness, and care that Tiffany and her team has used to build out their curriculum really brought this to life in the various classrooms they have worked with. In their courses, the Fulphil team includes examples of popular culture icons, films, relevant phenomena like the Black Lives Matter movement and Roe v. Wade. This team has brought the classroom learning experience to life while at the same time engaging students to be creative and problem-solvers.

Particularly with the school districts I've been engaged with, the entire staff of business and marketing teachers have benefited from the classroom presentations and curriculum Tiffany and the Fulphil team have designed. This has helped them teach their students to become compassionate problem-solvers and leaders to take on the new millennium. From their success, the Fulphil team has transformed their scaled curriculum into books with the vision of equipping all to have the tools they need to be inspired to make a positive impact on the world.

My hope for this book is that it will inspire people both inside and outside the classroom—no matter what stage of life they are in—to make a positive difference in the world and that it will equip them with the tools to do so. In these pages, I hope you find as much fulfillment and hope as I have working with Tiffany and her team.

Preface

By Tiffany Yau

Entrepreneurship is like jumping off a cliff and learning how to build a plane on the way down. Before even making the jump, you get an idea, and you go to your friends and family to talk about it. "Mom, I'm going to go to the highest cliff around, jump off, and build a plane that will soar unlike any other. I'll be the first to ever do it and succeed, making history." Chances are, you'll think your idea is brilliant. Chances are that the people around you will tell you that your idea is silly or not worth pursuing. You take their comments to heart and think about what they said, maybe even questioning your idea too for a bit. You realize there's some truth to what they said *but you do it anyway.*

You do the best you can to learn how to build a plane (probably, most realistically, from YouTube) and go to your local supply store to get all the parts you need. You buy everything and load your bag full of parts to assemble once you get to the cliff. You get to the cliff and then you build… and you jump—but as you jump, you realize you probably missed a lot of steps. Now? You're falling at breakneck speed and doing your best to be hacky and make all the tweaks needed as you plummet, knowing all too well that you could end up on the ground.

If you're an entrepreneur or are trying to become one, I bet you know exactly what this feels like. This very accurately describes how we all feel every day. We, entrepreneurs, feel this from the moment we wake up to the moment we fall asleep. *But we do it anyway.*

If you're not into scrappiness, this is probably not the thing for you. Entrepreneurship is all about the thrill of scrappiness. Every entrepreneur jumps off that cliff with uncertainty and at least a bit of ignorance. Often, they'll have absolutely no idea what they're doing when they jump—they simply don't know what they don't know. But they do it anyway for the thrill of it and hope for the best. Entrepreneurship comes with a lot of uncertainty and risk, but when it comes to *social entrepreneurship* there's even more. With social entrepreneurship, also comes lots of growth from learning by doing, but there is an even more complex layer added on—the urgency to solve a pressing social issue through the *impact* of your own innovation. This is exactly what sparked my interest and drew me into the world of social entrepreneurship.

When I first learned about the concept of social entrepreneurship, I was fascinated by its unique nature to drive an empowering sense of *urgency* and *contingency* behind one's actions to create a tangible impact. As Bill Drayton, founder of Ashoka says, "social entrepreneurs are not content just to give a fish or teach how to fish. They will not rest until they have revolutionized the fishing industry."

For social entrepreneurs, there is always more impact that can be made. There is a refreshing beauty in this relentlessness. In a way, we've normalized seeing and accepting the world as it is, as opposed to seeing it through the lens of how it *could* be.

And this is by no fault of our own. People have so much potential. We are all natural-born problem-solvers, but when we allow the size of the world and the massive systemic problems that plague it overwhelm us, it can feel as though things are happening *to* us, completely outside our control. It is easy and valid to feel helpless, perhaps even more so the deeper our knowledge about these complex systemic issues grows. Whether we're learning more about these big problems through the news, quick Google searches, or our break-time TikTok feeds, it's far too easy to get bogged down. When we lose hope and optimism, our motivation to problem-solve diminishes, and eventually, so does our desire to make some kind of difference.

It's unfortunate.

I've always believed that everyone has the potential to make a difference in the world—and not just any difference—a *real*, meaningful positive difference. The problem is, many of us often don't know how or where to start, which effectively causes us to feel overwhelmed and incapable of making any impact at all. The idea of making an impact can then feel *unrealistic*.

This dilemma, paired with my fascination of social entrepreneurship, made me realize the vast potential behind teaching social entrepreneurship to people. There is a certain degree of idealism that one must embody if they choose to pursue social entrepreneurship.

Pursuing social entrepreneurship is a way for giving *permission* to those who undertake it to *be stubbornly and unapologetically idealistic.*

This realization is what inspired me to create Fulphil. This organization has grown from a dorm room hustle I started in 2018 during my time studying at the University of Pennsylvania into an education nonprofit that creates fun and engaging educational content to inspire society's youth to make an impact and, in the process, become career-ready and equipped to succeed in this 21st century of work as compassionate and impactful problem-solvers and changemakers of tomorrow.

Build With Impact is based on the social entrepreneurship curriculum our Fulphil team has created for schools across the country. In addition to this, all the other books in our series are also based on our courses. All our courses and books have come together as a five-year-long feat in effort to provide access to equitable and inclusive educational content teaching students across the country to build compassion, instilling the idea that everyone has the potential to make a positive difference in the world.

I hope this book inspires you to envision and embody the impact that you are capable of making and to nurture compassion, just like it has for or students. This is *everything*—once an individual sees the impact she is capable of making, it is hard and perhaps even impossible to unsee it. Based on our team's experience with our students and teachers, we believe with all our hearts that this is the key to changing the trajectories of the future of our youth, our communities, and the world. And we can't wait for you, our readers, to be part of this journey!

When I first began working on the idea of Fulphil, I surveyed over 680 high school students who participated in a Fulphil workshop. The results from that survey revealed that many students care about making a positive social impact and also want to begin their own businesses. But it also revealed that these students did not know how or have the confidence to do either of those things.

As I sat with those findings, I found that the difference in these numbers proved to be even more pronounced in lower socioeconomic status communities—62% of students lack access or cannot afford an entrepreneurship education at their schools. I saw this as an opportunity to create equitable access to an *impactful* entrepreneurship education course.

Since 2019, the content from this book has been taught to a few thousand students nationally in business, marketing, and entrepreneurship classes—while also weathering the challenges that the COVID-19 pandemic presented to education systems across the world.

After having successfully implemented our curriculum nationally in various school districts from Philadelphia to the Bay Area, we're proud of our students' outcomes: 70% report feeling more invested in their local communities, 84% report feeling more motivated to use their future careers to make a positive social impact, 80% report increased confidence in their ability to overcome obstacles, 80% report increased belief in their ability to make a tangible impact on the world, 86% report increased confidence in their ability to start an impactful business, and 70% report having learned new skills that will help them succeed in their future careers.

Although the content from *Build With Impact* was initially created for youth across the country, I believe that anyone who is interested in building a socially impactful business can benefit from the material and also apply key lessons to their own personal life pursuits. *Build With Impact* will teach you how to build a social enterprise, but more importantly, it will teach you how to build a social entrepreneurial mindset. I believe that developing a mindset driven by our potential and ability to problem-solve is the key to succeeding in our future careers and cultivating influence wherever life takes us. My sincere hope is that this book makes learning social entrepreneurship a fun, relevant, inspiring, and empowering experience for every reader so they can do *well* and do *good*.

This book is designed as an actionable guide, so I encourage you to skip around to the sections you believe will be most helpful to you as you build out the business model for your social enterprise. *Build With Impact* is divided into five parts. Here is an overview of what you can expect from each part and the chapters they contain:

Part 1, "Redefining Impact, Entrepreneurship, & Yourself," covers the first three chapters which explore the building blocks that will set you up for success as you embark on your social entrepreneurial journey. Chapter 1 redefines the meaning of social impact and entrepreneurship using Fulphil's sociopsychological lens to look at these concepts in a new light that makes them more feasible and relevant to the world. Chapter 2 continues the conversation of social impact and the different forms it takes in the business world. You'll learn about how this concept has evolved over time to become what social entrepreneurship is today in addition to the foundations and promises of social entrepreneurship and what distinguishes it from other business models in addition to learning from an array of social enterprise case studies in both the nonprofit and for-profit sectors. Chapter 3 introduces the concepts of the entrepreneurial mindset and social entrepreneurial mindset. You will be guided to reflect on the accomplishments that excited or challenged you and leverage those through interactive learning activities to define your core values, motivations, and *social entrepreneurial mindset*.

Part 2, "Designing Your Impact," takes you step-by-step through the process of intentionally creating your social enterprise through the iterative design thinking methodology. Chapter 4 introduces the innovative framework of design thinking and why it's important as you build out your social enterprise. Chapter 5 focuses on problem-finding—to be a successful problem-solver, you need to know how to be an effective *problem-finder*. Here, you'll learn how to narrow down on the social problems you are hoping to solve to ensure your impact can be as actionable as possible. Chapter 6 covers problem-solving but more specifically ideation. In this chapter, you'll explore the interactive process of ideation to help you think of some exciting business ideas for a problem you hope to solve. Chapter 7 dives into prototyping. Here, you'll learn everything you need to understand the process of prototyping so that you can create your own minimum viable product. Chapter 8 then branches into the concept of product-market fit. Without the superpower that allows you to read other people's minds, can you still develop a product or solution that others want? Absolutely! Well, sort of. First, you need to understand your own biases and assumptions. In this chapter, you'll define your assumptions, conduct user interviews, and validate your prototypes and assumptions by testing them out like a scientist!

Part 3, "Getting Down to Business," outlines what you will need in order to assemble a business plan. Chapter 9 guides you step-by-step through the process of defining and quantifying your market and understanding how much potential your business has. This metric is vital for helping you decide how much time you want to pour into your social enterprise and determine how attractive it will be to investors and funders. Chapter 10 explores the concept of competition. Try to think about an industry where competition does not exist. It is hard to come up with anything because almost every company has competitors. In this chapter, we will explore different types of competition by analyzing Blockbuster vs. Netflix, Taylor Swift's music, and more. Chapter 11 introduces the topic of marketing. In this chapter, you'll learn how to effectively leverage all the information you've gathered from your users and customers in Part 2 and learn how to sell your product or solutions! The chapter opens by introducing some marketing metrics and commonly used marketing strategies, setting the groundwork for Chapter 13. Chapter 12 teaches you about pricing strategies. If you have ever been curious about how businesses set their prices, you will be able to relate to this chapter! Here, you'll learn the three pricing strategies most commonly used today: cost-based pricing, market-based pricing, and value-based pricing. Try out different pricing strategies to find what works best for you and your company by reflecting on the customer information you've collected from your user interviews. You will also learn how to create three different types of financial statements.

Part 4, "Getting It Out There," is where we'll bring it all together. This section covers chapters on marketing strategies and branding and will unveil everything you need to be able to breathe life into your idea. Chapter 13 takes a deep dive into more marketing strategies. We will have an in-depth discussion on social media marketing with examples from the top social media platforms, including TikTok, Instagram, and Twitter. Here, you'll learn about Spotify's marketing strategies and how they've managed to be a sticky brand over the years. Chapter 14 focuses on building your brand. Branding is all about what people say about your company when you are not around. In this chapter, we will introduce the four components of branding. From aesthetics to content, we compiled a comprehensive overview of the power of effective branding, including case studies covering companies like Nike, Starbucks, Airbnb, and Uber.

Finally, Part 5, "Manifesting Your Impact" focuses on measuring and showcasing your progress and impact, as well as building your essential business documents and presentations. This section is the bookend that brings together everything you'll learn throughout this book. Chapter 15 teaches you how to measure your success—this includes operational success, financial success, and impact success. Here, we will cover key performance indicators (KPIs) and objectives and key results (OKRs), which are used to determine how well your business is doing in terms of strategic and operational goals. In this chapter, we will talk about different types of KPIs and effective goal-setting tactics to help your business stay on track using frameworks like logic models and the balanced scorecard developed by Harvard Business School to keep you on track! Chapter 16 helps you build your essential business documents, which include executive summaries, pitch decks, and business canvas models. This chapter also focuses on helping you craft your pitch and public speaking skills and storytelling.

Beyond these chapters, we have additional resources—including our cheat code recap, glossary, cited sources, and downloadable worksheet activities—that can help supplement your learning experience. If you are interested in teaching the content from this book to a class or group, we also have turnkey slideshows available for download on our website that our team and teachers across the country have vetted.

From the bottom of my heart, thank you to my co-authors Aditya Desai and Brooke McCormick and to all of our students, teachers, board of directors, supporters, team, and contributors, including Emma O'Neil, Riley Gonta, Sam Stern, Grace Coughlan, Erin Flannery, Ashley Han, Elizabeth Guan, Emma Gould, Tyler Dickens, Geethika Koneru, Yunling Huang, Freya Busser, Jenny Tan, Abhi Suresh, April Zhou, and Osase Edogun. Thank you for all your effort and unconditional support to inspire and produce the first iterations of our curriculum, which provided the foundation of this book.

Part I:
Redefining Impact, Entrepreneurship, & Yourself

Chapter 1

Making Sense of Impact & Entrepreneurship

Written by: Tiffany Yau, Aditya Desai, and Riley Gonta

"Little strokes fell great oaks." —Benjamin Franklin, ***Poor Richard's Almanack***

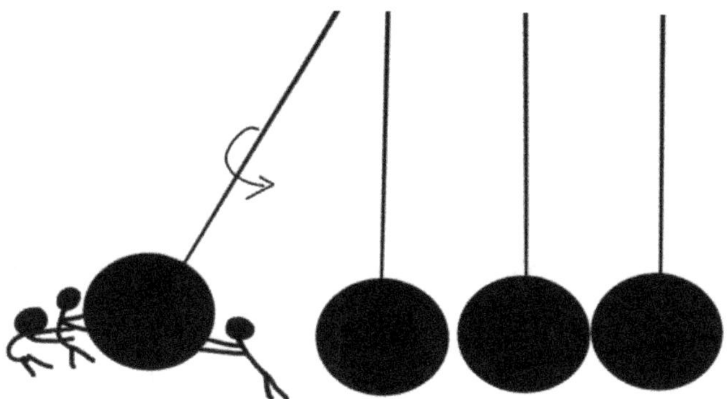

I. Redefining Impact

Let's first take a moment to answer a few questions:

- What is the *biggest*, craziest, wildest thing you could do to make a difference and impact on the world? It doesn't matter if you think this thing is out of reach—for now, don't think about how you'll get there. Be bold and honest!

- Got it? Now, what is the *smallest* thing you could do to make an impact? Something so small that it requires a minimal amount of effort but still makes a difference?

These are the first two questions we pose to Fulphil students when they begin our curriculum. We've received answers as big as curing cancer, ending world hunger, or starting a nonprofit. Students have also responded with answers as small as smiling at a stranger, helping a friend or family member, or joining a volunteer club at school.

Your answer to the first question may feel quite grand, distant, and maybe even impossible, whereas your answer to the second question should feel stress-free and easy to execute.

But *that's* the problem!

As a society, we're led to believe (by no fault of our own) that impact always needs to be *big*. When we think of social impact initiatives, the first thing that might pop up is the variety of well-funded initiatives in developing countries that empower vulnerable populations. *Big* problems likely require *big* solutions! In Tiffany Yau's TEDx talk in 2020, she explained that media conditions us at a young age to believe that for us to have any impact, we must be making a direct and tangible difference on big problems.[1] It can even be paralyzing to think about the extent we must go to bring our impact to life. The issue with impact is the stark contrast between what we *think* we need to do and what we can actually do to make a difference.

---

1 Yau, "Dream Big, Think Smaller," 2020.

After all, it's the stories of global initiatives that build wells to increase access to clean drinkable water or of local communities that clean up beaches to decrease plastic pollution that make the most eye-catching and heartwarming stories. In the same vein, the people we usually hear most about and associate with social impact are people like Bill Gates, who is eradicating poverty and life-threatening diseases and happens to also be able to read over 50 books annually, or Greta Thunberg, who was nominated for the Nobel Peace Prize at seventeen-years-old for inspiring seven million people to strike against climate change.[2] We think of these high-profile people—Gandhi, Mother Teresa, Ben Franklin, Elon Musk—and consider them *superhumans*. They aren't your average person. And we believe we need to be like them to be able to make a difference—we might as well have superheroes who fly through the skies sucking the excess of carbon out of the air, dropping food from out of the sky to food deserts, and creating airborne cures to lethal diseases.

The thing is, impact doesn't have to be big! **Social impact** is the net effect of actions on a community and the well-being of individuals, families, and society. Read that again: social impact is the *net effect* – it is not a singular action but rather our collective efforts. Because of this, impact can come in all sorts of shapes and sizes. And in fact, the smallest things can make the biggest impact. For example, if every American recycled just one plastic water bottle in a single day, 54

---

2 StackCommerce, "Whether You Love Him or Hate Him," 2021; Buli and Fouche, "Nobel Peace Prize: Is This Greta Thunberg's Year?" 2021.

million T-shirts or 6.4 million fleece jackets could be produced.[3] Isn't that incredible?!

You might be thinking, "But I can't control the actions of every American." Well, technically, you can—beginning with yourself!

If you were to spend just one minute less showering every day, you would save five gallons of water every day. If you multiply that by 365 days, you would conserve approximately 1,825 gallons of water annually—and that's just from your shower alone! Now *that's* what we call impact. Not only can impact be small but it can also happen right in your own community, beginning with you and the decisions you make.

Whether it's the seemingly small daily decisions you make or the company you decide to build, what matters is being able to impact someone at some level. Even if your action or idea seems insignificant, there are people—whether it's one or many—who could benefit from what you have to offer.

Let's look at some real-life examples to give you an idea of what's possible. Below are some examples of what former Fulphil students have created due to what they learned from our curriculum about solving problems they care most about:

- **The Health & Rights of Animals:** This is for the dog lovers out there! Freya created a junk-free dog treat company called Anubis in response to her experience trying to feed her dog

---

3 May, "What Would Happen If Everyone Recycled?" 2017.

who was diagnosed with cancer and could only eat limited ingredients.

- **The Representation of Gender-Nonconforming Individuals:** Shia created a gender-nonconforming and plus-size clothing line because Shia kept saying to himself "that looks so cute, just not on me" over and over again when they would go shopping.
- **Inclusive Beauty:** Tiara created Twisted Spirit, a hair product company that caters to women of color and those with curly hair.
- **Environmental Justice:** A group of three young ladies in our class created biodegradable cafeteria trays that are embedded with seeds. When the trays are composted, trees are planted. This created a more sustainable solution than the trays made of Styrofoam they saw being thrown away in their cafeterias.

First-hand experiences with the problems in our communities equip us with the depth of knowledge and familiarity to solve them. But even more importantly, our experiences *drive* us. We care because we are affected by the problems in our communities, and when we share experiences, we act out of compassion. We embody meaning in our experiences.

The people closest to the problems are closest to the solutions.

We care more about tackling issues close to home, and consequently, we are more emotionally invested in the solutions addressing those problems. On the flip side, we *don't* work hard for things we don't care about. It makes the most sense to address the problems we've been affected by or the hardships we've endured so that others don't have to experience the same problems or so that they have the resources necessary to better overcome them. This is what impact is all about! This is what makes it so exciting. And this is what makes *you* the right person to make an impact and solve the problems closest to your heart.

Oftentimes, however, we get sucked into the idea of becoming the next Steve Jobs, Bill Gates, Oprah Winfrey, or Michelle Obama. We get stuck thinking we are too small to make a difference or too unimportant to ask big questions. We get stuck in a state of "analysis paralysis," overanalyzing the issues we strive to solve to the point of not being able to move forward.

Impact comes in all shapes and sizes. The one thing Bill Gates *doesn't* have is your life story. He's *not* you. He doesn't have the unique compassion, empathy, or level of care you do toward the problems closest to you. It's about discovering your "*why*" (what motivates you to make a difference) and leveraging that.

In this book, we teach you what we know best: **entrepreneurship**!

II. Why is entrepreneurship important?

We'll admit it, entrepreneurship is a *big* word! Seriously! It's sixteen letters long and the average English word only has, on average, five letters. Just like spelling out "entrepreneurship" for the first time, the field itself can be a little tricky—but that is why we've written this book.

We define **entrepreneurship** as the act of creating one or more business entities with the hope of creating value *and* making a profit while taking on financial risk.

Entrepreneurship plays a key role in society. Entrepreneurship creates businesses. Businesses create jobs, which stabilize and grow economies and provide a route for collaboration toward global innovation. All of this is a result of entrepreneurship! Entrepreneurship *really does* have the potential to create social and economic value.

Job Creation

Because of entrepreneurship, people can create businesses and organizations that exist to provide jobs and career opportunities for individuals in a local community. This, in turn, empowers individuals to care for their families, pay their bills, and more. According to the Small Business Administration, small and new businesses added 1.9 million net new jobs in 2018 alone.[4] There are 30.2 million small businesses in the United States, which employ 47.5% of the state's private workforce! Those are some major numbers and percentages!

Economic Success

Entrepreneurship supports the growth of the local economy. When everyone in a community has a job, the community earns more money as a whole and the people in it are able to both support themselves and give back to the local economy. When you support local businesses and mom-and-pop shops in your community, many

---

4 U.S. Small Business Administration, "Small Businesses Drive Job Growth in United States," 2019.

benefit: the business owners, those who work for the business, and the community. According to Amy Hartzler, director of communications for the Business Alliance for Local Living Economies, as cited in a *Forbes* article and various research studies, for every $100 spent at a small business, $68 stays circulating in the local economy compared to the $48 that remains local if you were to spend $100 at a national chain.[5] Supporting local businesses means money stays in the community and raises the overall level of economic activity, leaving more margin to pay higher salaries and building the local tax base.

Globalization and innovation

When local economies grow, the businesses involved often scale beyond their regions. This process builds momentum and gives rise to globalization. **Globalization** is the process by which businesses or other organizations develop international influence or start operating on an international scale.[6] Globalization leads to the ever-changing era we live in today, making us more interconnected as individuals, as nations, and as a world. This interconnectivity promotes a global diffusion of knowledge and cross-pollination (think bees!) of technology, distributing it and making it available worldwide. Countries that receive new technologies gain the opportunity to advance their own research and development. With new innovations often comes greater opportunities, with new types of jobs that never existed before. Think about it: jobs in cybersecurity or social media would never have existed if the internet or smartphone weren't

---

5 Wirthman, "CenturyLink BrandVoice: 5 Benefits of Shopping Locally on Small Business Saturday," 2017.

6 Pologeorgis, "How Globalization Affects Developed Countries," 2019.

invented. The momentum behind scaling local economies is the first of many steps to forging into their national economy, and eventually, the global economy.

Because of this economic and global progress, there are now many available jobs in the field of *impact*. Companies are hiring more roles to ensure they are engaging in conscious capitalism—roles like director of corporate social responsibility, head of people, chief

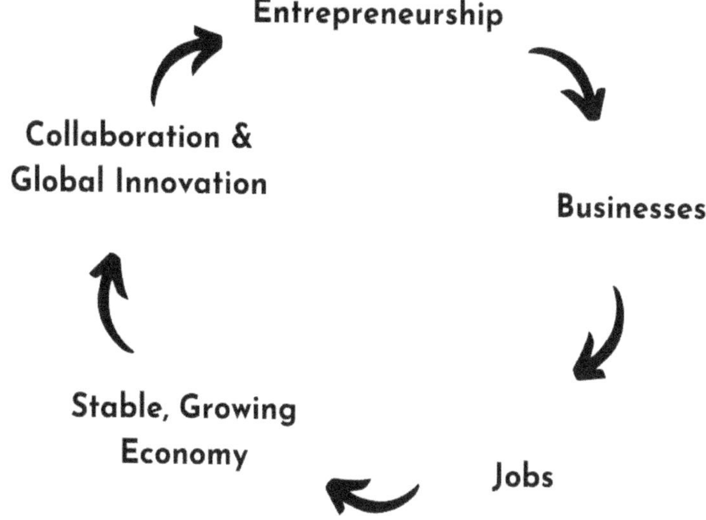

impact officer, and more. Roles like this never existed until recently, and as companies continue to become more intentional about their mark on the world, opportunities abound!

Creation of invaluable problem-solvers

Entrepreneurship does a lot for society, but it also makes an impact on us as *individuals* when we choose to pursue it. Specifically, undertaking entrepreneurship empowers us to embrace critical thinking, creativity, and problem-solving in order to create value in the world through our businesses.

Entrepreneurs must think out-of-the-box, analyzing the world from a variety of different perspectives and questioning the **status quo**—the current situation or the way things are—to envision what the world *could* be. Entrepreneurship thrives when critical thinking is involved because it is essential that we can imagine and see the world not as it *is* but how it *could be.*

As a result, entrepreneurship is all about problem-solving, and problem-solving is about finding innovative and creative ways to do and make something *better.* The best entrepreneurs are the most proactive problem-solvers because they can not only identify problems on the spot but also come up with appropriate solutions that may or may not be conventional.

Entrepreneurship thrives on creativity, opportunity identification, and critical thinking to come up with unique ideas and disrupt the current way of thinking, thereby advancing societal, business, and technological problems. Without critical thinkers, our world would be without the innovation that makes it what it is today.

Finding the balance between value creation and profit

There is always a risk with entrepreneurship. Entrepreneurship involves finding the balance between risk and reward. In this case, the reward is profit and value creation.

Value creation is the process of turning hard work and resources into something that meets the *needs* of others. Really, value creation is exactly what it sounds like—creating *value* for others.[7] To be successful, businesses must be maniacal about creating value for their stakeholders.

A **stakeholder** is any individual or entity that has an interest or concern in something.[8] Think of a stakeholder as anyone who has a *stake* in what you are doing. Stakeholders for entrepreneurs can be anyone from the people who invest money into their businesses to the customers that entrepreneurs are serving.

The stakeholders who put the most pressure on entrepreneurs are the ones who are keeping them and their businesses afloat. This is typically board members, investors, or donors. They are the ones betting on the entrepreneurs with their own money. When we put this into perspective, it puts a lot more at *stake*. For these individuals, it is important that they have a good **return on investment (ROI)**. ROI is the metric investors use to determine how effective their investments are. Traditionally, effectiveness is measured in the form of money (or profit). An investor might ask, "How much is this entrepreneur able to grow the money I gave them? Can they double it? Triple it? 4x it? 10x it?" This is why profit is important to consider.

Obviously, investors don't want to see their money go to waste, especially if they are investing several thousands to millions into a business—it already feels horrible when we see a few dollars go to waste when we play at the arcade and lose or when our lottery

---

7 Dieffenbacher, "Value Creation Definition, Model, Principles, Importance & Steps," 2022.

8 Fernando, "What Are Stakeholders: Definition, Types, and Examples," 2023.

tickets don't have the winning numbers. Profit is important, but balancing profit and value creation is where things can get tricky for entrepreneurs.

Entrepreneurs have a tall order: somehow, they must figure out a way to maximize both profit and value creation without compromising either one. There are a lot of heated discussions around some businesses' inability to balance the two: when value creation is prioritized over profit, a company may face the challenge of not having enough money to keep the business afloat, whereas when profit is prioritized over value creation, companies run the risk of making unethical decisions for the benefit of the bottom line. "Unethical" can mean a lot of things in the world of entrepreneurship, such as leveraging child labor or using unsustainable materials, which ultimately pollute either our society or the environment, respectively. On top of it all, seeking to act in an ethical manner invites even more stakeholders into the process. How you operate your business has the potential to influence individuals' wellbeing, contribute to socioeconomic mobility, and environmentally impact the planet—this can be either positive or negative. The work you engage in as an entrepreneur goes beyond your business' contribution to capital markets and consumers. Even if these stakeholders are not financially tied to your work, you have a moral responsibility to the people who pour their time and effort into your business, and also those who might be impacted by your work—both intentionally and unintentionally. It can certainly get tricky but that's where the idea of *social entrepreneurship* comes in.

III. Cheat Code Recap

1. Impact can look different, depending on the context.
2. The people closest to the problems are closest to the solutions.
3. Entrepreneurship can create social and economic value.
4. There is a fine balance between maximizing profit and value creation in entrepreneurship.

Chapter 2
Defining Social Entrepreneurship

Written by: Tiffany Yau, Aditya Desai, and Tyler Dickens

"Build your business around being the most helpful to the world and don't ever forget why you started giving back." —Todd Grinnell, Co-founder of This Bar Saves Lives

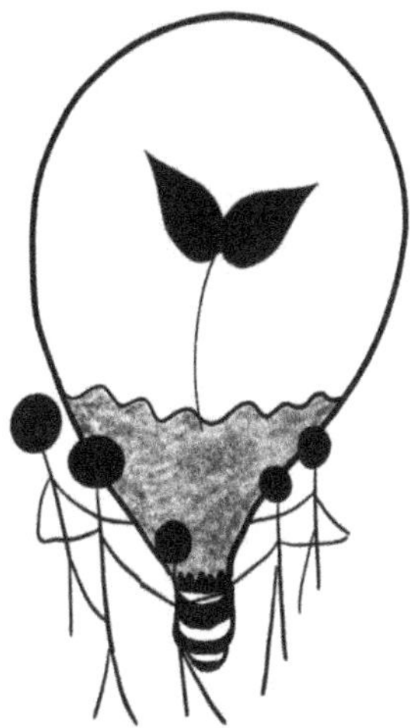

I. What is social entrepreneurship?

Now, imagine if businesses were used as a force for good. How would our world change? That's the basic idea undergirding **social entrepreneurship**—not only do we want businesses to be profitable but also difference-making! Social entrepreneurship has always been broadly defined because social enterprises take many different forms.

At Fulphil, we define a **social enterprise** as a self-sustaining for-profit or nonprofit business entity that intends to have a positive impact on humanity or the planet. To put it another way, a social enterprise is a business that has a positive impact and also makes money to employ conscious capitalism. The focus isn't just *profit* but also *purpose*.

When we think of traditional entrepreneurship, profit is important, but more specifically, it's the *net profit* that really matters. The **net profit** is how much money a business gets to keep after it deducts all costs and expenses from what it earned. Oftentimes, net profit is referred to as the **bottom line**. However, as social entrepreneurship has gained more popularity, so have the priorities and complexities of fulfilling a "double bottom line" and a "triple bottom line."

A double bottom line is a fancy phrase for a company's measure of its social impact in terms of both its commitment to society and its efforts to make a positive difference for people. Furthermore, the **triple bottom line** goes another step beyond that; in addition to the two factors used to measure the double bottom lines, a company also must measure its efficacy on the planet by how it practices sustainability. The triple bottom line is all about people, profit, *and* the planet.[9] You can think about it like this:

- Bottom line → Profit

9 Miller, "The Triple Bottom Line: What It Is & Why It's Important," 2020.

- Double-bottom line → Profit + People
- Triple-bottom line → Profit + People + Planet

It's not just about your net profit but also your *net impact*.

Pretty cool, right? Social entrepreneurship, if practiced effectively, can cause a rippling effect for good on society and the planet. The topic of being more intentional about social impact in business has dominated more and more conversations over the past few years—not because it's the "new trendy thing to do" but because it's the right and moral thing to do if we *truly* want to create a better and brighter future. After all, isn't that what innovation is for?

The Origins of Social Entrepreneurship and the Spectrum of Impact

Social entrepreneurship is rooted in the need for balance between making money and making an impact, which can be traced as far back as the 1880s with Andrew Carnegie's idea of **corporate philanthropy**—yes, you might recall him from your U.S. history class! Carnegie wrote "The Gospel of Wealth," a piece that challenged rich people to support social causes. In this article, he voiced his belief in giving away wealth during the course of one's lifetime. One of his famous quotes from this article says, "The man who dies thus rich dies disgraced." Ultimately, he advocated that extremely wealthy individuals like himself have a responsibility to benefit the greater good and close the wealth gap.

His message continues to resonate with us today, but it played a significant role in inspiring John D. Rockefeller—another famous philanthropist you might recall from your history class—to donate more than half a million dollars.[10] This was a huge deal at the time because Rockefeller was the wealthiest American at the time through the success of his business, the Standard Oil Company. The fact that the wealthiest man promoted and advocated for philanthropy was an eye-opening signal for other individuals and businesses to reconsider their contributions to society.

While corporate philanthropy is still relevant today, how we think about benefiting the greater good through business has evolved. In the 1950s, the idea of **corporate social responsibility (CSR)** arose, and the term was coined by Howard Bowen in his book *Social Responsibilities of the Businessman*, which popularized him as the "father of CSR."[11] CSR is defined as the practices and policies undertaken by corporations that are intended to have a positive influence on the world. Not surprisingly, the idea has continued to expand, becoming a hot topic in the twenty-first century.

It is important to note that there is a *difference* between CSR and corporate philanthropy. CSR is about the overall attitude and efforts of companies at large in promoting social impact, whereas corporate philanthropy is solely about giving financially to benefit social good in some capacity. An example of corporate philanthropy is an act like a *company match* for donations (whatever an employee donates to a charitable organization, the company will match the amount so that the charitable organization receives double the donated amount).

---

10 History.com Editors. 2018. "John D. Rockefeller." HISTORY. A&E Television Networks. September 20, 2018. https://www.history.com/topics/early-20th-century-us/john-d-rockefeller.

11 Bowen, *Social Responsibilities of the Businessman*, (1953) 2013.

There is even an entire holiday dedicated to this called Giving Tuesday—the Tuesday right after Thanksgiving (yes, after all the splurging happens on Black Friday, Small Business Saturday, and Cyber Monday). Another example of corporate philanthropy is corporate sponsorships, where companies will donate grants of money to support charitable causes. Corporate philanthropy can even exist outside of entrepreneurship in the traditional sense, with celebrities, including creators and music artists, who commit to donating a portion of the profits from their own creative work to support the charitable cause of the foundations they've created. For instance, Shawn Mendes created the Shawn Mendes Foundation, which seeks to amplify, empower, and uplift youth changemakers, their organizations, and their work. Selena Gomez created The Rare Impact Fund as part of her makeup company Rare Beauty's commitment to raising awareness and promoting mental health and wellness. Leonardo DiCaprio also created a foundation, the Leonardo DiCaprio Foundation, dedicated to the protection of wildlife, threatened ecosystems, and climate change issues. Jeff Bezos, the founder of Amazon, donated $100 million to Dolly Parton, an influential pop culture icon, to benefit causes in literacy and education as part of the "Courage and Civility Award."[12]

CSR, on the other hand, is more general—corporate philanthropy is a *type* of CSR. CSR can include any general initiative outside of the company's business operations that gives back or benefits a social good. For instance, a company might coordinate a food drive

---

[12] Chappell, "Dolly Parton Gets $100 Million from Jeff Bezos to Spend on Charity," 2022.

donation driven by its employees or might organize a beach cleanup that any of its employees can volunteer for.

Beyond organizing things outside of a company's core operations, CSR initiatives have been increasingly intertwined with the work itself. For instance, Spotify actively advertises its diversity, equity, and inclusion initiatives to "uplift marginalized voices and amplify important causes." For instance, for underrepresented artists and creators, Spotify makes an effort to feature their content to be more accessible to listeners to create more equity. Also, for the 2022 midterm elections, Spotify actively promoted efforts to motivate its listeners to vote and make their voices heard through their Play Your Part campaign.[13] This included featuring resources to help listeners know where to vote, creating playlists to keep their listeners some company while they stood in line to vote, creating more incentivizing messages for young first-time voters, curating podcasts to inspire civic engagement, and more.[14]

CSR has gained a lot of momentum over the years. Approximately 90% of companies on the S&P 500 index published a report on their CSR in 2019, which is a big improvement from just 20% in 2011![15] CSR has been successfully executed with the help of trusty partners that are more familiar with the people and causes that corporations are trying to benefit—after all, *the people closest to the problems are closest to the solutions.*

---

13 "Social Impact," Spotify, accessed February 14, 2023.

14 Spotify, "Spotify Encourages Eligible U.S. Voters to 'Play Your Part' by Registering for and Voting in the 2020 Election, "Spotify, 2020.

15 Global Giving, "17 CSR Facts You Need to Know," 2022.

Beyond CSR, we also have the idea of social entrepreneurship. Around one century after Carnegie's article, Bill Drayton coined the term "social entrepreneurship" (*finally*, right?!). Drayton is the founder and CEO of Ashoka, the leading organization for cultivating changemakers (including social entrepreneurs!)

When we compare social entrepreneurship to traditional entrepreneurship, the former prioritizes the impact a business has just as much as its generated revenue. For example, TOMS was started in an effort to solve the problem of providing shoes to children in Argentina. TOMS matches every pair of shoes purchased with a pair of new shoes for a child in need. Similarly, Warby Parker has a Buy a Pair, Give a Pair program for their glasses.[16] Social entrepreneurship is a dedication to finding ways to solve issues in society that the **market economy** has failed to address.

The market economy is more casually known as "the market." You can think of the market as the overall ecosystem where businesses interact with consumers. This isn't like your neighborhood farmer's market but is better compared to the entirety of transactions of every kind between businesses and customers.

When we talk about the market, we are generally referring to this idea but in a broader relationship to our economic system. When we talk about the market in entrepreneurship, we are referring to the *ecosystem* that surrounds the transaction process between businesses and consumers, which includes investment, production,

---

16 Peters, "Toms Made Buy-One, Give-One Famous. Now It's Updating the Model," 2019.

and distribution—all of which are affected by forces like supply and demand.[17]

Thus, when we refer to disrupting the market economy through social entrepreneurship, it might sound somewhat similar to socially responsible businesses practicing CSR, but the main difference to keep in mind is that impact for social entrepreneurship is *proactive*, whereas for CSR it is *reactive*. For enterprises created through social entrepreneurship, impact is in the DNA of the organization, whereas with businesses who practice CSR, impact is woven into the organization but is not a core element of the business itself. So, if we think about Spotify, their social impact efforts aren't elemental parts of their business model, but everything they do promotes the impact they desire to have, which is a nice (and very appreciated) add-on. By our definition, they are not a social enterprise because the mission to have impact was not the reason why the company was founded. In comparison, impact was the reason for companies like TOMS and Warby Parker.

Social entrepreneurship is about making impact an essential part of the *core* of its business. CSR is about adapting a company's existing business model to feed into the disruption, but social entrepreneurship is about *being* the disruption to the underlying dynamics that create demand for the products and services we crave.

---

17 Investopedia, "What is a Market Economy and How Does it Work?" 2022.

Scopes of Social Entrepreneurship

Social entrepreneurship seeks to find an optimal balance between profit and value-creation. However, like a balance scale that has two sides that need to be level, the crux of social entrepreneurship is finding that stasis between profit and value-creation. Because it can be challenging to *perfectly* balance the two, there are various expressions of social entrepreneurship, which is why it is often hard for people to define exactly what a social enterprise is. For our purposes, we define a social enterprise as *a self-sustaining for-profit or nonprofit business entity that intends to make a positive impact on humanity or the planet.*

There are two key parts to our definition:

- The first is the need to be *self-sustaining*: Social enterprises must have a business model of some sort to stay afloat and cannot solely rely on external funding.
- The second is the *intention*: Was impact the reason for the creation of the enterprise? Or was it more of an afterthought? Social enterprises will always be created with the intention of having an impact.

For our more visual learners, we've created a framework we like to refer to as the **Fulphil Profit-Impact Matrix**, which visually frames these variables to help our students understand social entrepreneurship and how it fits in with the world of impact in business and philanthropy.

The matrix consists of a four-quadrant system, like the graphs you've probably seen in your algebra classes. On the *x* axis, we have our self-sustainability variable, where the left side represents entities that need a constant inflow of money from outside sources to support their operations, whereas the right side represents entities that earn their own revenue.

Meanwhile, the *y* axis measures the intentionality of the business entity's impact. If the reason for the entity's inception was for the sole purpose of creating a positive social impact, it falls above the *x* axis. If it was not created with that intention, it falls below the *x* axis.

FULPHIL PROFIT-IMPACT MATRIX

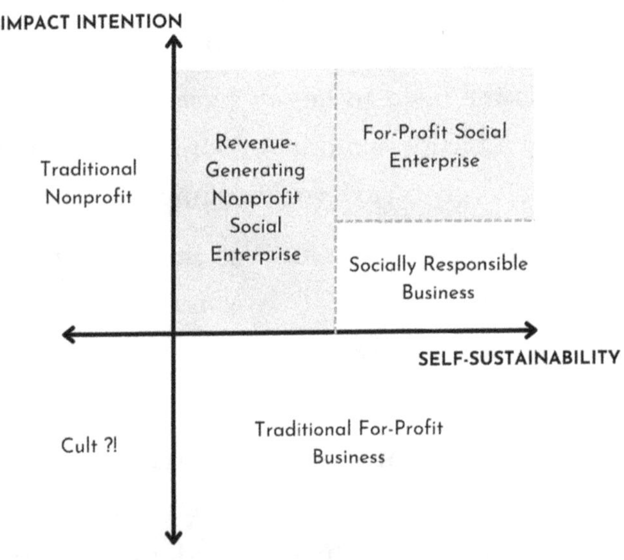

The top left quadrant includes nonprofits that operate more traditionally by relying on grants and donations as the primary source of revenue. They have a less self-sustainable business model but are created with the intention of making an impact.

The top right quadrant includes for-profit social enterprises, socially responsible businesses that practice CSR, and revenue-generating nonprofit social enterprises.

We should point out here that the term "nonprofit" is a bit of a misnomer. Nonprofits *can* make profits. The reason they are called nonprofits is because they cannot return a profit to their shareholders (donors) as for-profit organizations do for their shareholders (investors). For nonprofit social enterprises, it is more about the return on *impact,* whereas for-profit social enterprises focus on both a return on impact *and* a return on investment. With this, notice that our social enterprises (both for-profit and nonprofit) are highlighted.

The bottom right quadrant includes traditional for-profit companies. This includes businesses that are solely focused on their bottom line and are not devoting attention to their social impact.

Lastly, the bottom left quadrant includes nonprofits that do not intend to create a positive impact—a category that would probably include cults (which we discourage you from exploring).

Among all these types of businesses, the main distinctions are their method of sustainability in earning revenue and their intentionality regarding impact. Hopefully, this visual model helps you remember that a social enterprise is *a self-sustaining for-profit or nonprofit business entity that intends to make a positive impact on humanity or the planet.*

Scales of Social Entrepreneurship

Beyond the foundational business models of social enterprises, Dr. Joe Johnson asserts they can also exist at different scales.[18] Each of the following is often differentiated by its scope of work, yet you might find that they blend into one another – a single social enterprise can identify with a variety of these categories, and so can your work as a social entrepreneur!

- A **community social entrepreneur** is one who creates an organization to serve the niche needs of a very specific geographic area. Think of the people who run organizations like your local community center.
- A **nonprofit social entrepreneur** is one who prioritizes their organization's social well-being over traditional business needs. Any profits earned are reinvested back into the business.
- A **transformational social entrepreneur** is one focused on creating businesses that can meet the social needs that governments and other businesses aren't currently meeting. This is essentially the personality of the for-profit social entrepreneur but can also include more advanced and evolved nonprofit social entrepreneurs.
- A **global social entrepreneur** bases their success on their work around transforming an entire social system worldwide. Think of groups like the Bill & Melinda Gates Foundation or the Chan Zuckerberg Initiative. In the case of these two examples, they funnel their profits from Microsoft or Facebook to their

---

18 Group, "Types of Social Entrepreneurs," 2018.

philanthropic work—Microsoft and Facebook are practicing corporate philanthropy as a form of CSR as their own entities, and that money transfers over to the founders' nonprofit work. Global social entrepreneurship can also include for-profit and nonprofit social enterprises.

As we mentioned, impact really does happen in a variety of ways! As you continue reading, keep in mind how you hope to make a difference—there are lots of routes to choose from!

II. The Promises of Social Entrepreneurship for the World

The Promise for Prosperity

Former Harvard Business School professor and author Clayton Christensen advocates that businesses and development programs at large must focus on addressing the "prosperity paradox," which he terms as the phenomenon that describes how lasting wealth and development is not the result of creating urgent solutions to poverty but rather building self-sustaining prosperous ecosystems.[19] In his study of the most prosperous nations, he found that innovation and entrepreneurship had more potential than antipoverty initiatives to create prosperity. For instance, companies like Sony, Toyota, and Canon were some of the big players that helped Japan build its

---

19 Christensen, Ojomo, and Dillon, *The Prosperity Paradox*, 2019.

economy post–World War II, and the same can be said for others like South Korea thanks to Hyundai, Kia, and more.

One of the biggest takeaways from Christensen's research is that an innovation-focused strategy is humanity's best shot at creating lasting prosperity. An innovator (and social entrepreneur—yes, that's you!) is in a better position to address gaps in the market and to make an impact than governments. Governments have the power to make an impact on sectors at an extremely high level, but social entrepreneurs create innovative solutions that can accelerate that impact and bring it to fruition. With this, social entrepreneurs need to think even more intentionally about value creation by dedicating more thought to the effects that their businesses have on people and the planet.

If we want to create prosperity as social entrepreneurs, we must measure value based on both the return on *investment* and the return on *impact*.

In the previous chapter, we mentioned the importance of making ethical decisions when it comes to building with impact. The social responsibility of decision-making is not limited to your customers and investors, as in the traditional entrepreneurial setting, but includes your beneficiaries and anyone you choose to engage with when building and executing your solution.

It is not just about the impact you're *set* on creating but also those you impact *along the way*.

One model of social entrepreneurship that empowers marginalized communities is **asset-based community development (ABCD)**.

This model speaks to the fundamentals of groundbreaking impact that starts in local communities and builds to the global level. ABCD is a bottom-up methodology that communities follow to develop sustainably; the community development process is executed by those who are directly affected. This methodology largely focuses on the assets and strengths of a community rather than on the deficits and problems. It seeks out ways to tap into those strengths to further empower the community and all those in it.

Now, THAT's radical. You won't look at "ABCD" the same again! When we look at social entrepreneurship through the lens of ABCD, it is easier and a lot clearer to see that that people *can* make a difference and marginalized individuals *can* achieve personally defined success—and most importantly—the people closest to the problems are closest to the solutions.

A poster child social enterprise example that embraces ABCD is Homeboy Industries. Homeboy Industries is a social enterprise based in Los Angeles and it is the largest gang rehab and re-entry program in the world.[20] Based on their reports, over 10,000 former gang members all over Los Angeles come through Homeboy Industries' doors every *year*.

The organization leverages ABCD through workforce development, namely, training people to build the skills they need to succeed in the workplace. They have an eighteen-month program that focuses on empowering people to heal from trauma and be able to fully contribute to their families and communities by reducing recidivism,

---

20 Homeboy Industries, "Our Mission," 2019.

reducing substance abuse, improving social connectedness, improving housing safety and stability, and reunifying families. The organization creates a strong sense of community and kinship, and it offers a wide spectrum of services that range from tattoo removal to anger management and even parenting classes. In this process, they are employing beneficiaries who work for Homeboy Industries' chain of businesses, which includes electronics recycling, silk screen and embroidery services, catering services, and a variety of bakeries and cafes across Los Angeles.

Homeboy Industries' founder, Father Gregory Boyle, launched the organization because he wanted to reduce gang violence in his community, which was at an all-time high at the time. Having personally witnessed the damaging impacts of gang violence through his community members, his solution was "to treat gang members as human beings." Father Greg sought to truly empower the gang members who joined Homeboy Industries and tap into them as *assets* who could drive even greater community impact by creating sustainably run businesses that could employ even *more* beneficiaries and support them in their rehabilitation journey. There were various ways he could have created a solution to solve the problem of gang violence, but he chose the ingenious ABCD model, which has resulted in a prosperous, self-sustaining ecosystem that leverages business as a force for good to yield a net profit that can continue to support and sustainably create a positive *net impact*.

To provide another example of ABCD in social entrepreneurship on a different community scale, let's look at the company Zaaf in the fashion industry.

The fashion industry still has room to improve, especially in regard to their impact on stakeholder groups and the environment. Many Americans donate their unwanted clothing in the hopes of doing good, but many are unaware of what happens to the clothing they donate and the market it creates.

About fifteen million clothing items are imported into Ghana every week from North America and Europe. Most items are donated, including from charities, and about 40% of the items are considered low quality and are dumped in a landfill.[21] These landfills are harmful to the environment—the clothing pollutes the water, air, and soil, and it can take hundreds of years for the clothing to biodegrade.

This industry has risen due to the mass second-hand clothing imports. Ghanaians buy the donated clothing and sell it in local markets. The imports of clothing can decrease Ghana's need to create their own local textiles and also decrease the demand for local textiles; however, while this is not solely responsible for the decline in local textile industries, it has contributed. Some argue that the reselling industry is fair because it is providing jobs.

However, various stakeholders are deemed to have low importance by the retailers of these clothing items, namely the local community, environment, and second-hand sellers. The international retail reuse-and-resale industry at large tends to prioritize profits to the detriment of the local community and its environment.[22] Several

---

21 Besser, "'It's an Insult': In an African Clothing Market, a Bale of Used Clothes Donated by Australians Is Opened," 2021.

22 Bearak and Lynch, "African Nations Are Fed up with the West's Hand-Me-Downs. But It's Tough to Keep Them Out," 2018.

social enterprises have emerged in an effort to creatively rethink and disrupt this systemic problem to empower their local communities. This includes Zaaf, whose founder, Abai Schulze, an Ethiopian adoptee who was raised in America, sought to start a business in East Africa. Zaaf is an Ethiopian brand that specializes in handcrafted luxury bags and was founded with the intention of creating long-term economic opportunities in Ethiopia.[23]

Schulze was intentional in how she developed her business concept, especially in regard to how her business would impact local Ethiopians. She works with the local community to create entirely handmade purses using indigenous materials and practices that she hopes to keep alive by incorporating them into the company.[24] Schulze challenges the perception that the best way to help impoverished communities in Africa is through charity. Instead, she proposes that these communities lack the opportunities needed to be self-sustaining. Rather than making charity donations, Schulze advocates in her TEDx talk that we should invest in these communities and support their local businesses so that they may thrive like brands from other countries.[25]

Schulze's focus on economic development is what has allowed Zaaf to make a tangible and dignifying impact on the community and empower its people to grow their prosperity potentials. Oftentimes in social entrepreneurship, it is easy to become so wrapped up in the

---

23 "A Little Bit about ZAAF…." ZAAF, accessed January 9, 2023.

24 "Abai Schulze, the Founder of ZAAF on CNN African Voices," ZAAF Collection, 2018.

25 Schulze, "'Made in Africa' - the Power of Shifting Perceptions," 2019.

idea of the impact we are set to make that we often forget about the people involved in the process. Consequently, even when we start with good intentions, we can negatively affect the world of social impact and social entrepreneurship. As social entrepreneurs, we can't afford to overlook the people involved; we need to think very intentionally about the impact we're having on everyone in the entire process. How will *you* make a meaningful, positive difference for and truly empower the people you are trying to help through your business?

The Promise for Empathy and Citizenship

Like Father Greg was motivated to solve a problem he witnessed, we are all more invested in solving the issues that we face in our own lives and know in our own communities. When we care about things, we want to help and improve what is around us. After all, **empathy**—the ability to understand and share feelings and experiences with other people—is an important part of being an effective social entrepreneur.[26]

To better understand what empathy can look like in context, we've always taught our students the importance of embracing global citizenship. **Global citizenship** is the idea that we as individuals do not identify as a member of a state, nation, or tribe but rather as a member of humanity. A **global citizen** is an individual who is aware of the world and his or her role in it.[27] According to Ron Israel

---

26 Greater Good Magazine, " What Is Empathy," 2009.

27 United Nations, "Global Citizenship," 2022.

with the Global Citizenship Initiative, "A global citizen is someone who identifies with being part of an emerging world community and whose actions contribute to building this community's values and practices."[28]

Global citizenship is not only about awareness but also about participating in the community, problem-solving, and respecting and valuing diversity. The values of global citizenship include helping individuals understand pressing issues of the world (social, political, economic, or environmental), their place relative to them, and what they can do about these issues. With this, it's no surprise that **UNESCO** (United Nations Educational, Scientific and Cultural Organization)—a special agency of the United Nations aimed at promoting world peace and security through international cooperation in education, arts, sciences, and culture—ranks global citizenship as one of the top three priorities in education.[29] That's a pretty high priority!

But to become a global citizen, we must learn how to be a local citizen of our community first. This helps us take action for local issues that are also present on a global scale.

Some of the world's greatest social challenges are found in our very own cities. This could range from homelessness and food insecurity to transportation inefficiencies and so much more. The possibilities for social impact (and social enterprises) within our own communities are endless! Being aware of these social issues in your own community can help you empathize with people around the

---

28 Israel, "What Does It Mean to Be a Global Citizen?" 2014.

29 Unesco, "Global Citizenship Education," 2018.

world who experience similar challenges on different scales, which makes you a better global citizen who can identify with humanity as a whole.

An article in the Harvard Business Review discusses the power of engaging with local issues. "Collaboration must happen at a local level, where all relevant actors in business, government, and civil society must be brought together to create systematic change."[30] This alludes to our earlier point in Chapter 1: the people closest to the problems are closest to the most viable solutions. Therefore, there is great power in bringing together multiple stakeholders at the community level who have an understanding and connection to the local needs.

Even though the local needs of our communities are a small fraction of the world's needs, they are needs nonetheless and must be addressed. Being able to put this into perspective can help open our minds to see that even if our contributions to society on a local level feel small and insignificant, they are still contributing to making a broader positive difference.

Global citizenship advocates for everyone in the world to act as a citizen of their community; by doing so together, we are citizens of the world. Global citizenship can seem like an overwhelming concept, but it starts small and begins with you in your community. As individuals, we each know more about issues closer to home, and it is through this intimate and powerful local action that we grow an

---

30 Kramer, Pfitzer, and Mahne, "How Global Leaders Should Think about Solving Our Biggest Problems," 2020.

authentic connection to the global community—where similar issues are also present in their own unique ways. The more you connect with problems in your community and connect them to global issues at large, the more you grow in your awareness of the global environment.

As you think about your local and global environment, consider reviewing the **United Nations Sustainable Development Goals (SDGs)**. The United Nations created these SDGs for all people in order to accomplish the 2030 Agenda for Sustainable Development.[31] The SDGs encapsulate high-priority issues:

- **Goal 1: No poverty**—"End poverty in all its forms everywhere."[32]
- **Goal 2: Zero hunger**—"End hunger, achieve food security and improved nutrition and promote sustainable agriculture."[33]
- **Goal 3: Good health and well-being**—"Ensure healthy lives and promote well-being for all at all ages."[34]
- **Goal 4: Quality education**—"Ensure inclusive and equitable quality education and promote lifelong learning opportunities for all."[35]

---

[31] United Nations, "The 17 Sustainable Development Goals," 2015.

[32] United Nations, "Goal 1," 2020.

[33] United Nations, "Goal 2," 2022.

[34] United Nations, "Goal 3," 2021.

[35] United Nations, "Goal 4," 2021.

- **Goal 5: Gender equality**—"Achieve gender equality and empower all women and girls."[36]
- **Goal 6: Clean water and sanitation**—"Ensure availability and sustainable management of water and sanitation for all."[37]
- **Goal 7: Affordable and clean energy**—"Ensure access to affordable, reliable, sustainable and modern energy for all."[38]
- **Goal 8: Decent work and economic growth**—"Promote sustained, inclusive and sustainable economic growth, full and productive employment and decent work for all."[39]
- **Goal 9: Industry, innovation and infrastructure**—"Build resilient infrastructure, promote inclusive and sustainable industrialization and foster innovation."[40]
- **Goal 10: Reduced inequalities**—"Reduce inequality within and among countries."[41]
- **Goal 11: Sustainable cities and communities**—"Make cities and human settlements inclusive, safe, resilient and sustainable."[42]

---

36 United Nations, "Goal 5," 2022.

37 United Nations, "Goal 6," 2015.

38 United Nations, "Goal 7," 2022.

39 United Nations, "Goal 8," 2021.

40 United Nation, "Goal 9," 2021.

41 United Nations, "Goal 10," 2021.

42 United Nations, "Goal 11," 2021.

- **Goal 12: Responsible consumption and production**—"Ensure sustainable consumption and production patterns."[43]
- **Goal 13: Climate action**—"Take urgent action to combat climate change and its impacts."[44]
- **Goal 14: Life below water**—"Conserve and sustainably use the oceans, seas and marine resources for sustainable development."[45]
- **Goal 15: Life on land**—"Protect, restore and promote sustainable use of terrestrial ecosystems, sustainably manage forests, combat desertification, and halt and reserve land degradation and halt biodiversity loss."[46]
- **Goal 16: Peace, justice and strong institutions**—"Promote peaceful and inclusive societies for sustainable development, provide access to justice for all and build effective, accountable and inclusive institutions at all levels."[47]
- **Goal 17: Partnerships for the goals**—"Strengthen the means of implementation and revitalize the Global Partnership for Sustainable Development."[48]

Acknowledging these SDGs is the tip of the iceberg to help you become more aware of global events at large. Doing so can help you

---

43 United Nations, "Goal 12," 2022.

44 United Nations, "Goal 13," 2022.

45 United Nations, "Goal 14," 2021.

46 United Nations, "Goal 15," 2020.

47 United Nations, "Goal 16," 2021.

48 United Nations, "Goal 17," 2021.

develop and drive your own insights about issues affecting millions not only in your own community but also all around the world—whether it's the lack of access to clean water, gender inequality, or something else. As a social entrepreneur, working to solve problems in your own community that you have a stake in brings you closer to truly connecting with and eventually solving those problems in the global landscape.

What challenges does *your* community face? How can you, as an individual, make an impact on your community? Which problem do you care to solve in your social entrepreneurial journey? As you read the rest of this book, be sure to keep these questions in mind.

The Promise for the Future

Ultimately, whatever impact we choose to make today *matters*. William MacAskill, Cambridge professor and researcher, asks in his book *What We Owe the Future*, "How would our priorities change if we truly took future lives as seriously as our own?" and advocates for the theory of *longtermism*, which is a philosophy proposing that humanity has a moral obligation and responsibility to positively influence our distant future and the future generations who will live in it. [49]

MacAskill proposes that the future is uncertain, and that humanity has the potential either to create a great, bright future or to turn it upside down and create a dystopian one (similar to what we see in sci-fi movies or in disconcerting episodes of *Black Mirror*). The future is *full* of possibilities, and those outcomes can either be full of promise

---

49 Macaskill, *What We Owe the Future*, 2022.

or despair. And just like what we see in the movies, with more advanced technology, innovation, and interconnection, the degree of either of those could be exponential.

The future of humanity can depend on whatever we do today and whatever impact we choose to make on the world—no matter how big or small. That's what makes the idea of social entrepreneurship all the more exciting and hopeful for the future!

III. Cheat Code Recap

1. Social impact takes on different forms in business.
2. A social enterprise is a self-sustaining for-profit or nonprofit business entity that intends to make a positive impact on humanity or the planet.
3. Social entrepreneurship revolves around ways we can disrupt issues in society that the market economy has failed to address.
4. Social entrepreneurship can happen at different scales, depending on its scope of work (community, nonprofit, transformational, global).
5. The promises of social entrepreneurship in the world include prosperity, empathy and citizenship, and the future.

Chapter 3
Build with Impact: Aligning Your Values and Purpose

Written by: Tiffany Yau, Aditya Desai, Sam Stern, and Riley Gonta

"Passion is energy. Feel the power that comes from focusing on what excites you." — Oprah Winfrey, American talk show host and philanthropist

I. Introduction to the Entrepreneurial Mindset

It's Time to Get Building!

Remember our metaphorical plane? The one we built after we jumped? Well, we're still falling. Our idea seemed pretty great when we were 1,800 feet up, but now that we're falling at 9.8 meters per second squared... well, let's just say we're starting to freak out a bit.

Your mind is probably racing with thoughts.

Should I have jumped? Should I have waited for more equipment? Should I have asked a friend to jump with me? If only I'd asked Sam; he might have jumped with me... no, wait, Sam has band practice on Wednesdays so that wouldn't have worked out....

HELLO! HI! Snap out of it. You're still falling and it's time to get *building*!

The Journey is Long

"If you stand for nothing Burr, what do you fall for?" - Alexander Hamilton (Broadway Musical)

Look, let's be real: entrepreneurship is hard, and social entrepreneurship is just as challenging, if not more so. We're not trying to scare you away from your mission, but even writing those words does not do the statement justice. Social entrepreneurship is *hard* and you need to know how to stay resilient when the going gets tough!

Remember the core values we mentioned earlier? You need to be grounded in your core values. Social entrepreneurship is about standing for something. And to stand for something, you need to stand on something. This "something" you stand on is your set of core values.

Fail Fast, Fix Faster

Failure—the F-word! Remember, we told you to take this word out of your vocabulary, but just in case you need some help doing so, let's translate it into something a bit more meaningful and helpful! The world of innovation revolves around the 4 F's: Fail Fast, Fix Faster.

There will be times when you'll feel like something you did was a total failure. You'll probably be stressed *out of your mind,* trying to pivot—and pivot *well* at that! Believing in what you're doing and having a firm sense of optimism will be imperative on this journey of social entrepreneurship. These two things are what will make the difference between giving up and pushing through. You can do it. We believe in you, so now it's your turn to believe in yourself.

Your goal throughout this process is not to solidify your mindset. It's not to find it, claim it, and carve it in stone. Instead, this is the start of a lifelong journey of exploring your social entrepreneurial mindset, and how much of it you can apply to your everyday life.

II. The Social Entrepreneurial Mindset

Before diving into the *social* entrepreneurial mindset, we should first understand the entrepreneurial mindset. The entrepreneurial mindset is a bit difficult to define; if you look it up, you'll probably find fifteen or more different definitions.

Like any soldier, an entrepreneur might have the strength and speed to keep up with their battalion when they're fresh out of the gate.

But what happens when deployment reaches day 124 and they're surrounded by an unfamiliar world with new threats and challenges?

An Entrepreneur's Way of Thinking: What does it really take to make it?

In the Olympics, we watch top-performance athletes compete against each other for their countries and themselves. They break world records, Olympic records, personal records, and *record* records!

But what we don't see is the decade of training it took to get them to that event. We don't see the athletes up at 4:15 a.m., training on their thirtieth Saturday in a row. We don't see them agonizing over what seemed right then to be a career-ending Achilles fracture. We don't see bitter losses to rivals whom they desperately wanted to beat. No, we don't see any of the fight it took to reach the pinnacle of their sport. Instead, we see the athlete winning that race they've been training for in the *blink* of an eye. A culmination of a lifetime of training, all in the blink of an eye.

Successful athletes have a set mindset, one that is very similar to an entrepreneurial mindset, actually. Athletes need this quality of mind to operate at peak performance, especially when the going gets tough. It is cultivated, trained, rehearsed, and learned. In this section, we are going to dig into the mindset we need to succeed as entrepreneurs, defining who we are and what we stand for.

The **entrepreneurial mindset** is an entrepreneur's way of thinking. Specifically, it is an established set of attitudes that includes grit, resilience, accountability, passion, and persistence to overcome obstacles and achieve results.

A Social Entrepreneur's Way of Thinking: Where Impact Is Front and Center

The **social entrepreneurial mindset** is a term we've coined at Fulphil to describe the characteristic of being not only an effective problem-solver but more importantly one who does so with the intention of making a positive impact.

social entrepreneurial mindset = being impact-driven + being a problem-solver

Similar to the concept of an entrepreneurial mindset, the social entrepreneurial mindset is a mentality that is *not* exclusive to the field of entrepreneurship. We at Fulphil have always emphasized that this mindset as one that our students can carry over into all aspects of their lives.

Being an impact-driven problem-solver will help anyone excel in whatever field they choose. But it doesn't stop there. Utilizing this mindset can help you with the smaller decisions in your life too—small decisions and actions like helping a neighbor or colleague with a small favor or shortening your showers by a minute.

Exploration takes time. We cannot set out to hike a mountain and expect to reach the summit in an hour. It's not what you'd call a fun process. Exploration is about growing 1% every day.

It's about the journey over time, not the destination. It's about challenging ourselves to listen, learn, reflect, and ask questions. It's about fighting complacency, not taking "no" for an answer, and being worthy of loyalty and trust. Growing 1% each day leads to exponential effects and an ever-evolving personal conviction.

You don't need to pull off something big and grandiose to have an impact. Taking on the social entrepreneurial mindset and creating a bigger impact in the world starts with the altruistic decisions you make every day and ingraining this attitude into your habits. The social entrepreneurial mindset is really all about living your life with high moral standards and following them. It's about being impact-driven above all else. The more you govern the way you live your life—with the intention of making a difference bigger than yourself—the more likely it is that you will make more impactful decisions for yourself and others.

III. Your North Star

Designing Your Life, a book written by Stanford professors Bill Burnett and Dave Evans, recommends defining the idea of your "North Star."[50] We found this inspiring and reference it all the time with our students whenever we get the chance!

Your North Star is out there! It exists, even if it doesn't seem obvious, and all you need to do is find it. Start by looking between where your identity, purpose, and will live. We all have unique stars

---

[50] Burnett and Evans, *Designing Your Life*, 2018.

so we all have to spend time defining them for ourselves! Your North Star is where your gut senses it to be.

In this section, we're going to dig deep. We'll dissect our identity, find our core values, and then define our purpose. Many of us don't reflect this way often, so if it feels weird, *great*! If it feels uncomfortable, *even better*! It takes courage to search within and actively listen to yourself. Don't worry, we'll be with you the whole time.

Defining Your Motivations

Why are you here? Yes, *you*. Why are *you* here?

It's a loaded question. But really think about it.

Why did you choose to buy this book?

Are you ready? (We hope the answer is "heck yeah!")

Why are you here?

Take the time to think about and write (in your notebook or on our downloadable worksheet) about why you decided to pick up this book. Why did you choose this book over binge-watching your favorite Netflix series or playing your favorite game?

Your answer should address the following:

- Why are you reading this book?
- What do you hope to get out of this book?
- What makes what your goal *worth* it?

As you respond to these questions, keep in mind that your responses don't need to be perfect! Whether you've written your answers in a notebook or computer document, keep them somewhere safe but also somewhere you can access them with ease. We'll return to your responses often throughout this book to help you stay on track with your personal expectations.

Why are we the way we are?

Now that you've explored why you picked up this book, let's dig a little deeper! It's time to define your core values.

Does the term **symbolic interactionism** sound familiar? It probably doesn't! And that's okay. This is the term for a theory in sociology that explains the phenomenon of how we as individuals embody and *symbolize meaning* from our *interactions* with things, people, and experiences. It explains why certain things resonate with us more than others and why certain things that are so special to us may mean little to our friends.

Our past experiences shape us into becoming the people we are today. More importantly, they shape what we believe. Maybe the smell of banana bread is special to you because it reminds you of your mom's baking; or perhaps the Lion King is special to you because you have a fond memory of the people you watched it with for the first; or maybe you like watching reruns of your favorite show (even though you've seen it dozens of times) when you are upset because it reminds you of a more comforting time.

There are several factors that shape our core values, which are what dictate how we choose to live our lives.

Core Values

If you've ever watched the classic Disney movie *Pinocchio*, you can think of your North Star and motivation as Pinocchio's desire to be "a real boy" and your core values as whatever Jiminy Cricket (i.e., your conscience) tells you to follow. Your core values help you navigate and stay true to your motivations and North Star.

Your core values are the set of beliefs that guide your decision-making based on your judgment of right versus wrong. Your core values ultimately define your priorities and empower you to make purposeful judgments.

Important, right? Now if we, as individuals, have core values that guide us, why shouldn't we, as leaders, also have core values? This is especially true of leaders of soon-to-be social enterprises! Core values determine both your own priorities *and* the priorities of your company.

Without further ado, let's dive into a little interactive activity to get our gears turning! You can find downloadable worksheets on our website. The goal of this activity is to help you define what direction you want to take your social enterprise. But to figure that out, you'll need to start by defining your core values and motivations. Let's get started!

ACTIVITY: Defining your core values

Step 1: List Your Experiences

Let's start with your experiences!

Ask yourself, "What are some moments and experiences in my life where I have been extremely happy and my fullest self?" In other words, what are your *peak* experiences?

For example, a peak experience in your life could've been when you scored the final point in a championship soccer match or passed a class with a better grade than expected. A peak experience is one that fills you with extremely positive emotions and makes you feel the most alive and engaged with the present moment.

On the flip side, it's just as important to note moments that are the complete opposite.

So, ask yourself: "What are the moments and experiences in my life where I've been extremely unhappy and not my fullest self?" In other words, what are my *low* experiences?

For example, a low experience in your life could've been when you turned in a group project that you didn't feel so hot about or a time when you were deeply embarrassed about a mistake you made. These moments most likely filled you with great unhappiness and made you feel disconnected from who you are.

Step 2: Categorize

Now that you've answered those questions, let's take a step back and move away from the small granular details so we can identify bigger-picture ideas!

Consider the themes that arose from the moments and experiences you wrote about.

For example, some common themes in happy moments are time with your family or being on the receiving end of validation. Success is another common theme.

Do this for the unhappy moments you wrote about. When you start dissecting your unhappy moments, you may notice that the values involved might be "flipped" from your responses about your happy moments. For example, some of your unhappiest experiences may have involved being away from your family or failing in some regard. This flip-flop is perfectly normal!

Now, try to identify some patterns and create as many categories as you can for the peaks and lows. Once you have these categories, it's time to narrow the list! Try refining your list of values under each category. The goal is to end this process with your top three to five core values that you identify with most.

Step 3: Find the "*Why*" behind the "*Why*"

Now that you've found some common denominators, let's figure out *why* you care about these values. In other words, why do you value what you value?

It's easy to find other people who share similar values, but the motivation behind why you hold those values may differ quite a bit. This might seem confusing at first, but we promise it'll make more sense as we start to flesh this out.

For instance, referencing the earlier example, ask yourself *why* you care about family. The answer can't simply be "because they're family." Dig deeper! *Why* do you value family? Maybe it's because they've always cared for you? Answers will vary from person to person, so it's important that you define this now. This is the fun part! Ask yourself *why* again.

Why does it matter that they've always cared for you? Perhaps it's because you wouldn't be where you are today if it weren't for them. Explore *why* it matters that they're always there for you at the end of the day. Maybe it reassures you, knowing you always have people to rely on.

This might be difficult the further you go. Finding the right words may be harder than before, but don't be afraid to give it your all! This is the most exciting part because new, deeper values will likely start to arise as you uncover the "why behind the why."

Let's dig a bit deeper: *why* does it matter that you're where you are today because of their support? Is it because you value *giving*? *Why* does it matter that you have people to rely on? Perhaps it's because you value *trust*. There is no limit to where you can go with this simple exercise.

Step 4: Connecting Your Values to Your Everyday Life

Does the line of reasoning you explored align with how your values fit into your day-to-day life?

Seeing how your values play out in your everyday life is powerful. It makes them tangible and easier to track. I guess you could say it brings them to life—pun intended!

In the previous example, we defined some possible values as *giving* and *trust* after asking why a couple more times. If you value giving, you may see it in real life when you're always the first one to help a friend if they're stuck on a homework problem. If you value trust, you may notice your circle of friends is smaller than most because you are careful with who you choose to trust.

Now that you've defined some real-life examples of moments or experiences where you've seen your values play out, how would you rank yourself on how well you live out your values? Is it a 10?

For most of us, it's not. And that's totally fine! The next stage should inspire you to start acting more in line with your core values.

Once you have a list of categories, spend some time reflecting on them and how these categories align and show up in your day-to-day life and environment. You don't need to dwell here too long; just take a moment to reflect!

Step 5: Turning Core Values into Personal Statements

You made it to the last step! We're calling this one the "synthesis stage," which is a fancy way to describe the process of taking all the information we've gathered and to create some powerful personal statements.

Through these personal statements, you'll take ownership of your values and be able to act on them more readily. How cool is that?

Let's start by using this template: "I am someone who values X because Y."

Using the example from the previous step, the statement might look something like this: "I am someone who values *giving* because *it means a lot to me when people give me their time and attention when I need it most and I hope to give to others.*"

The purpose of writing one cohesive personal statement is to help you to make sense of it all. By mapping your values in this way, you're 1) owning your values as part of your identity (you are someone who values X, Y, and Z) and 2) you're directly *connecting* your *values* to your *experiences*.

A Gentle Reminder

On your social entrepreneurship journey, you'll often find yourself straying from your path or mission as you make progress.

Your North Star may flicker or even fade over time and with it your sense of direction or purpose. It's in these moments that you need to refer back to these activities to redirect. It will be crucial to ask yourself, "Am I still following my North Star? Am I staying true to my core values?"

Review your North Star and your core values over and over again as you continue on this path you've chosen to pursue to minimize the chances of losing your focus.

It'll make all the difference as you navigate your journey and solve problems.

IV. Cheat Code Recap

1. The entrepreneurial mindset is an established set of attitudes that includes grit, resiliency, accountability, passion, and persistence to overcome obstacles and achieve results, and can be applied outside of the scope of entrepreneurship.
2. Social entrepreneurial mindset = being impact-driven + being a problem-solver.
3. Your North Star provides your sense of direction and purpose.
4. Your core values define your moral compass, which will guide your actions and decisions along your journey.

Part 2:
Designing Your Impact

Chapter 4
Introduction to Design Thinking

Written by: Tiffany Yau, Aditya Desai, Emma O'Neil, and Freya Busser

"Becoming isn't about arriving somewhere or achieving a certain aim. I see it instead as forward motion, a means of evolving, a way to reach continuously toward a better self. The journey doesn't end." – Michelle Obama, former First Lady, author of *Becoming*

I. What is Design Thinking?

If you want to be an effective problem-solver, you need to embrace design thinking. According to the Interaction Design Foundation, **design thinking** is defined as a "non-linear, iterative process that teams use to understand users, challenge assumptions, redefine problems and create innovative solutions."[51]

We know, that is a *lot* to unpack. Despite its rise as a common buzzword, design thinking is an important concept to understand. Essentially, it is a process for solving complex problems by thinking like a *designer*.

Why? Because all good designers prioritize user needs. Great designers will rarely create a product that is not useful for its target audience. Creating a good solution begins with understanding the needs and wants of the people you're designing for; after all, people are more likely to apply a solution to their lives if it solves a problem they're dealing with. Design thinking can be best applied to **wicked problems**. As the name implies, wicked problems are complex situations without an obvious fix—perhaps even for our wizard friends like Harry Potter!

Design thinking is also **iterative**, meaning the process repeats itself to gather continuous feedback in order to best meet user needs. It involves pinpointing a problem to solve; observing the needs, gaps, and context around the problem; following up with some solution prototyping; and repeat testing to get feedback to improve and discover the best solution.

A core principle of design thinking is its emphasis on a human-centered approach at each stage of the process.

---

[51] Interaction Design Foundation, "What Is Design Thinking?" Accessed February 14, 2023.

II. Five Steps of Design Thinking

There are five main steps in design thinking. As a result, the five steps of the design thinking process are:

- Empathize
- Define
- Ideate
- Prototype
- Test

Everything starts with empathy. If you can't see things from the customer's perspective, how can you design a product that will be optimal for them? The short answer is you *can't*! Empathy is the tool that allows you to take control of your business, your product, and your solutions by allowing the users themselves to drive your decisions as the creator.

Person → Need → Solution

Neat concept, right? To create an effective solution, you must identify a need, and to identify a need, you must identify the person who has that need. Don't build a product you *think* people want. Let them *tell you* what they believe a good solution would be and use that feedback to inform what and how to innovate. Build what the people want!

However, these five steps don't occur linearly. Remember that we described design thinking is an *iterative* process. Instead of going from Step 1, to 2, to 3, to 4, to 5 and being done there, you might go from Step 5 back to Step 3 and then Step 1 to Step 2 and back to Step 1—then on to Step 4! To be iterative means you can jump around to different steps, depending on the feedback you receive after testing things out. Design thinking (and impact as a sector!) are *nonlinear* processes—and that's what makes them so exciting! The process doesn't always work out exactly like you expect it to.

1) Empathize

As with anything in life, always start with empathy.

This is the human element that makes the design process and innovation as a whole so personable. At this stage, it is important to understand your users' beliefs, values, and needs. You do this through *observation* and *interaction*. Consider the following and jot down your notes:

- Who are your customers?
- What do they do?
- How are they thinking?
- What do they want?
- What motivates them?
- What discourages them?

Your goal is to gain a stronger understanding of your users and their perspectives so you can design a product that they love and cannot live without!

Above all, your job here is to *understand* and *listen*. Many businesses and development initiatives flop because they get this first step wrong. Our "Hunger in Nicaragua" case study illustrates this point well—their initial approach was to educate about nutrition when what the people needed, in fact, was nutrition accessibility.

When working through this step, question everything you think you know and listen with an open mind. Be curious and let new knowledge soak in as though you are a sponge! Going back to the iterative aspect of design thinking, remember that empathy is *not* a one-time thing. You must *always* empathize and try your best to understand, learn, be willing to unlearn, and relearn everything all over again.

2) Define

With this step, you are creating your point of view. Taking the observations you gathered from your potential users during Step 1, compile what you have learned into insights and patterns. This is the time to pinpoint the problem you are seeking to solve—you must problem-find! Yes, if this is beginning to sound familiar to you, you are onto something! You've done this already through root cause analysis and by leveraging divergence and convergence to effectively problem-find.

This step of design is all about defining the problem statement.

3) Ideate

This is the time to let your ideas run to test the limits of your problem-solving potential! How can you address the user needs you identified in the Define step? Come up with as many solutions as possible. Don't be afraid to include them even if they sound ridiculous.

If you can, ask others for input on your potential solutions. Avoid being critical of yourself and your ideas during this phase. Braindump everything; the need for critical review will come later.

Taking the time to think through as many possibilities as you can in this phase will help prepare you for the next.

4) Prototype

Now comes the fun part! It's time to try out different solutions! This is your chance to answer the questions, "Will it work?" and "How will it work?"

When you prototype, you are creating a simple test model. This is also the time to determine the feasibility of some of your ideas as you come closer to the tangible solution.

Let's take a look at Zappos, for example. Zappos was one of the first online shoe retailers. Founder Nick Swinmurn wasn't sure whether customers would buy shoes online (considering it was a very new concept), so he used a **minimum viable product (MVP).** An MVP is a version of a product or service with just enough features to be usable by early customers who can then provide feedback for future product development. He used his MVP to test his hypothesis that consumers would buy shoes online. He took pictures of shoes from local shoe stores and posted them on a website. If customers placed an order, Swinmurn himself bought the shoes at full price from the store and delivered them directly to the customer. From these simple tests, he proved that customers were interested in this concept. Using his MVP, Swinmurn minimized the time, effort, and resources it took users to buy shoes and ultimately came to the conclusion that he could turn his idea of Zappos into an actual business.

5) Test/Validate

This step is the time to **test** and **validate** your solution in some scale to the problem to see how effective or wanted it actually is. This does not mean you have to do a full-fledged product launch; this step is meant to measure its efficacy on a smaller scale. For instance, if you're creating a food company, you can rally a small group of people to get some taste-tasting; or if you are building an app, you can get a small group of people to try using it to see how they use it.

Another example is Dropbox, the file transfer service. Dropbox also started exploring user needs with an MVP, which was a three-minute screencast showing customers what Dropbox would do. Through this test, Dropbox received valuable feedback from consumers, proved that this was in demand for customers, and gained an initial audience through a waiting list. The feedback gained through forming hypotheses and testing them allowed Dropbox to create a product that actually fulfilled customer needs. And now, Dropbox has over 500 million users worldwide!

This is why the iterative nature of design thinking is crucial for success. Get feedback from your users! Consider the following:

- How is the user experience of interacting with the prototype?
- How do customers react to the product?
- Does this solution meet their needs?
- Has it improved their lives in measurable ways?

And if you feel like you need to, revisit any step as needed.

Testing your product may lead you back to any of the steps. That's okay, don't get frustrated. This is a *good* thing.

- Maybe you did not define the problem accurately.
- Maybe you do not understand your audience.
- Maybe you need to refine the prototype to better match user needs.

But there is no need to worry! Iteration is crucial in the creation of worthwhile products that consumers love.

III. A Broader Look at Design Thinking: Hypothesis-Driven Entrepreneurship & Lean Startup Method

Design thinking in entrepreneurship is also known by other names, like **hypothesis-driven entrepreneurship** or, more commonly, the **lean startup methodology**.[52] They are the same general idea but reframe the steps in different ways. For the remainder of this book, we will continue to stick to the design thinking framework for

52 Blank, "Why the Lean Start-up Changes Everything," 2013.

consistency, but it's important that you are aware of the ideas behind the lean startup methodology.

Organizations that follow design thinking or a hypothesis-driven approach are called lean startups. Companies use the hypothesis-driven approach to minimize the risk of launching an unsuccessful product or business. This approach focuses on experimentation, testing, customer feedback, and validation. The goal is to create a sustainable business without investing huge amounts upfront.

The Power in Iterative Design

We should not underestimate the power of design thinking. There are lots of benefits, including the following:

- It helps you *identify unmet customer needs.*
- It *reduces the risk* associated with the launch of new ideas.
- It helps you *build entrepreneurial skills* like creativity, problem-solving, and self-confidence by requiring you to brainstorm a wide range of potential solutions and then narrow these down to the best-fit solution. After all, *you must solve problems to add value.*
- It helps you *redefine your value proposition* when the market shifts or there is a change in consumer behavior. The times are always changing, and you don't want to be left behind the trend!

The design thinking approach also taps into abilities that might be underutilized if a traditional problem-solving approach is used.

Design thinking relies on your ability to be intuitive, to recognize patterns, and to recognize design with emotional meaning as well as functionality. It forces you to *experiment* and seek out solutions without fear of failure. It blends the emotional and the analytical by emphasizing empathy to solve problems. It also enables you to better define your *go-to-market strategy* and effectively *brand* your company later in the game by clearly defining your value proposition.

As a practical approach to problem-solving, design thinking increases your chances of success by helping you optimize your potential to create a product that transforms lives.

PepsiCo's Chief Design Officer Mauro Porcini sums up the approach with this: "Design is more than the aesthetics and artifacts associated with products; it's a strategic function that focuses on what people want and need and dream of, then crafts experiences across the full brand ecosystem that are meaningful and relevant for customers."[53]

IV. Cheat Code Review

1. Effective problem-solving requires design thinking.
2. Design thinking, according to the International Design Foundation, is defined as a "non-linear, iterative process that teams use to understand users, challenge assumptions, redefine problems and create innovative solutions."

---

53 de Vries, "PepsiCo's Chief Design Officer on Creating an Organization Where Design Can Thrive," 2015.

3. The five nonlinear steps of design thinking are empathize, define, ideate, prototype, and test.
4. Iterative design is powerful because it identifies unmet needs, reduces risk, builds entrepreneurial skills, and redefines/refines your value proposition.

Chapter 5
Problem-Finding: Digging into Our Roots

Written by: Tiffany Yau, Aditya Desai, and Riley Gonta

"The important thing is not to stop questioning. Curiosity has its own reason for existing." — Albert Einstein, theoretical physicist

We live in an extremely unique time because every global crisis on this planet is a *human-generated problem.*

Ice caps are melting, certain animals are getting closer to extinction, and certain countries are becoming the world's dumping grounds.

Although we've entertained the idea of uprooting our entire civilization and relocating to Mars, deeply problematic social issues like discrimination remain the silent epidemic that limits 62 million girls from equitable opportunities to attend school while also depriving marginalized communities from obtaining equal pay and living opportunities.[54]

We live in a world of big human-generated problems that can really only be solved with *human-generated solutions.*

I. Don't Start with Problem-Solving

Life is all about problem-solving. Whether it's as big as solving pressing global existential problems to more trivial ones like forgetting your keys, letting your phone battery die, or only having one month left to get your grade up in calculus—AHH! —you are always solving problems.

All the problems in our everyday lives demand solutions, but a critical part of that problem-solving is often overlooked: problem-finding.

It's so easy to get excited about cool solutions and want to dive head-first into creating them. But there's a catch: you may end up solving the problem, but you won't get to the **root cause** of the problem.

---

54 The White House. "FACT SHEET: Let Girls Learn - A Comprehensive Investment in Adolescent Girls Education." 2016. https://www.usaid.gov/sites/default/files/documents/1869/USAID_LGL_FactSheet.pdf.

For instance, let's say you woke up later than you were hoping today because you stayed up really late last night to watch your favorite Netflix series, *Stranger Things*. We've all been there! It's easy to think that the real problem is you oversleeping or taking too much time to relax last night, when the root problem may be how you prioritize your time. Whether it is something as trivial as watching too much Netflix or solving a systemic social issue, it is important to dig deeper to get down to the root and solve from there.

It's important to remember that problems have their own **causes** and **effects**. It's your job to locate the ***root*** of these issues. Not only would it suck to work really hard and make a lot of progress on a solution only to realize you were solving the wrong problem but solving the root problems is the *key* to having a meaningful and prosperous impact! Deciding which problems, you want to focus on will be one of the most important decisions you make as an aspiring social entrepreneur.

Problem-solving begins with problem-finding.

In his TED Talk "Start with Why," Simon Sinek talks about our "what," "how," and "why." Sinek suggests that people don't care about *what* you do or *how* you do it, but they care about *why* you do it.[55] Creating good, implementable solutions depends on how well you know how to pick apart problems in a logical way. In this chapter, you'll discover that the problem you initially set out to solve will often not actually be the true root problem. On the surface, it's easy to define certain problems. But the purpose of this section is to

---

55 Sinek, "How Great Leaders Inspire Action," 2009.

help you dive much deeper so you can truly understand the causes and effects of the problem you're trying to solve.

II. Root Cause Analysis: Roof vs. Bucket

A great example to demonstrate the importance of understanding a problem's true causes and effects is what we like to call the *Roof-Bucket analogy*.

Imagine yourself in the comfort of your own home. It's a rainy afternoon. You sense the droplets of water weaving down your windows, and you're doing something relaxing like reading, watching TV, playing video games, or napping.

Suddenly, much to your dismay, a small droplet of water splashes onto your hand. Confused, you look up and see a splotch of water leaking through your ceiling.

This is a problem: Water is dripping through your ceiling from the rain. Every problem has implications. Because water is dripping from your ceiling, you can't focus on the activity at hand. You're asking yourself, "Where did the water come from and why is it now dripping through my ceiling?"

Problems prolonged over time "snowball" into larger consequences. Because water is dripping through the ceiling, your roof as a whole, the carpet underneath, and eventually the wooden floor are all at risk of getting wet and growing mold over time—that is, if no one does anything about it!

These potential consequences demand immediate solutions to the problem, to which there are many!

So, why is the water leaking through the ceiling? What's the root?

It's the rain. But rain can't be stopped unless you can master the rain dance in ten minutes (and even that is a dubious solution). Bill Burnett and Dave Evans, authors of *Designing Your Life,* would define this situation as a "**gravity problem**"—the effects of gravity are inevitable owing to the laws of physics.

***"If a problem is not actionable, then it's not a problem. It's a situation, a circumstance, a fact of life. It may be a drag (so to speak), but, like gravity, it's not a problem that can be solved." — Designing Your Life,* Bill Burnett and Dave Evans**

In the same way, stopping the rain is not actionable, so it can't be the *real* problem.

Good solutions must be *feasible* and *relevant,* meaning they will actually solve the cause/problem. The two most common solutions to this rain scenario we've received from our students are the following:

- *Use a bucket:* Use a bucket under the leak to catch the water
- *Fix the roof:* Fix the roof with the leak

Although both options relieve the problem in some capacity, these options solve different problems:

- *Bucket:* Prevents the water from dripping onto the carpet/wood floor
- *Roof:* The water can no longer seep through the ceiling

The most feasible problem will come to light when you ask yourself, "*Why* is the water leaking?"

Putting a bucket underneath the leak acts more like a band-aid solution than an actual fix to the root problem. It's a solution for the *effect*—often also known as a "**symptom**" in design thinking that we will cover more in a later section. You can think of effects and symptoms similarly as you would think about diagnosing a health issue. If you are sneezing at someone else's home, you can assume lots of different things: maybe you are allergic to their cat or the meal they served you, or maybe there is pollen blowing through their open window. You have a whole world of potential problems! However, your sneezing is not the problem; it is a *symptom* of something else, not a "sneezing disease."

Fixing the roof in our rainy day scenario is a solution for the *cause* of the leakage rather than a solution to the effect or symptom, like the bucket.

The roof vs. bucket problem is a bit more visually straightforward, so it might be harder to properly pinpoint the *root cause* of a real-world issue.

Root cause analysis (RCA) is a formal process of effective problem-solving that we can use to understand how to solve the root cause as opposed to the root effect.

Understanding this directly impacts your soon-to-be social venture because it you must have a deep understanding of the causes and effects of the problem you set out to solve.

Developing a deep understanding of the relationship between causes and effects will enhance your ability to define problems and, in return, create robust solutions.

III. Root Cause Analysis: In Action

Effective problem-solving begins with *problem-finding*. As mentioned, RCA is an effective way to do just that.

We've included an activity that will help you go through the process of RCA yourself for your own idea! You can also find a worksheet online (available for download) to help guide you through it.

Step 1: Identify a problem you care about in your local community.

Example: A lot of homeless people have mental health disorders in Philadelphia.

Step 2: Is the problem you defined really the root problem or is it a symptom? Ask yourself "why does this problem exist" three or more times to boil it down.

Example:

Problem statement: A lot of homeless people have mental health disorders in Philadelphia. Why?

Why 1: Homeless people feel lonely and isolated.

Why 2: Homeless people are stigmatized by society.

Why 3: Homeless people don't have the resources they need to lift themselves out of homelessness.

Root problem: Homeless people lack accessible mental health services in Philadelphia.

***Note: The real root problem could arguably be the fact that we need better ways to prevent people from becoming homeless. There is no "right" answer when it comes to defining which problem you want to solve. Ask yourself, is this a problem that I care about solving? Is there something I can feasibly do about it?*

Step 3: From what you wrote above, identify the following:

Who: *Who does this problem impact?*
Where: *Where exactly is the problem focused? Is it in your city? Your region? Your state? This should help you understand the scale of the problem you are addressing.*
Root cause: *What is the root problem exactly?*
Effects/Symptoms: *What are the effects/symptoms of this problem?*
For example:

- *Who: Homeless people*
- *Where: Philadelphia*
- *Root cause: Access to effective mental health resources*
- *Effects/Symptoms: isolation, loneliness, stigma, mental health problems*

Step 4: Reframe your problem statement in the following format:

Due to [root cause], [who] are experiencing [effect] in [where].

Example: Due to a lack of access to effective mental health resources, homeless people are experiencing isolation, loneliness, stigma, and mental health problems in Philadelphia.

IV. Case Study: The Importance of Problem-Finding

In these activities, you used RCA to dig deeper into the problems burdening your community.

In the coming sections, you will work step by step to build viable solutions to these problems, including one very important step: **validation**.

It's easy to conduct RCA from the outside looking in using observation and internet research. However, it is vital that these observations and research be tested. By conducting user interviews, described in a later section, you will test those assumptions by taking your proposed solution to those it could impact.

Maybe your solution is exactly what the world has been waiting for, or maybe you will find that it's time to revisit the drawing board.

Either way, validation is an essential step in the problem-finding process.

Here is a case study of an event seen all too often in the impact sector: spending a lot of time and resources to solve the wrong problem.

Case study: Hunger in Nicaragua

What's the Problem?

This example is based on a discussion in the research from *Competing Discourses on the Political Economy of Hunger* by Andria Timmer.[56]

On the West Coast of Nicaragua lies the city of Puerto Cabezas, a city like the rest of the coast, beautiful to the eye yet socially paralyzed by cyclical poverty. Many government programs, nongovernmental organizations, and health care organizations abroad were becoming particularly concerned with the malnutrition that plagued the youth of the West Coast.

After conducting research using digital databases and through the observations of foreign medical workers in the region, the researchers found that children were being fed unhealthy food at home, such as processed meals and soda.

With the goal of improving the nutrition of local children, the public, private, and nonprofit sector joined forces to develop education and feeding programs that

- educated mothers on health and nutrition in the household, and
- gave students a glass of milk during recess for cognitive and physical development.

Solving the Wrong Problem

Great, right?

Wrong.

---

56 Timmer, "Competing Discourses on the Political Economy of Hunger," 1–13.

Millions of dollars were spent to deploy these programs, but it turns out they were trying to solve the *wrong* problem.

After locals began rejecting the humanitarian services, they realized the problem was not a lack of education. Mothers already knew that Instant Noodles were worse for their children's health than fresh produce. The real problem was the lack of access to nutritious food.

"But how?" International organizations were confused. Fruit trees were plentiful around Puerto Cabezas and chickens roamed everywhere!

As it turned out, these goods were owned by large businesses and food corporations that shipped products to the east coast of Africa or abroad. Thus, to buy a mango that was grown on the trees of Puerto Cabeza, one would have to pay triple the price after it had been exported and reimported to their own economy. For similar reasons, the one glass per day program was not sustainable as mothers could not provide this nutrition while their children were at home. International players realized they had to solve nutrition accessibility, not education, and found themselves having to execute the proper RCA they skipped.

You just learned how to find problems—not any problem, but *the* problem—that cause a conflict to exist in the first place. Be sure to apply the process of RCA and problem-finding when you begin to determine the social problem you want to solve!

V. Cheat Code Recap

1. Effective problem-solving begins with effective problem-finding.
2. Problems have root causes and effects (or "symptoms").
3. Root cause analysis is a formal process of effective problem-solving in which we can understand how to solve the root cause rather than the "root effect."
4. Validation is an essential step in the problem-finding process to ensure you save yourself time and money by trying to avoid solving the wrong problem.

Chapter 6

Innovating & Designing Great Solutions

Written by: Tiffany Yau, Aditya Desai, and Riley Gonta

"One idea lights a thousand candles."—Ralph Waldo Emerson, American philosopher, essayist, and poet

I. What Makes a Good Solution?

So, you've created your problem statement? Great! You're on the right track to creating the best solution to a problem. In other words, it's time to *problem-solve*!

If you're excited about the big problem that you're going to tackle, we're excited with you! But wait—do you feel it? That small, lingering part of you that feels terribly uncertain. Yeah, we've felt it too.

We as human beings naturally have this problem with the concept of "big" things. When we see *big* problems, we want *big* solutions. And it's not that big solutions are necessarily bad! However, when we invest a lot of time and energy thinking about the size of these problems, we get stuck and lose sight of the big difference we could make by starting with small ideas. The size of the problems can be daunting and overwhelming, making us feel small and helpless.

In the shadow of the bigness of these problems, we forget that small actions and efforts add up. We get stuck in a state of "analysis paralysis"—but there's hope! The neat thing about human beings is our minds' capacity to solve problems despite big challenges.

Throwing it back to the Stone Age

Let's take, for example, the domestication of fire. Fire is and always has been a natural part of life on earth. Yet through mankind's adaptation, how to use fire was one of the earliest forms of innovation.

In other words, fire is a (literal) Stone Age technology. It's the ultimate technology that marked the beginning of our rise to the top of the food chain in spite of our scrawny (compared to those of our predators) physiques.

Fire symbolizes what makes us truly unique: the ability to tackle complex challenges with innovative, evolutionary solutions. The transformations of the use of power from then to now are many. What our ancestors used as a source of heat to keep them warm is the legacy of what we know as our modern heaters. What they used for roasting archaic creatures and nut crops we now use to enjoy fondue.

As you know, our use of fire evolved over time because we domesticated it! Fire demonstrates the amazing capacity of humankind for disruptive innovation and, more importantly, our timeless capacity to create solutions to solve big problems. But these big solutions, such as light bulbs and ovens, were not created overnight nor were they created by one person.

Fire was once only a way to create warmth, yet it has been built upon over generations of changemakers to become the disruptive technologies it is today. It was once one small idea, one small moment of time, yet it changed the course of history over hundreds of thousands of years. Whether the problem that demands to be solved is protection from a saber-toothed cat or climate change, the solution doesn't have to be big to make a difference—just like fire.

Impactful solutions come in all sorts of shapes and sizes, whether it's creating a torch of fire or recycling! When you recycle one bottle today, the impact might seem so small it's not worth undertaking. Yet if you recycle one bottle every day for the next year, the impact suddenly increases exponentially. Small-impact solutions can turn into bigger-impact solutions in the long run. Don't forget that!

"Good" Solutions Aren't Always the Same Size

By now, it's well-established that solutions will vary in size. However, what characterizes a *good* solution? Good solutions answer the following questions:

- Does it tackle the problem?

- Is it feasible?
- Is it scalable?
- Is it something that aligns with my values (think North Star)?

It maybe come as a surprise, but it's not about finding the right solution. Anything can be right. It's about finding what's right for *you*!

Our goal at this stage is not to get to the "perfect" or "right" solution. Our goal is to develop as many potential solutions as possible. Let's broaden our mindset! Be curious about all the interesting solutions you can come up with! And, who knows, maybe your "right" solution is hiding somewhere in that creative mix.

How do we do this? We achieve this through *ideation*.

II. How to Ideate

Ideation is a cool word, and what it means is even cooler! **Ideation** is the creative act of generating innovative ideas. Once you figure out an idea you are excited enough about, you can bring it to life through a process known as **prototyping**. Prototyping is the process of building an early sample, model, or release of a product for the purpose of testing a concept or process.

The prefix *prot-*, or *proto-*, comes from the Greek language and translates to "first in time" or "first formed."[57]

---

[57] *Meriam Webster*, s.v. "prototype (*n*)," accessed February 14, 2023, https://www.merriam-webster.com/dictionary/prototype

Entrepreneurship is all about trying things out for the first time. It's a process of *constant* iteration. In other words, ideation isn't a one-time thing that you do at the start of your idea; it's a process that you'll return to over and over again once you've validated or implemented a solution.

Through ideation, you'll overcome your startup's top challenges. After all, you don't overcome challenges by immediately finding a perfect solution; you overcome them when you keep an open mind and make yourself available to as many solutions as possible. Ideation is all about producing lots of ideas. We value *quantity* over quality in ideation.

"All you need is the possibility that one might be good. You don't know too much about a specific solution until you actually pursue it and start it, so create all the options you can." — Bill & Dave, authors of *Design Your Life*

How Do You Start?

Stage 1: Write Your Problem Statement

It's time to put your idea on paper! Start by writing down your problem statement that you created in Chapter 5. You can also use the downloadable worksheet from our website.

Example: Philadelphia's homeless population lacks proper access to mental health resources.

Stage 2: Reframe

This next step is a very simple and subtle one: reframe your problem statement ever so slightly to make it into a question, starting with the words, "How might we…"

Using "How might we" at the beginning of your problem statement creates a sense of optimism about solving the problem you are hoping to tackle. It also gets your mind thinking about how to be more actionable about the problem!

Example: How might we improve access to mental health services for homeless people in Philadelphia?

Step 3: Brainstorm

Write down as many jottings (brief informal notes) for any ideas you have that solve the problem you've defined. Aim to note at least ten things! Here, you're going for quantity over quality.

This step is about *brainstorming*! When you brainstorm, you shouldn't be worrying too much about the ideas themselves. That'll come. In this part of the process, you're giving yourself as many options as possible.

It is most effective when your jottings are five words max. Don't erase or delete any ideas

How might we improve access to mental health services for homeless people in Philadelphia?

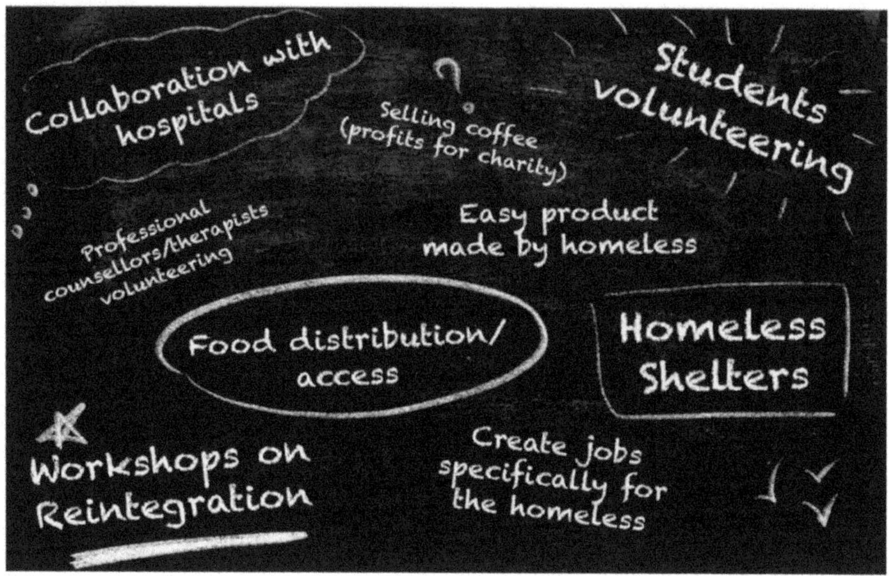

Step 4: Filter

Great! You might not know it, but you just engaged in a design thinking process called *divergence*! Tim Brown, executive chairman of Ideo and author of *Change by Design*, references this as **divergent thinking**.[58] You did this by creating as many different choices to choose from as possible. Now, it's time to *converge* (**convergent thinking**) and narrow down your options!

---

58 Brown, *Change by Design*, 2009.

Ask yourself, "Which of these notes stirs up the most compassion and/or excitement? Which seems doable?"For instance, perhaps you picked the following:

- Students volunteering
- Workshops on reintegration
- Opportunities for the homeless population to create easy-to-make products
- Homeless shelters
- Collaboration with hospitals

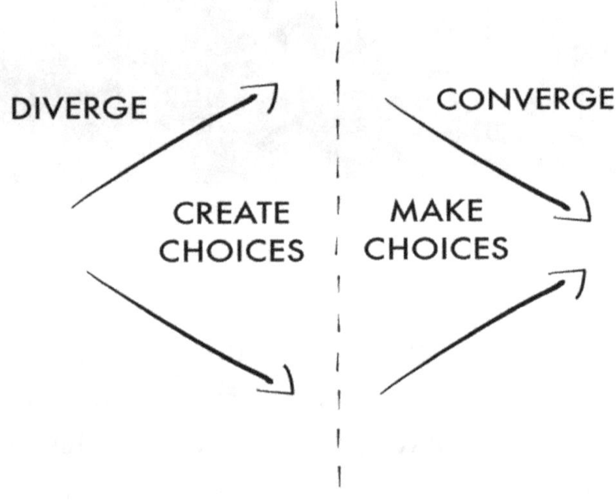

Step 5: Daydream

Daydream? Yes, you heard right! Now that you have a few options that excite you, it's time to daydream. We want to flesh these ideas out by letting your imagination run wild!

We wouldn't have planes if the Wright brothers hadn't let their imagination run (fly?) wild when they were thinking about defying gravity. Now *that's* a crazy idea! Can you imagine a world without planes? Now is the time to get creative! Get imaginative and think of any scenarios where your idea could work. Here are some examples if you need some inspiration:

Scenario 1: Create a service where university students could volunteer to lead professional development workshops at homeless shelters.

Scenario 2: Create a service where clinicians could volunteer during off-hours to meet with homeless people at shelters.

Scenario 3: Create a product or service where a percentage of the profits go to helping homeless shelters access mental health resources.

Step 6: Pick a Solution

There are lots of exciting and fun solutions you decide to pursue, but frankly there is not enough time or energy to be able to pursue everything at once. Think very intentionally about what your solution should be.

Step 7: Reframe it into a Value Proposition

Whichever idea choose to run with, you need to know how to reframe your solution into a value proposition. A **value proposition** is a single statement that explains *why* your customers should come to you over another company. It is exactly what it sounds like. What specific *value* is your social enterprise offering to them?

We create value when we *solve* problems. A value proposition should be a statement that ties together your problem statement, which you learned how to develop in the last chapter.

For example, the problem statement from the last chapter was as follows:

Due to lack of access to effective mental health resources, homeless people *are experiencing* isolation, loneliness, stigma, and mental health problems *in* Philadelphia.

(Remember, this follows the problem statement format of ***Due to [root cause], [who] are experiencing [effect] in [where].)***

Let's say you chose Scenario 1 as a solution. Your value proposition would be something along the lines of the following:

"For *homeless people* who are experiencing *isolation, loneliness, stigma, and mental health problems* in *Philadelphia*, [Your Company] *provides mental health resources* through *its service where university students volunteer to lead professional development workshops at homeless shelters."*

The format for a value proposition is as follows:

For [who] are [effect/problem] in [where], [Your Company] provides [rephrased root cause of the problem] through [solution].

With this format, you can concisely tie your problem statement together with your solution and demonstrate that you are addressing the root cause of that problem.

If you chose the other scenarios, your value propositions might look something like this:

- Scenario 2: "For *homeless people* who are experiencing *isolation, loneliness, stigma, and mental health problems* in *Philadelphia,* [Your Company] *provides mental health resources* through *its service where clinicians could volunteer during off-hours to meet with homeless people at shelters.*
- Or Scenario 3: "For *homeless people* who are experiencing *isolation, loneliness, stigma, and mental health problems* in *Philadelphia,* [Your Company] *provides mental health resources* through its product or service where a percentage of the profits go to helping homeless shelters access mental health resources.

Step 8: Map out the Customer Journey (recommended time: 20 minutes)

Now, it's time to map out the **customer journey**! This is your chance to imagine your customer's path, step by step, through your product or service. How would they use it?

Mapping out your customer journey can help you:

- **Visualize** the logical order of what needs to happen in order for you to deliver your product/service
- **Demonstrate** how your beneficiaries are interacting with your business
- **Identify** gaps you need to address

For practice, let's apply the customer journey framework to Scenario 1. Below are some examples of the steps that might be involved in the customer journey:

- University students see an opportunity to volunteer
- University students sign up
- Students are grouped into teams to determine what kind of workshop they want to lead
- Students deliver the workshop at a homeless shelter
- Homeless people are empowered to take steps to develop their professional skills

Many questions will unfold as you map out the customer journey. With the example of our first scenario, this might include questions like:

- Where will the students see the opportunity to volunteer?
- How will you get to the students?
- How will they sign up to volunteer?
- How do you determine who is an acceptable volunteer?

- How will you group the students and determine the kinds of workshops to lead?
- Will this be a one-time workshop or will there be follow-up workshops?
- Will the students create the content or will you?
- How will you hold people at the shelter accountable?
- How will you get in touch with the shelter?

Don't get too caught up on the specific details or questions that pop up. It's important that you first get down the basic steps of the customer journey. You will flesh out the rest later!

Now, congratulations! You're on your way to gaining a general sense of the product or service you plan to offer in addition to areas you need to think about and work on.

Lots of questions will pop up, but don't worry, we're here to guide you through it all!

III. SCAMPER

It's time to SCAMPER. And we don't mean scampering like a squirrel! We mean the amazing design thinking methodology created by Alex Fackney Osborne in 1953 and enhanced by Bob Eberle in 1971.[59]

This tactic is still relevant today and has helped the world's top organizations solve their most pressing problems.

---

59 Serrat, *The SCAMPER Technique*, 2009.

SCAMPER is a useful acronym that maps out different types of thinking techniques you can use to help you work through the potential solutions you've gathered.

Innovators are free to choose one or all seven techniques for their design thinking needs. Think outside of the box! SCAMPER stands for the following:

Substitute

Combine

Adapt

Modify

Put to another use

Eliminate

Reverse

Let's flesh the acronym out:

Substitute

- What materials or resources can you substitute or swap to improve the product?
- What other product or process could you use?
- What rules could you substitute?
- Can you use this product somewhere else, or as a substitute for something else?

- What will happen if you change your feelings or attitude toward this product?

Combine

- What would happen if you combined this product with another to create something new?
- What if you combine purposes or objectives?
- What could you combine to maximize the uses of this product?
- How could you combine talent and resources to create a new approach to this product?

Adapt

- How could you adapt or readjust this product to serve another purpose or use?
- What else is the product like?
- Who or what could you emulate to adapt this product?
- What other context could you put your product into?
- What other products or ideas could you use for inspiration?

Modify

- How could you change the shape, look, or feel of your product?
- What could you add to modify this product?
- What could you emphasize or highlight to create more value?
- What element of this product could you strengthen to create something new?

Put to Another Use

- Can you use this product somewhere else, perhaps in another industry?
- Who else could use this product?
- How would this product behave differently in another setting?
- Could you recycle the waste from this product to make something new?

Eliminate

- How could you streamline or simplify this product?
- What features, parts, or rules could you eliminate?
- What could you understate or tone down?
- How could you make it smaller, faster, lighter, or more fun?
- What would happen if you took away part of this product? What would you have in its place?

Reverse

- What would happen if you reversed this process or sequenced things differently?
- What if you try to do the exact opposite of what you're trying to do now?
- What components could you substitute to change the order of this product?
- What roles could you reverse or swap?

- How could you reorganize this product?

Use SCAMPER whenever you need a fresh jolt of inspiration.

Now that you are familiar with design thinking as a concept and not just a buzzword, try applying it! Try out the worksheet on our website. It will ask you to recall the five steps of design thinking and apply them to the problem you are interested in solving. Whether or not you are able to directly empathize or test with users, try your best to conduct a virtual design thinking sprint.

IV. Cheat Code Review

1. Good solutions tackle the problem, are feasible, scalable, and aligned with our values.
2. Ideation is the creative act of generating innovative ideas. Quantity > Quality
3. A value proposition is a single statement that explains why your customers would go to you over another.
4. SCAMPER is an effective problem-solving/ideation method.

Chapter 7
Prototyping

Written by: Tiffany Yau and Erin Flannery

"I do not think there is any thrill that can go through the human heart like that felt by the inventor as he sees some creation of the brain unfolding to success." —Nikola Tesla, Serbian-American inventor

I. What is Prototyping?

Let's dive a bit into prototyping! In previous chapters, you have explored the first few stages of design thinking: defining the problem and ideating solutions. By choosing one or a combination of solutions you now have an idea of what to prototype or create.

A **prototype** is a *preliminary* model for a venture, machine, or invention. It is an important step because it allows you to *troubleshoot* and build in a *low-stakes* situation before you fully scale a product or service to market.

Think of architects. Before they go ahead and build a whole building with construction companies and millions of dollars worth of materials, they build tiny models of the buildings they hope to build using small pieces of wood. Before even making tiny models, architects have to draw the building plan out on paper and make sure everything is in proportion. And they probably had to draw and erase, draw and erase again, and maybe even throw out a few initial designs and start all over again—and repeat!

Just like an architect, you will go through a lot of prototypes before you get to a main solution. You may have thousands of prototypes before you get to market. Imagine making 1,000 versions of a product that weren't manufactured properly! Prototyping allows you to get out all of the kinks and design flaws of your idea. The beauty of prototyping is that there are no rules and you can build or sketch them out with anything. Prototyping makes you think deeper about your original solution so that you can make it your best work.

This is a rollercoaster of a phase. You very well might find a peak solution that fails. You will *have* to fail (or fall—*rollercoaster,* remember?) fast and try harder.

Prototyping Basics

When prototyping, it is important to recall the concept of the **lean startup**. When you utilize the lean startup methodology, you can flush out design flaws rapidly through the prototyping and innovation phases to see if a product will be viable enough to make it to market. Lean startups are open to criticism, change, and innovation. Their agile nature is what makes them often successful.

We prototype because it allows us to visualize and interact with an idea (just like our architect friends with their blueprints and tiny models). We continue to improve prototypes through iteration, or repetition, of the process.

Phew! That was a lot. Here are some key takeaways to remember:

1. *Prototypes will fail:* If you bring your first prototype to market, it will surely not be your best work. This is why it's important to continue to get feedback and remodel what you're building.
2. *Prototypes help us troubleshoot:* Prototypes are inexpensive generations that bolster your ideas. They allow you to interact with and visualize your ideas.

Case Study: Instagram and Its Early Prototypes

In order for you to get a better sense of the world of prototyping, let's take a look at Instagram and its journey as a company.[60] Instagram was acquired by Facebook in 2012, but the founders went through a lot of prototyping practice in the three years before this acquisition.

---

60 Blystone, "The Story of Instagram: The Rise of the # 1 Photo-Sharing App (FB)," 2022.

The journey started in 2009, when Kevin Systrom, a 27-year-old Stanford graduate working at Nextstop, had an idea for a web app, "Burbn," to share check-ins, plans, and photos of fine whiskey and bourbon. While time-sharing and plan-sharing apps were common at this time, the photo-sharing feature of Burbn was unique.

Systrom had previously worked at Google and Odeo (a company that later evolved into Twitter). He gained recognition from receiving venture capital investments in Silicon Valley to further his entrepreneurial ventures. He built a low-resolution version of the app to show some venture capitalists the general idea of what he was trying to make with Burbn. This was his prototype—a bare skeleton of the coded versions of some of the check-in, posting, and photo-sharing features the app would support. (Remember, prototypes just need to convey the gist of your idea!)

The app took a pivot after venture capitalists got on board. Partnering with Mike Krieger, an engineer and software designer, the two founders refocused the app as a photo-sharing platform instead.

Then, another pivot happened when the pair reevaluated the field of social media at that time. They stripped Burbn down to *just* the photo-sharing technology and added in liking and commenting functions.

The prototypes informed them that they needed to pivot. **Pivoting** is an important part of entrepreneurship. It is to switch gears or mechanisms so that you can reach your end goals. It's pretty common for an idea to turn out less than its creator hoped, but sometimes all it takes for success is shifting to another point of view.

They then renamed the app: Instagram. After eight weeks of fine-tuning a high-resolution prototype, they gave it to their friends to try it out in exchange for feedback. After getting feedback and correcting some errors in the software, Instagram was launched.

Throughout the years, Instagram has continued introducing new features and versions of their app as social media changes.

Now that you have seen some examples of how other entrepreneurs in the field built and tested their prototypes, how might you build your prototype?

The Importance of Empathy in Prototyping

When you get excited about a venture or product and begin to build within your own vision, you risk missing out on an important piece of the puzzle. You can't afford to overlook the preferences of your users and customers. Remember, this is about *human*-centered design. When you interviewed potential stakeholders and customers early on in this process, it was to learn what those potential customers or users want so that you can design a product suitable for them—leverage that knowledge.

Jot down everything you know about the problem and your proposed solution. You have empathy, so remember to use it. What have you learned from your observations and interviews? What are the stakeholders' needs or wants? You need to prototype and build for *them*, not for yourself.

It is important not only to engage in empathy as you plan but also to be agile. If you can focus on quick deliverables and consumer feedback, you will do well for yourself. Customers expect timely and constant deliverables in this day and age.

This is quite a process, so if at this point your vision has shifted and your idea has taken another form, it will be beneficial to go back to the drawing board and conduct some more user interviews (which we will cover in the next chapter) to get the best vision for your design. Additionally, you will want to continue communicating with your stakeholders throughout the design process. Aside from empathy, these individuals will be helpful for feedback on your prototype.

II. Low-Resolution & High-Resolution Prototyping

Building a low-resolution prototype

There are so many different ways to prototype, but for our purposes, let's focus on two broad fields of prototyping: **low-resolution** and **high-resolution prototyping**.

Beginning with the low-resolution variety, this will be the type of prototype you use to tackle your first product iteration. This is your first prototype, a sketch of sorts. Whether it's a physical product or service, the object of this step in this process is to sketch out or **storyboard** your venture in detail. **Storyboarding** is the process of detailing each step of the user and customer journey .

When storyboarding, it is encouraged that you make something like a comic strip – a series of boxes that represent a sequence of events to capture all of the important details.

Remember Instagram's low-resolution prototype was Burbn, which was completely different from the end result! Low-resolution prototyping will allow you to work through bumps in the road in a cost-effective and creative way.

If you need help getting started, visit our website for a downloadable worksheet that will guide you through storyboarding. If you are feeling adventurous, grab a stack of sticky notes, popsicle sticks, pens, or other household/classroom items to make a 3D version of your low-resolution prototype.

When you are finished with your low-resolution prototype, find a few people to test your work. You can present your prototype to them. Ask for feedback and record it. This feedback is the material you need to build your next iteration.

Feedback and Iterations

Once you create your prototype, it is important that you show it to people who can give you helpful feedback.

Here are some ideas for how you can think about conducting your feedback:

- Rather than explaining the prototype first, let users experience the product.
- As your users test the prototype you created, you can seek feedback on how to improve their solution and take that feedback to continue to prototype.

- If possible, let your users compare multiple prototypes. This will help you form a concrete understanding of where your design needs improvement.

Receiving feedback can be fun but also challenging. A helpful way to optimize your feedback collection process is to organize it into three main categories: 1) I like, 2) I wish, and 3) I wonder. Doing this can be helpful because it allows you to identify what people like about your product ("I like"), problems ("I wish"), and ideas easy or hard to implement ("I wonder").

Take a moment to copy this chart (or use the downloadable version on our website) to organize the feedback your prototype receives.

"I Like"	"I Wish"	"I Wonder"

Fail Fast, Fix Faster!

Point of view: you just finished some tests on your low-resolution prototype and the feedback wasn't what you expected. IT'S OKAY!!

When you are prototyping, you will FAIL. We know, it's a huge bummer, but this is totally normal. Design thinking certainly keeps you humble. It is inevitable that you will come across faults in your action plan or will encounter engineering issues. As you go through prototype iterations, remember that failure and discovery are both part of the journey. Think of this saying every time your prototyping journey is falling flat:

Fail fast, fail forward, fail early, fail often.

This is a reminder to keep moving forward through failure. If you fail often and early in your prototyping journey, you are learning what *not* to do and developing an understanding of how you can fix the problems in your process. The whole point of human-centered design is the learning experience, and feedback from others is an essential part of this experience.

High-Resolution Prototyping

Once you have finished your first phase of prototyping, you are ready to move forward to a high-resolution prototype. This will be a more refined version in the medium of delivery and will look closer to what you want your product/project to look like in real life. High-resolution prototyping requires *major* attention to detail.

Ask yourself these questions:

- What have you learned in previous testing?
- What do people like?

- What do you want to refine?

High-resolution prototyping is a lengthier process. You want your medium of delivery to be the actual version you plan to use/market. We call this version of the product the **minimum viable product (MVP)**. The goal of high-resolution prototyping is to end up with an MVP.

Remember, Instagram produced a high-resolution prototype to send out for beta testing. Consumers came through with feedback, and after incorporating it, Instagram's MVP was launched.

Remember to ask yourself reflective questions throughout the process. Think of your interviewees and what they said would work for them. Design composite characters to walk through your build. Then move on to testing again!

When building your high-resolution prototype, take a few days (at least) to do so. This could be a Google Site with a thought-out business plan or just a better mockup of your original model project. Prototypes come in many different formats.

Make sure you get yourself into a great headspace before you prototype: Do something you enjoy. Go for a walk or dance around your room for a little. Work in a setting that helps you focus! Set yourself up for success. Set realistic goals and clear expectations. Good luck!

Here's a list to review what makes for effective prototyping:

1. **Embrace empathy** and write down key takeaways from your interviews/research that are necessary for your solution.

2. **Build a low-resolution prototype** or storyboard to get all the kinks and details worked out.
3. **Get feedback** on this low-resolution version by conducting tests.
4. **Build a high-resolution prototype** that resembles your desired end result.
5. **Conduct tests and gain more feedback** for your next model.
6. **Create your MVP.** This version should be your best prototype or something that you would send to market.
7. **Conduct beta testing with your MVP** and get feedback from users and make final tweaks to your prototype.
8. **Launch your idea**!
9. **Continue to iterate and test** after you have launched your product—your work is never finished!

If you've noticed, these steps basically follow the pattern of listening, building, getting feedback, and listening more, building again, and repeating. Prototyping is the part of entrepreneurship and innovation that makes your idea actually begin to come to life! If you've made it this far, congratulations!

In the next chapter, we will go more in-depth to understand what testing and iterating your product really entails.

III. Cheat Code Recap

1. Prototyping is an iterative process that allows you to troubleshoot and build in a low-stakes situation before you fully scale a product or service to market.
2. Prototypes will fail and help us troubleshoot and pivot.
3. Empathy is important in prototyping because we are creating solutions that meet the needs of people. Effective prototyping involves listening, building, getting feedback, and listening more, and building again.

Chapter 8
Testing for Product-Market Fit

Written by: Tiffany Yau, Aditya Desai, Emma Gould

"Don't find customers for your products, find products for your customers." – Seth Godin, American entrepreneur, author, and public speaker

When creating a business, you are identifying a *specific* area that you believe needs improvement in that particular moment but which lacks a proper solution.

You are ultimately addressing a specific need that you believe is significant in the world with a solution that is not yet available. In other words, you are addressing a specific need in *the market*.

But *how* do you know others will agree that that need must be addressed or that your creation will provide that resolution? Or...

How will you know how to target those people?

How do you know the different specific situations they will use what you have to offer?

How do you understand people's needs?

That's a lot of *how*'s, huh? Don't worry, there is a simple solution: feedback. Feedback is arguably your most powerful tool. Always search for feedback on your product or service. It will help you identify what you're doing right, what you're doing wrong, and ways to improve it. To elicit good feedback, you must become an expert in product-market fit and testing assumptions!

I. Product-Market Fit

Product-market fit is when a product generates high demand from the market because it addresses a specific customer need within that market. In other words, it is how your product *fits* the demands of the market. When customers like your product and want to use and buy it, the product will be very successful on the market—this is product-market fit!

To determine whether your solution has product-market fit, you first have to understand your customers.

Defining Your Customer: Customer Profiling and Segmentation

The process of defining your customer in detail is known as **customer profiling**.

Details in customer profiling can be anything. Maybe they are typically between 18 and 30 years old. Perhaps your customers are mostly women, and maybe they typically spend more money on self-care. Maybe they spend their free time on TikTok and Twitter rather than other platforms. The possibilities are endless!

There are a variety of ways to define and segment your customers, including the following:

- **By demographic:** What is their gender? Age? Education level? Ethnicity? Nationality? Income level? Occupation?
- **By geography:** Where in the country do they live? Are they in the city? Where do they go for fun?
- **By behavior:** What do they tend to buy and how frequently? What do they typically look for in products? What do they like? How does their lifestyle influence their behavior and interests?
- **By values:** How do they live? What do they value? What do they do for fun?
- **By social media:** Where do they linger online? Why do they use certain platforms over others?

Knowing how to create customer profiles is so important. It can help you understand how to cater to their needs and market to them in a way that makes it compelling for them to buy into your product or service.

Beyond that, these profiles can be a helpful tool to help you rally partners, collaborators, and potential funders because you're able to define who you're serving. For instance, imagine that you're pitching a product to provide healthy school lunches to kids:

Meet Sydney. Sydney is nine years old and lives in the suburbs with two busy working parents who don't have the time to make her lunch every day. As a result, her only options are to eat school food, which she still barely touches, or to visit the vending machines for junk food. After surveying 50 kids across Pleansanton, I found that 79% of students face this same problem.

Or imagine you're pitching a pet-sitting service that employs people who are looking for passive income:

Meet Mike. Mike just graduated from college and has three months before he starts his first job out of school. He can't afford to travel anywhere and is trying to save up and find something easy and fun to do during his in-between time. Mike follows lots of dog TikToks and Instagram reels, and he often takes care of his neighbors' pets when they are out of town. After distributing a survey to 100 recent college grads, he noted that 68% of them face the same issue of wanting to find some form of passive income.

When you can personify those traits and show your audience that your customer is an actual person with real needs, you're able to demonstrate that you are solving a real-world problem (backed by your own research!) that demands a solution.

The question is, does your product or service fit the greater needs of others in the market you're pursuing? Do you have product-market fit?

II. Assumptions

The fact is, we can't *really* know if we have product-market fit. It's hard to know if your future customers—not counting your mom and best friend—will actually like and buy what you plan on selling if you aren't already selling! The only thing you're left to do is *assume*.

Within the scope of design thinking, an **assumption** is a statement that you presume to be true without concrete evidence to support it. In the business world but particularly in entrepreneurship, assumptions are used to allow companies to plan and make decisions despite inevitable uncertainty.

You create these statements knowing that they must be true for your product or service to be successful. You can think of an assumption as being like a hypothesis (remember the scientific method you learned in school?).

For instance, for Airbnb to be successful, guests have to be comfortable staying at a stranger's apartment and hosts have to be comfortable with strangers at their home.

For Uber to be successful, there must be drivers who will willingly offer car service in return for pay and passengers who wish to use a quick and convenient alternative form of transportation to get to their destinations.

Just like scientists do with hypotheses, you must *always* test your assumptions. If assumptions are things that *must* be true for your social enterprise to succeed, it is vital that you test and validate them. Thankfully, the testing and validation stage of design thinking can happen simultaneously with the empathy stage as well—after all, design thinking is a nonlinear process!

What are some assumptions that your social enterprise needs to address? Feel free to download the worksheet for this exercise from our website.

Testing our assumptions

Now that you know what assumptions are, you may be wondering, "How do we determine whether our assumptions are true?"

The answer is to test it by conducting your own experiments!

Think like a scientist!

Entrepreneurship is more similar to the scientific process than you might think, as it follows its own kind of scientific method. In any science experiment, there are a few essential first steps:

- **Make an observation** about the problem.
- **Research** the topic area more deeply.
- **Create a hypothesis,** which is a tentative, testable answer to a scientific question. It is tentative because the true answer is still unknown, and it is testable because you must be able to determine whether the hypothesis is right.

- **Test the hypothesis.** Is your hypothesis true or false?
- **Analyze** the reasons why your hypothesis was proven true or false.
- **Draw conclusions** to refine the hypothesis and plan next steps.

Let's say you are in a lab and want to answer the following question: does fertilizer make a plant grow bigger?

Before conducting the experiment, you create your hypothesis, "Plants need many types of nutrients in order to grow. Fertilizer adds those nutrients to the soil, allowing plants to grow more."

Therefore, based on your hypothesis, you predict that if you add fertilizer to the soil of some tomato seedlings but not others, the seedlings that got the fertilizer will grow taller and have more leaves than the non-fertilized seedlings.

With this prediction, you can test your hypothesis by running the experiment and seeing whether the results support or fail to support your hypothesis.

So far, you should have *already* defined your problem and made your own observations from your past experiences. On top of that, you've already formed your own "hypothesis" on what must happen in order for your experiment to run smoothly. Now, it's time to get some feedback to test your hypothesis.

The results of the feedback you seek will leave you with three main options: to *persevere, pivot, or perish.*

- **Persevere**: If the tests and feedback **confirm** your assumptions, you can continue on the current path!
- **Pivot**: If the tests and feedback **reject** or **confirm** your assumptions, but some points of feedback suggest they might be more successful with **changing direction**, you can pivot to a different path. Pivoting means keeping some parts of your business and changing others, based on the feedback you received.
- **Perish**: If the tests and feedback **reject** your assumptions and there is **no place to pivot**, you might consider abandoning the new business.

Gaining direct feedback from your target customers is the key to knowing what direction to go in when developing and launching a successful product. So, *how* can embracing the customer discovery process help set you up for success as an entrepreneur?

It allows entrepreneurs to understand the customers' desires.

It minimizes the amount of time, money, and effort spent on an idea that is not valuable to customers.

It provides proof of a product-market fit.

Validating assumptions at the idea stage

If you are at the **idea stage**, potentially without a product or service ready to sell, your goal is to *understand*.

You need to *really* understand your user's perceptions, past experiences, and various factors of their everyday lives that contribute to their interaction with the problem you are solving. On the flip side, if you're past the idea stage and you have created your prototype and are seeking ways to improve it, your goal is *still* to understand.

Learning NEVER stops! You will continue to validate assumptions of all sorts even when you are running your social enterprise. You should always be learning about your customer because you should always be testing and validating different assumptions! Thinking back to our five steps of design thinking, you must *always* be in "empathize" mode.

For instance, if you were to reorganize the layout of your large retail store, you may survey customers on their way out to find out whether they found the new organization easier to navigate, resulting in a more positive shopping experience.

If you were to update the user software of your mobile app, you may analyze new customer reviews to determine whether the update was positively received and determine new directions for product development.

As entrepreneurs, it is essential that we understand the needs and wants of our customers before we put a new product on the market. The biggest risk entrepreneurs face is producing a product that customers do not want. Many entrepreneurs fail because they waste resources and time creating a product before truly understanding their market and customers.

Google Glass is a good example.

Google Glass is a wearable device that looks like a pair of glasses but displays information directly in front of the user's eyes, like something you would see in sci-fi movies, like Tony Stark's glasses in *Iron Man*!

Now, this product may *sound* very cool, but this innovative product failed quickly! Why? It failed because the creators did not understand their users' desires and did not clearly define what problem they were trying to solve. Instead, they just *assumed* it would sell itself. Some creators may luck out when using a process built on untested assumptions, but it's more likely that this way of thinking will lead to failure.

So, how do you prevent this from happening to you? After all, you can't read minds! This is why customer profiling (also called **customer discovery**) is critical when developing a new product or startup. Customer discovery is the process of defining exactly who your customer is and what they care about in addition to validating any assumptions you might have about your customers.

Earlier, you defined an *idea* of who your ideal customer might be. Now, it's time to put that idea to the test and see if it's actually true. Time to test your assumptions!

User Interviews

We validate assumptions so we can create a great **user experience**. This includes everything you do for your business from branding to design to usability to function. To create a great user experience, it is important to understand how to solicit feedback from users to understand what they actually want. This is where user interviews come in.

User interviews are typically conducted before you have a design to inform assumptions, during the contextual understanding phase, and at the end of your product/service uses. Keep in mind that you can validate your assumptions at any time (so you can have user interviews at any time)!

User interviews are important to conduct because they help you understand whether your product will be successful based on how your target market perceives it. Successful user interviews will give you insight into knowing what your users want, as well as what they like about your offering and what they don't like about it. With this knowledge, you can figure out which direction to take your enterprise. Remember, people won't buy something they don't need or want. To make a product successful, you must cater to the customer needs with evidence-based decisions!

While they describe their problems to you, your users might even explain how they created their own solutions. With this, you can gain a better understanding of how you can add value to their lives.

But what about all of the potential competitors?

User interviews can actually help with those. By providing feedback, users are likely to reference other products or services. These references can help you understand how and what they think of your competitors—and specific components of your product that you can improve on to gain a competitive advantage.

We know you're eager to get out there and hop on those interviews, but there's still one more core benefit to conducting these interviews! With interaction between business owners and potential customers, you are allowing people with external perspectives to participate in decision-making within your business.

As a result, they will feel like they are part of the decision-making process and can be converted into customers when you launch. Oftentimes, your first customers are those with whom you cultivated strong relationships.

How to conduct your user interviews

Get your toolkit ready—it's time to learn how to conduct a successful user interview.

Set a goal. What does a successful interview look like to you? What do you hope to walk away with? Define a specific, concise, and concrete goal. It should be more than to just learn about your customers!

Make the user feel comfortable. Reach out ahead of time, show empathy, find a convenient location, start with easier questions, and simply wait for the user to complete his/her thoughts!

Ask specific questions. Don't ask either closed-ended questions that only elicit "yes" and "no" answers or leading questions that prime the user by suggesting a response. Remember a user interview, or usability tests, are not any old interview. These interviews are opportunities to get the most direct insight from potential customers. These interviews allow you to answer all of the following:

- Why is your design easy or difficult to use?
- Why would people want to use your design?

- When would people see themselves wanting to use your design?

Jot down as many questions you can think of that you would ask during a user interview.

User interviews and Validation

Let's return to the concept of validation. (We take it very seriously around here, stay with us!) User interviews could be considered the pinnacle of validation—they're a straightforward way to test whether future customers would be interested in your product and how they might benefit from it.

Assumptions, assumptions, assumptions. It's the name of the game.

For every assumption you make, such as "my product will be most popular with middle-school students," you need to back it up with evidence. The ability of an entrepreneur to gather real data from user interviews to validate—or upend—their assumptions will prevent overinvestment and commitment to one idea.

What are some assumptions you have made for your social enterprise? How do you plan to *validate* those assumptions, proving them right or wrong?

Try out our online worksheet if you need help identifying and testing out assumptions.

More Validation and User Interviews Tips

Keep in mind that user interviews don't always have to be conducted with actual users. If this is your case and you've found it challenging to get precise market research because you're still not 100% sure about who your users might be, you should start by reaching out to existing entrepreneurs in the same industry or segment. How can you validate your idea if you don't know who to target?

Also, refrain from conducting informal "user interviews" with your friends and family. Your friends may be genuinely interested, but their opinions shouldn't be taken as true validation. They may just be telling you what you want to hear! Instead, you'll need to target more objective people for your interviews.

If your social enterprise is a bit further down the road, testing your assumptions may look a little different, including putting up a launch page online for your product or service and seeing how people are signing up by analyzing your web traffic.

A/B Testing

A/B testing is the process of comparing two or more variations of something and statistically comparing which variation performs better. When we apply this to the design thinking framework, it can be incredibly useful!

A/B testing allows you to isolate the elements of your product, service, or marketing strategy you want to get feedback on to understand what works in your business and what doesn't. Successful A/B testing produces real quantitative data and allows you to accurately test your assumptions. For instance, you can test which web page on your website is more attractive based on its click rate or conversion/sign-up rate metrics. Another example is to experiment with the time you send out marketing emails to your customers.

For instance, you can send the same exact email out at 9 a.m. and at 12 p.m. to see which performs better. With user interview questions like "what does your daily routine look like?" or "what time do you usually check your personal emails or texts?" you can obtain information that informs your execution strategy.

For example, let's say that your customers are working adults. They may be likely to read their emails around lunchtime because they are too busy in the morning with school drop-off and only have time to look at personal emails during their lunch break. Or if your customers are teenagers, you might find that the ideal time to engage with them is after school hours. You might find that teens with no extracurricular activities look at their personal emails or texts earlier than those who are busy with after school athletic or academic extracurricular activities. Based on the feedback you receive, you can continue to test to determine the best way to cater your product, service, or marketing strategy to your customers.

After you've performed enough research and assumption-validation to know who your ideal customers are exactly, you can consolidate your findings and fully define your customer based on what you learned. Once you do so, you will be able to build out the rest of your business model!

Case Study: Rent The Runway

To bring it all together, let's look at the example of Rent the Runway. Rent the Runway is an online platform that allows customers to rent, subscribe, or buy dresses. Co-founders Jennifer Hyman (Jenn) and

Jennifer Fleiss (Jenny) used the hypothesis-driven approach to help turn their vision into a successful company!

Hypothesis- Driven Entrepreneurship	
Steps	Example: Rent the Runway
Empathizing	Jenn and Jenny identified their root problem—buying fancy dresses can be very expensive.
Defining a problem	Jenn and Jenny discovered that women empathized with the root problem. What if there were a way to rent designer dresses instead of buying them?
Ideating	They had an idea: an online service customers could use to rent designer dresses at a lower price.
Testing: Defining assumptions	They tested many different hypotheses/ assumptions to find out if their idea would actually work: - Will women want to buy dresses without trying them on? - Will women want to wear previously worn dresses? - Will women like the idea of renting a dress?

Prototyping & Testing	Rent the Runway held two trunk shows to see if women would rent dresses. They hosted pop-up shops on Harvard University's campus (the university Jenn and Jenny attended) and invited undergraduate students to borrow these dresses.
More Testing & Feedback	They continued to host trunk shows, hear from customers, and gain feedback. The results showed that one-third of attendees from the first trunk show rented dresses, and three-quarters of the attendees from the second trunk show rented dresses without being able to try them on while at the event. This proved that women would wear previously worn dresses and return them on time without any damage. These tests also allowed them to collect information about size, styles, colors, etc. Overall, their peers were so excited about this new concept!

In this case, Jenn and Jenny persevered! After seeing the excitement from their customers and proving their hypothesis, Rent the Runway was born! Rent the Runway demonstrated great product-market fit. Jen and Jenny and other team members worked hard to get the Rent the Runway website up and ready to launch on November 10, 2009. These days it still runs and is even a publicly traded company in the stock market!

Bringing It All Together

We can't build effective products and services until we validate how we plan to solve a specific problem and exactly whom we're bringing value to. Design thinking is a process you'll need to continually embrace as you embark on your entrepreneurial journey.

Our biggest takeaway for you is this: *always listen and always iterate.* Always remind yourself to learn from minimum viable product (MVP) tests and receive and incorporate feedback. You may need to change some parts of your product or service after evaluating feedback from the MVP tests, but that's okay! This is the part where you keep iterating and tweaking your product or service, even after multiple rounds of feedback, until you have proof it's ready to push out to the world!

In entrepreneurship (and social entrepreneurship), it is all about achieving great product-market fit—this is what separates great companies from good companies. And you can only achieve it by embracing design thinking and always listening and iterating.

IV. Cheat Code Review

1. Product-market fit is when a product generates high demand from the market because it addresses a specific customer or user need within that market. This begins with an in-depth understanding of the customer.
2. Assumptions are statements that you presume to be true without concrete evidence to support them. It's important to identify the assumptions you're making for planning and

decisions-making purposes, despite the inevitable uncertainty, but these assumptions must be tested and validated to proceed successfully with your social enterprise.

3. User interviews can help you understand if your product will be successful based on how your target market perceives it.

Part 3:
Getting Down to Business

Chapter 9
Defining Your Market

Written by: Tiffany Yau

"It's only by saying 'No' that you can concentrate on the things that are really important." —Steve Jobs, American entrepreneur, co-founder of Apple Inc.

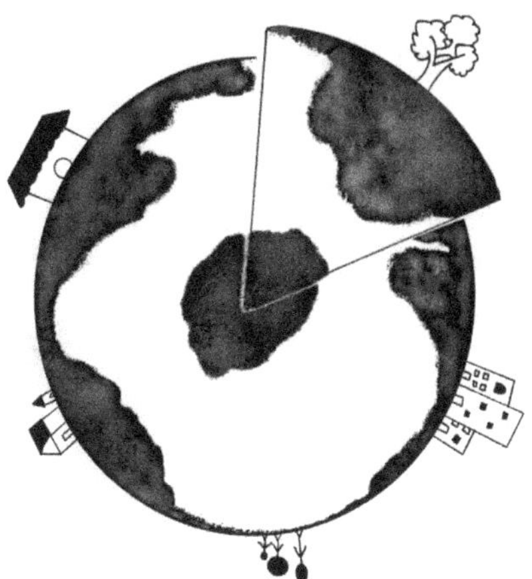

Up until this point, you've learned how to figure out the needs and desires of your potential users, which is perhaps the most important part of starting a business. Next, you'll need to get down to business and turn everything you've learned into an actually viable business model.

To start, you need to define your market. Beyond defining who your customers are, you also need to quantify the potential for success of your social enterprise.

I. Segmenting Your Market: TAM, SAM, SOM

As mentioned previously, "the market" in traditional business lingo is defined as the ecosystem around the transaction processes between businesses and consumers. So far, we've done a fair amount of work to define a lot around our consumers and their wants and needs.

But as you continue to learn, it is important to quantify this and assign a monetary value to it. When you are building and growing your social enterprise, you might consider seeking funding. If you're pitching to investors, you'll absolutely need to know how to quantify your market by defining your **market size**.

Your market size is defined as the total number of customers you can expect to have over a given time period. Investors care about defining the market size of a business because it gives them an idea of how big the business can get and how successful it can be. This is part of their own market research process and **due diligence**. This is the formal process that investors and funders go through when they are in the process of deciding whether or not to fund a company. (Think of this as a chance to learn how they do it and get an idea of how they think!)

When defining the market, you must segment it into three main categories:

- Total addressable market
- Serviceable attainable market
- Serviceable obtainable market

Your **total addressable market (TAM)** is the total overall market that your business can potentially serve. This is the north star goal you should be going after. If a business captured their TAM, that means *everyone* who could ever have the potential to be a customer *is* a customer that uses your product or service. Let's say you are looking to start a coffee shop chain. Your TAM here, if you were to own 100% of your market, is everyone in the United States (or the world, depending on your goals) who drinks coffee regularly.

Your **serviceable attainable market (SAM)** is the portion of your TAM that you can realistically and logistically serve based on your business model. When business owners talk about their "niche," they're usually talking about their SAM. Using our coffee shop chain example, let's say this is all the regular coffee drinkers of California.

Your **serviceable obtainable market (SOM)** is a portion of your SAM (thus an even smaller portion of your TAM) that you can realistically win in the short term. Continuing with our example, your SOM might then consist of all the regular coffee drinkers in Southern California.

In this example, we used the idea of geography to segment our market, but that isn't the only way. For instance, Airbnb segmented their market by the style of booking trips:

- TAM: People in the world who go on trips
- SAM: People who book budget and online trips
- SOM: People who book budget and online trips and are willing to try alternative non-traditional options for lodging (AKA people who use Airbnb!)

Your SOM is the main market within your niche market that you should pursue.

II. Doing the Math: Two Methods for Market Sizing

There is no straightforward way to know how many total potential customers you could have, so you will need to make some estimates based on existing data. When searching for data, it's best to seek trustworthy publicly available sources, like U.S. Census data. Given this, it's important to acknowledge that your market sizing calculations will never be 100% accurate—there is no way to know with absolute certainty. The point of calculating your market size is to get a general idea of how big your market is.

Calculating your TAM can help you understand how much revenue you might be able to generate from your market and how you could compete with other similar businesses in your market. Calculating your SAM can help you understand what success looks like for your niche market. How much revenue can you expect to generate from your niche market? And lastly, your SOM can help investors understand how successful your business is even if you are only able to capture a tiny portion of your SAM. After all, your SOM is a percentage of your SAM.

To understand your social enterprise's potential for money-making, there are two methods of analysis you can use to quantify your TAM, SAM, and SOM, and, ultimately, the monetary value amount of your business that is traditionally used to help investors evaluate your company's value:

- Top-down market sizing
- Bottom-up market sizing

Top-Down Market Sizing

Top-down market sizing is one of two approaches you can use to analyze the current market. It takes a macro approach, starting with the largest possible market size estimate, then reducing it.

You must first begin by finding your TAM and asking yourself "What is the total amount of spending happening in X market today?" You can search research firms online to find some numbers.

To calculate your TAM with a top-down approach, you must first start with the total number of potential customers or purchase opportunities in the world, then narrow that down based on factors like geography and demographics until reaching the target market.

All of the top companies do this, including Airbnb in their initial 2008 pitch deck. They cited a TAM of 2 billion trips booked worldwide.

Segmenting that down, they defined their niche market, namely their SAM, as customers who are interested in booking budget and online trips. At the time, this number was 560 million budget and online trips booked.

They took a percentage of that to create their SOM. In their case, they chose 15% and ended up with a SOM of 84 million trips.

Let's go back to our imaginary coffee shop example.

Our TAM would consist of U.S. coffee drinkers, and according to IBIS World, the U.S. retail coffee market size is $47.4 billion.[61]

TAM = U.S. coffee drinkers

TAM = $47.4 billion U.S. retail coffee market size

Let's say we're going after coffee drinkers in California only. California accounts for approximately 15% of the U.S. gross domestic product (GDP).[62] To calculate our SAM, we need to multiply these two numbers, which is $7.1 billion.

SAM = California coffee drinkers

SAM = Total U.S. coffee drinkers × California market share

Total U.S. coffee drinkers = $47.4 billion U.S. retail coffee market size

California market share = 15% of the U.S. GDP comes from California

---

61 "The Retail Market for Coffee in the US - Market Size 2005-2027," IBIS World, updated April 26, 2021.

62 "List of US States by GDP, 2010-2021," Knoema, updated November 3, 2022.

SAM = $47.4 billion U.S. retail coffee TAM × 15% = **$7.1 billion SAM**

Companies in an earlier stage of development, especially if they are not earning revenue yet, don't have numbers to rely on for this. To provide the fullest picture, it is recommended they provide a range of percentages for best-case and conservative-case scenarios. A best-case scenario might be a 15% market share, meaning you are projecting to capture 15% of your defined SAM. A conservative-case scenario could be 2%, meaning you are projecting to capture 2% of your defined SAM. It is important to show a range because this is your chance to show your audience how big or small your company can become.

SOM = last year's market share × this year's SAM

Best-case SOM = Last year's best-cast case market share × this year's SAM

Last year's best-case market share = 15%

This year's SAM = $7.1 billion

Best-case SOM = 15% × $7.1 billion market size = **$1.1 billion**

Conservative-case SOM = Last year's conservative market share × this year's SAM

Last year's conservative-case market share = 2%

This year's SAM = $7.1 billion

Conservative-case SOM = 2% × $7.1 billion market size = **$142 million**

Meanwhile, companies further along the process will need to use their market share from last year to calculate their SOM. To do this, they will divide their revenue from the year before by their SAM.

Last year's market share = last year's company revenue/SAM

Bottom-Up Market Sizing

Meanwhile, bottom-up market sizing is calculated by estimating your current or potential sales to determine your market potential.

When conducting a bottom-up analysis for your TAM, you must multiply the number of customers by the average revenue per customer per year (i.e., the annual contract value [ACV]):

TAM = Total number of customers × ACV

Going back to our coffee business example, let's say we're trying to target people between 20 and 35 years old as the bulk of your customer base. That's approximately 66 million people in the United States.[63] Next, we have to make assumptions based on the reasonable data we can find online.

Let's assume that 30% of those 66 million people buy a cup of coffee every day—that's 19.8 million people who could be potential customers.

---

[63] Duffin, "Resident population of the United States by sex and age as of July 1, 2021 (in millions)," Statista, published September 30, 2022.

To calculate our TAM for this example, we must multiply 19.8 million people by the ACV. Assuming the average cup of coffee costs $4, and each one of these 19.8 million people is purchasing one cup of coffee every day of the year, that's a $28.9 billion market you're going after.

TAM = Total number of customers × ACV

Total number of customers = 19.8 million potential coffee drinkers

ACV = $4 per coffee drinker × 365 days per year

TAM = 19.8 million potential coffee drinkers × $4 per coffee drinker × 365 days per year = **$28.9 billion**

It is important to note that these are pretty optimistic numbers. Maybe an avid coffee drinker actually buys a cup of coffee three days a week instead of seven days a week. If that's the case, we'll have to factor that into our equation to calculate the true TAM.

To calculate our SAM, we might want to target 20- to 35-year-old residents of California.

SAM = Target segment of TAM × ACV

Because the target segment of our TAM here is residents of California within a certain age range, we should try to find that data online. In this case, it is 7.6 million people.[64]

SAM = Target segment of TAM × ACV

---

64 "CA Demographic Statistics," Infoplease, accessed February 14, 2023.

Target segment of TAM = 7.6 million potential coffee drinkers

ACV = $4 per coffee drinker × 365 days per year

SAM = 7.6 million potential coffee drinkers × $4 per coffee drinker × 365 days per year = **$11.1 billion**

To calculate our SOM, we will take a percentage of our SAM as we did for our top-down approach (using both best-case and conservative-case scenarios):

SOM = Last year's market share × this year's SAM

Best-case SOM = Last year's best case market share × this year's SAM

Last year's best-case market share = 15%

This year's SAM = $11.1 billion

Best-case SOM = 15% × $11.1 billion market size = **$1.7 billion**

Conservative-case SOM = Last year's conservative market share × this year's SAM

Last year's conservative-case market share = 2%

This year's SAM = $11.1 billion

Conservative-case SOM = 2% × $11.1 billion market size = **$222 million**

It makes sense to wonder which method is better. But we want to note that they are both important. You'll know that your calculations are accurate when the numbers align.

III. Every Industry Has a Different Standard for Market Size

Once you size your market, you should have a rough idea of how big your market is. It is important to keep in mind that different markets have different sizes. Some markets and businesses have more potential to grow faster than others owing to the nature of the industry they're in—different needs for different businesses allow them to thrive in their own individual markets.

For instance, the health care market is a very big market that's worth a lot of money, but it can take quite a while to implement solutions owing to the nature of policies and regulations. Furthermore, the education market is a smaller market because of limited funding but is also slow-moving to implement solutions because of the bureaucracy in schools. A successful company in education will look different than a successful company in health care simply because the market potential of each sector is different to begin with.

Calculating your TAM, SAM, and SOM can give you a better idea of what you should realistically expect from your social enterprise. The bigger the market size, the better—big companies are only possible because of big markets. If you find you're pursuing a smaller market than you initially intended, you have the opportunity to reevaluate whether you want to continue to pursue this market opportunity or rethink your strategy.

It is important to succeed in your SOM before you even think about expanding your product or service to other market opportunities. The best companies start with their original SOM, and from that success, they expand. For instance, Crocs found their start by dominating the boat shoe market. They created value with their comfy, slip-resistant, waterproof, and breathable design, but were able to expand beyond their original TAM to serve the everyday consumer. Known for being ugly, it›s debatable whether Crocs would be as popular as they are today if they didn't first focus on their original SOM in the boat shoe industry.

Whether you're creating the next ugly, comfy shoe or launching a coffee business, it is important to be laser-focused on succeeding in and creating value in your SOM. This begins with understanding who else is in your market and finding ways to stand out, then figuring out how to best engage with those in that market—after all, you can't succeed until you know exactly what you're dealing with. We'll review the concept of competition in our following chapters.

IV. Cheat Code Recap

1. "The market" is the ecosystem around the transaction process between businesses and consumers.
2. Defining your market involves segmenting it into your TAM, SAM, and SOM.
3. You can analyze your market with either a top-down or bottom-up method.
4. Every market has unique standards and needs.

Chapter 10
Competition

Written by: Aditya Desai, Tiffany Yau, and Elizabeth Guan

"There is no such thing as a new idea. It is impossible. We simply take a lot of old ideas and put them into a sort of mental kaleidoscope. We give them a turn and they make new and curious combinations. We keep on turning and making new combinations indefinitely; but they are the same old pieces of colored glass that have been in use through all the ages." — Mark Twain

I. Finding Your Edge

As we've reviewed in our previous chapter, every market is unique. Some may be bigger or smaller, whereas others might be more crowded or slow-moving.

A **crowded market** is when there are a lot of competitors selling similar products or services. When a market is not crowded, it means the opposite—there is less competition.

For anyone who has lived in the twenty-first century, from Baby Boomers to Gen Z, we will almost instinctively think of technology-driven companies like Apple and Netflix as disruptive and revolutionary companies.

Let's take a closer look at a few of these companies.

Apple: The iPhone

Apple has a history of making quite an entry: In 1984, they entered the personal computer market; in 2001, the music market; in 2007, the mobile phone market; and they have influenced wearable technology, like watches, and smart home technologies.

The iPhone's introduction disrupted a completely unexpected market: the laptop market. It did not disrupt the smartphone market itself. Apple used the iPhone to usher in a new business model: letting developers create applications and connect directly with consumers.

The iPhone also possessed a first-of-its-kind sleek touchscreen, brimming with apps and a clear camera. The interface was user-friendly, colorful, and appealing to nearly all customers. Its clean, sophisticated packaging also made it stand out. The in-store experience, with minimalist tables, fun devices to test out, and a squad of Apple "geniuses" clad in blue-colored t-shirts made the company's purchasing experience enjoyable.

The iPhone changed the way people access the web and created a new market of app and phone users. As a result, smartphones become the most popular way to access the internet.

This only bolstered the sales of Apple's later devices, which are designed to work harmoniously with the iPhone, such as the Apple Watch and AirPods. Additionally, the huge success of the iPhone convinced scores of customers to become Apple devotees, which led them to buy the company›s computers and tablets almost without question.

Apple's relatively humble beginnings and explosive early products are worth studying as you hone your entrepreneurial skills. Their innovation and ambition can inspire even the most jaded businessperson.

Netflix: Video Streaming

Video streaming took the entertainment sphere by surprise, rising from the bottom of the market as a low-cost way to watch shows and movies to become the multibillion-dollar industry it is today—think Hulu, Disney Plus, HBO Max, Amazon Prime, and Crunchyroll!

Video streaming eventually disrupted the cable industry and drove nearly all video rental stores out of business. And Netflix? The company initially began by renting out DVDs by mail. A lot has happened since then. As of 2022, Netflix still remains the unquestioned king of subscription video streaming in the United States, having a global paid subscriber base of over 220 million users, even after losing over 1 million subscribers in the beginning of the year because of their monthly price increase.[65]

Nonetheless, it is important to remember that Netflix began serving customers in a niche market that consisted of movie lovers who did not care about new releases and did not mind waiting a few days for DVDs through the mail. Meanwhile, Blockbuster served a different type of customer, one who rented more impulsively and prioritized new releases.

A disruptive company like Netflix targets segments of the population that are often overlooked by its competitors and delivers a cheaper, inferior yet tailored alternative. Once the disruptive company is established, it adds what mainstream customers want and gradually drives customers away from its competitors—in Netflix's case, they were able to draw competition away from Blockbuster and eventually put them out of business.

Netflix was able to appeal to Blockbuster's core customers by providing a wider selection of content, characterizing it as an all-you-can-watch, on-demand, low-price, high-quality, and highly convenient service.

---

65 Maglio, "Disney+ Soars, Netflix Sinks: Here's How Many Subscribers 10 Key Streamers Have Now," 2022.

As with the rise of companies like Apple and Netflix, one reason why disruptive companies are often able to quickly capture the market is because their larger competitors overlook them.[66]

Competitors in the business context are organizations that strive to win or gain commercial or economic success in a market by establishing superiority over others who are in a similar sector and trying to do the same. The process and act of this is **competition**.

They often do not initially compete for the same customer base. We all want to be the next Steve Jobs or Elon Musk, illustrious visionaries of the digital age. Apple made computers an essential part of a modern lifestyle, Tesla produced a luxury electric car ecosystem, Netflix created an addictive and diverse streaming platform, and Airbnb provided a homey and less expensive alternative to the conventional hotel.

Were all of these companies *truly* innovative? While they, without question, introduced new products and services, were they inherently original?

Spoiler alert: They're not really *new* ideas!

What made Apple better than Nokia (another booming smartphone company)? How did Samsung beat Sony? All these companies had a similar vision in mind, but what was it that actually made one more successful than the others in its industry?

As entrepreneurs, we are always trying to create something better than anyone else to win the race against our competitors. While this

---

66 McAlone, "The Father of 'Disruption' Theory Explains Why Netflix Is the Perfect Example — and Uber Isn't," 2015.

may sound daunting, this chapter will outline some strategies you can use to stay competitive and thrive in a crowded market.

II. Types of Competition

When we talk about competitors in the entrepreneurial context, we are referring to your rivals—regardless of whether you're competing to win the same customers or your market at large. Your competitors sell similar products or services with the goal of earning more revenue and profit and more of the market share. Competition comes in many different shapes and sizes, but when you're the founder of a startup, competition will *always* exist for you.

Pinpointing exactly who your competition is can be *key* to your success. Most importantly, clarifying your competition allows you to define exactly what sets you apart from the rest. In entrepreneurship, there are three main types of competitors you should be familiar with:

- Direct competitors
- Indirect competitors
- Replacement competitors

Each of these are categorized by 1) the type of product or service they sell and 2) their targeted customer and market in comparison to yours.

Direct Competitors

The first kind of competitor we often think about is a **direct competitor**. Your direct competitors, as their name suggests, are the competitors who are targeting the *same audience* you are trying to target. They also sell the *same products in a similar market* and may distribute their products in a similar way. You are competing against your direct competitors in every way to get the same customers.

A prominent example set of direct competitors is one of our generation's favorite take-out options: pizza. Popular national chains include Pizza Hut, Domino's, and Papa Johns. All of these options sell approximately the same kind of product and target the same type of customer—the hungry night owl, the couples who don't feel like cooking on particular evenings, the group of friends who want to get together for a movie night or game night—all of whom want an easy, cheap, and quick food option.

Indirect Competitors

Indirect competitors are one degree distant from direct competitors. They *do not compete by selling the same product* but *can still take away your potential customers*. They're the kind of competitor you likely won't see coming!

Going back to our fast-food options, an example set of indirect competitors can be Pizza Hut and Burger King. Pizza Hut sells pizza and Burger King sells other kinds of fast food, particularly burgers and fries. These two competitors ultimately sell different types of products; however, they still share a similar customer: people who want a fast, easy, and cheap food option. While Pizza Hut and Burger

King are indirect competitors, Burger King is a direct competitor to other fast-food chains like McDonald's or Wendy's.

Replacement Competitors

A **replacement competitor** is another type of competitor who *can replace your product or service by providing a new solution.* These competitors are known to be unpredictable. They can create newer, faster, and more productive solutions, and there is not much you can do to prevent your customers from preferring their services (rough, right?).

A good example of a set of replacement competitors is the case of Netflix and Blockbuster. While younger Millennials and Gen Zers may be more familiar with the term "Netflix and chill," renting a movie or two from Blockbuster was the precursor to this concept, something Gen Xers and older Millennials may be nostalgic for.

Netflix positions itself as a media services provider and production company, whereas Blockbuster was a provider of home movie and video game rental services through a video rental shop. Blockbuster was founded in 1985 and it grew quickly, expanding internationally throughout the 1990s.

Blockbuster and Netflix both aimed to be a service that provides easy access to home entertainment. But why is Netflix more relevant today despite Blockbuster's rapid growth in the 1990s?

It goes back to the original problem they were trying to solve. Blockbuster was most focused on assuming the role of a video rental shop while Netflix has always been more focused on being a "media services provider." In the early 2000s, individuals could still rent DVDs from Netflix, but they had already begun the slow transition to direct video streaming. Netflix was no longer focused on being a DVD rental service but rather had stepped into their role as a media services provider. Consequently, this allowed Netflix to be more fluid in how it delivered its content. Because Netflix was focused on being a provider, regardless of medium, Netflix is still relevant today and Blockbuster dwindled from 9,000 stores to its last-standing brick-and-mortar store in Bend, Oregon.

Just as Netflix competed with Blockbuster, many companies out there attempt to solve the same problem in different ways, and this constant evolution of innovation is dependent on the needs and behaviors of its consumers.

Here is a chart to visually summarize the three types of competitors:

	Type of product/ service sold	**Type of audience/ customer**
Direct Competitors	Same	Same
Indirect Competitors	Different	Same
Replacement Competitors	Potentially the same, new type of solution	Potentially the same

III. Evaluating the Market

There are many competitors who sell a similar product or service, target a similar customer, or both. When we delve into replacement competitors, it gets a little more complex. Regardless, understanding your competitors affords you the following advantages:

- Allows you to understand what is already out there
- Enables you to allocate your resources efficiently
- Allows you to effectively design your communication and marketing plan
- Gives you an understanding of how to set your prices competitively
- Allows you to reduce risk and wasteful expenses
- Provides you with a better grasp of the size of the market and gaps in the market you can fill

After all, achieving marketing and business success is all about knowing your audience. If you know what customers are expecting and the options that are available to them, you can figure out how to differentiate yourself in a way that is truly meaningful to consumers. Here are some things to keep in mind as you get the lay of the land of your competitors:

Determine feasibility. Is there an unmet niche where your idea might take off? As an entrepreneur, understanding your competition can show you how feasible your idea is to implement. If the competition is too strong, you may need to reconsider your solution or your market. However, if there are not many competitors, your idea may be an exciting opportunity to pursue your dream venture!

Understand the do's and don'ts. Mapping rivals and their strategies to market their products/services will give you a better sense of what worked for them and what didn't work. Their marketing strategies and product features are often indicative of the existing wants and needs of the consumers you are trying to target. Doing your due diligence to understand what has been done successfully and unsuccessfully will play in your favor.

Learn as much as you can. Knowing the scene is impressive to investors because it shows that you did your homework to understand the demands and challenges of the market. While investors care about your solutions, they also value a keen founder.

Know that nothing is ever permanent. As the founder of a startup, you'll end up *pivoting* many times. Understanding your competition will help you figure out whether you should pivot to a different business model—and you may even identify models where there is less competition and more opportunity.

IV. Differentiation: Stand Out From The Crowd

But can a business successfully stand out from the crowd? Unfortunately, there is no formula, but there *are* components of successful business models that are useful in the challenging process of addressing your competitive landscape.

We know that competition is determined by the extent and alignment to which others are pursuing a similar solution or market. On an even deeper level, however, it all goes back to your customers' *needs* and *wants*. Remember, we care a lot about user-centered design: your customers and users define your competition.

Their preferences ultimately determine the market and how companies should be delivering their products and services to stay ahead of the competition.

Next, we'll talk about some strategies you can use to stand out from the crowd.

Make an impact.

You're likely already familiar with this strategy because you were inclined to pick up this book. But in the world of social entrepreneurship, how impactful you are and how effectively you're able to create value can truly make the difference between you and your competitors, especially if they are not focused on making a positive difference to the same degree as you are.

Beyond the attractiveness of marketing ideals of altruism, actively finding ways to make a positive social impact through your social enterprise is an excellent way to create value for your stakeholders.

Provide excellent customer service.

Serving your existing customers can take many forms. One type can revolve around tweaking your business model to include improved credit terms, discounts, and loyalty memberships that can allow you to solidify your customer base. After all, it is easier and less expensive to keep existing customers than to find new ones.

For example, Typeform—an online software-as-a-service company that specializes in online form building and online surveys—invests heavily in **customer retention** (i.e., a company's ability to keep a customer for a certain amount of time). They have six teams working to ensure customer success: support, education, customer experience, customer outcome, sales, and operations.

Customer retention is the outcome of *really* being there for your customers, online or offline. Being a reliable source for your customer ultimately helps build your brand and your customers' affinity toward your company. For instance, let's imagine that you are looking to buy a game at a store. When you walk into a Best Buy or Target's technology section, someone will often come up to you and ask how they can help you. This might not be the case for other retailers like Walmart. As a result, stores like Target offer a more pleasant shopping experience. However, Walmart stays competitive because of its low prices, making it even more important for other retailers to focus on their customer service!

Make your company a club.

Making your customers feel like they belong can go a long way in furthering customer satisfaction and steering clear of threats from competition.

If you have an American Express card, you are a *member* of a select card-carrying club. You have access to special customer service, exclusive tickets to concerts and sports events, and other perks, including insurance.

Invest in your employees to create a positive company culture. Skilled, motivated, and satisfied employees are the foundation of a thriving, growing business. Let's look at Facebook. In addition to receiving career guidance and quality training, Facebook employees are given the flexibility needed to set personalized work schedules, measuring progress by impact rather than hours.

Offer a guarantee.
Adding a type of assurance to your marketing message demonstrates to customers that you care about their satisfaction and stand by your word. But remember, you must back up the guarantee if and when the time comes.

For example, L.L. Bean notes that their products are "guaranteed to give 100% satisfaction in every way. Return anything purchased from us at any time if it proves otherwise."

Price it right.
There are many ways to stand out against the competition, but pricing is certainly one of the top strategies. For instance, some businesses are run on a **freemium model**, which is made possible by a company's other sources of revenue. Freemium models are the type of business model that offers a certain set of features for free but will charge for any additional features. This model is more commonly used

for subscription-based businesses. For example, Slack's freemium approach and streamlined onboarding process make it easy for new users to get started—and hard to say no when they discover the premium features.

On the other hand, products and services can be priced higher to signify exclusivity and quality This is called **premium pricing** in economics. For example, the steep prices for Tiffany & Co. products attract customers seeking high-quality, luxury jewelry. With premium pricing, more money signals better quality.

Have the need for speed.

Everyone wants things faster. Even with the same prices and quality, speed can win a customer over. Sometimes, even with higher prices, speed can still be the deciding factor.

Let's take Amazon. Amazon puts billions of dollars into distribution centers around the world, as fast shipping can often be the deciding factor when different distributors offer similar products. Beyond this, they even filed a patent for their "1-Click" ordering feature. The idea was that customers would only need to enter their billing and shipping information one time, to be saved for all future purchases. When they did that, all they needed to do to purchase something was to click the "buy now" button. This patent was finalized in 1999 and became the catalyst for an entire era of "hassle-free online shopping."[67] They even sued Barnes & Noble for infringing on this patent.

---

67 "Why Amazon's '1-Click' Ordering Was a Game Changer," Knowledge at Wharton podcast, 2017.

Customize.

Customers enjoy being able to connect their purchases with their sense of identity. For instance, people customize their own Converse sneakers or Crocs, tailoring them to their own sense of style. Customization also leads to more opportunities for profit. When Crocs acquired Jibbitz in 2006, they were able to use the low-cost/high-margin Jibbitz plug-in charms as an opportunity to boost their revenue, especially in their Millennial/Gen Z markets that place high value on self-expression.

Be sustainable.

Being the conscientious, ecofriendly brand in the industry can increase your sales and brand reputation.

For instance, Patagonia is an outdoor clothing brand that prides itself on its environmentally friendly production, which attracts nature lovers who seek to support brands doing good for the environment.

Support the solution of a global or local problem.

The effort to ameliorate a social issue can draw customers who care about corporate social responsibility (CSR). As mentioned earlier in this book, CSR is defined as practices and policies undertaken by corporations that are intended to have a positive influence on the world, where companies actively find ways to make an impact through their business models.

At the onset of the COVID-19 pandemic, Crocs created their "Free Pair For Healthcare" campaign and gave away 910,000 pairs to health care workers. This catalyzed an expansion of their initial market—they sure have come a long way from nifty boat shoes.

Redefine the experience.

Create a truly unique experience for consumers that enhances their day-to-day lives.

Starbucks differentiated itself from other coffee shops when it first opened because of everything *but* its coffee. They emphasized being a *third place*, meaning a place between home and work.[68] As of May 2022, Starbucks even published that they are seeking to be the *digital* third place. To do this, they are tapping into the promise of Web 3.0 by creating a series of branded non-fungible token (NFT) collections to further engage their community.

Deliver quality.

If you cannot compete on price or delivery, there is certainly no harm in putting all your efforts into creating the best quality product.

Apple charges premium prices, and the high profit margins enable the company to reinvest in marketing its brand and producing the highest-quality products.[69] It also allows the company to provide the kind of customer service its lower-priced competitors simply cannot match.

---

68 Simon, " Everything but the Coffee - Learning about America from Starbucks," 2011.

69 Nielson, "Apple's Premium Pricing Strategy and Product Differentiation," 2014.

Be laser-focused on design.

It is absolutely worthwhile to think about the design of websites, apps, and products—everything from user experience design and logos to packaging and the product itself.

ZipRecruiter, one of the top-rated job search apps, removes features by request if users do not use them frequently enough. By cutting out the complexity that does not deliver on solving user pain, they created a product that customers truly value.

In reality, understanding your competitive landscape is just a starting point for understanding how to best differentiate yourself. As you think about how you want your company to stand out from the rest, consider how you can manipulate common business factors to create a memorable brand.

Can you think of any other companies that leverage these and other strategies to differentiate themselves from their competitors? There will *always* be competition. After all, entrepreneurship, and especially social entrepreneurship, is all about creating *value* for your customers and your market. Now that you are in the know on some useful strategies, you can begin to think about how you might stand out from the crowd!

V. Competitive Analysis

Evaluating the Competition: A Checklist

Even if you believe you are going after a new market, you will still face competition. If this seems puzzling, start by thinking about what problem you are trying to solve. Remember, we must problem-*find* before we can problem-*solve*!

How have consumers dealt with this problem in the past? Many entrepreneurs often forget to think about the status quo as a key competitor. For instance, as search engine websites like Yahoo!, Bing, or Google grew more popular, one of their big competitors was local old-school libraries. They had to compete with the status quo of how people had traditionally searched for answers to their problems. Sometimes your greatest challenge will be to shift consumers from using other services that may be less efficient and useful.

In this section, we will review the four competitive analysis methods you can use to help you identify your competition, understand the market even more, and make sense of how you can stand out:

- Competitive landscape
- Competitive matrix
- SWOT analysis
- Porter's Five Forces

Competitive Landscape

The **competitive landscape** is a type of business analysis method that identifies direct or indirect competitors; at the same time, it helps you understand those competitors' missions, visions, core values, niche markets, strengths, and weaknesses.

Here is a very basic example of a competitive landscape:

	Netflix	HBO	Hulu	Your Business
Pricing	$6.99+ /month	$9.99+ /month	$6.99+ /month	[insert a quality you think would make you stand out]
TV Content	Releases season by season	Releases new episodes as they come out	Releases new episodes as they come out	[insert a quality you think would make you stand out]
Type of Content	Indie films, popular "blockbuster" movies, international content	Popular "blockbuster" movies, international content	Popular "blockbuster" movies, international content	[insert a quality you think would make you stand out]

What other points of comparison can you think of to analyze these three streaming services? What would the competitive landscape look like?

For competitive landscapes, you need to demonstrate to your audience why your social enterprise is better by aligning similar categories you share with other businesses—like pricing, features, or target market. There is a worksheet available on our website that can help you create a competitive landscape for different markets in which your own business idea exists.

What we showed above is an example of a descriptive competitive landscape. In the image below, we will show a categorical type of competitive landscape. Instead of using thorough descriptions, this competitive landscape simply indicates whether or not competitors meet the criteria you are defining.

	Business 1	Business 2	Your Business
Quality 1	✓	✗	✓
Quality 2	✗	✓	✓
Quality 3	✓	✗	✓

Competitive Matrix

Meanwhile, the **competitive matrix** is another type of analysis model that can help you map out your company's competitive advantage. It provides an easy-to-read portrait of your competitive landscape and your position in the marketplace. The matrix can be just a four-quadrant graph with two different axes, which represent the two main lenses of comparison. When companies create competitive matrices, they usually position their companies in the top right corner.

An effective competitive matrix will help you identify the following:

- Strengths and weaknesses of each brand in your industry
- Differentiators for your brand's uniqueness and how you can leverage that
- Gaps in your market segment that aren't currently filled

When creating a competitive matrix, it is recommended to identify key features that are important to your customers and identify where your company stands out. Some commonly compared attributes can often include some of the following:

- Quality of products or services
- Prices charged
- Marketing strategies to customers
- Distribution and delivery processes
- Strategies for enhancing customer loyalty
- Brand and design values (pay attention to this... they're more important than you think!)
- Staff members and the caliber of staff they attract

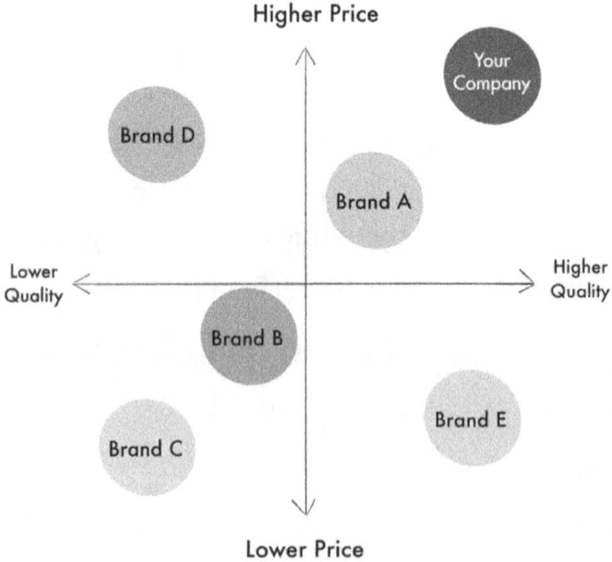

- Use of technology
- Ownership, specifically who owns the business and what sort of person he or she is—what is their personal brand? Check the annual report (if it's a public company)
- Customer base

What attributes will you use to identify your company's differentiation? Feel free to use our worksheet available on our website to help you create your competitive matrix.

SWOT Analysis

No, not like a SWAT team!

SWOT analysis allows you to build on **S**TRENGTHS, minimize **W**EAKNESSES, seize **O**PPORTUNITIES, and counteract **T**HREATS concerning your venture.

The S in SWOT stands for *strengths*. When it comes to strengths, we look at factors such as things your company or brand does well, the qualities that separate you from your competitors, and any advantage that you have over other companies in your industry. An artist like Taylor Swift (calling all Swifties!) is well known for her songwriting skills and her versatility as an artist, which anyone can see in the variety of music styles she's produced over the years. When analyzing your company, ask yourself, "What are some of my company's strengths?"

The W in SWOT stands for *weaknesses*. When we look at weaknesses, we observe factors like things your company lacks, things your

SWOT Analysis

	Helpful to achieving the objective	Harmful to achieving the objective
Internal Origin (attributes of the organization)	S Strengths	W Weaknesses
External Origin (attributes of the environment)	O Opportunities	T Threats

competitors do better than you, resource limitations, and areas that can be improved. A few years ago, Taylor Swift chose not to stream her music on Spotify. This became a huge weakness for her business, especially considering a large portion of the listener market uses Spotify—one of the only free music streaming services on the market. Can you think of some weaknesses that your own venture might have? They might be related to marketing, financing, team management, or lack of a unique value proposition.

The O in SWOT stands for *opportunities*. This is where indirect competition comes out to play. When evaluating the opportunities that your company might encounter, it is extremely important to understand your industry as a whole. You cannot simply observe your direct competitors alone because doing so will limit your potential reach in the future. When you look at your industry as a

Strengths (Internal Positive +)	**Weaknesses (Internal Negative -)**
- Qualities that separate you from your competitions - Internal resources like skills, knowledgeable staff - Tangible assets - intellectual property, capital proprietary technologies etc - Areas you overall do well or your competitive advantage - What business processes are successful? • What abstract assets do you have in your team, such as knowledge, education, network, skills, and reputation? • What physical assets do you have, such as customers, equipment, technology, cash, and patents? • What competitive advantages do you have over your competition?	- Things your company lacks - Things your competitors do better than you - Resource limitations - Unclear unique selling proposition to customers and stakeholders - Areas that could be improved - Questions to ask: • What business processes need improvement? • Are there tangible asssests that your company needs, such as money or equipment? • Are there gaps within your team? • Is your location ideal for your success?
Opportunities (External Positive +)	**Threats (External Negaitive -)**
- Underserved markets for specific products - Few competitors in your area - Emerging need for your products or services - Press/media coverage of your company -External factors that can contribute to your organization to grow and build up your strengths - Questions to ask: • Is your market growing and are there trends that will encourage people to buy more of what you are selling? • Are there upcoming events or changes in government regulations that may affect your business positively? • If your business is up and running, do your customers think highly of you?	- Emerging competitions - Changing regulatory environment - Negative press/media coverage - Changing customer attitudes towards your company - Potential risks caused by external factors that your organization may face (economic recession, natural disaster etc) - Questions to ask: • Do you have potential competitors who may enter your market? • Could future technological tevelopments change how you do your business? • Are market trends or consumer behaviours changing in a way that could negatively affect your business?

whole and study the consumers who make up your target market, you can discover emerging needs that consumers might have for which you can provide a product or service.

In addition, expanding your product or service line to reach underserved markets is another great move. Artists in the music industry will try to reach new markets or meet the changing trends of a preexistent market in order to make the most out of their opportunities. Taylor Swift saw her weakness with Spotify as an opportunity as well, and as a result, she continued to re-record her earlier albums that were originally produced by her former label, Big

Machine Label Group. In 2018, her contract with them ended, calling for an opportunity to re-record.[70] Her plans to re-record actually stirred up even more excitement amongst her fans since her old songs were revisited in a refreshed perspective and matured vocals. She also included released songs from her "vault," which created even more value for the new re-recorded albums, while gaining back rights and obtaining her full ownership. This also allowed her to put her music on Spotify and also succeed in reaching a larger market.

Just as Swift did, ask yourself, "How can I turn my weaknesses into strengths? What are some of the opportunities for my venture? Is there another market of individuals that I can meet? Are there changing trends that I think I can handle?"

Lastly, the T stands for *threats*. This is an extremely important part of the analysis, especially as it relates to indirect competition. In fact, indirect competitors are some of the *biggest threats* to any company. Threats can include any emerging competitor that could take away your customers at any time. Threats could also include your customer's altering environment, which may change their need for your product or service. One of Taylor Swift's greatest threats came during the Kanye West feud, starting all the way in 2009. During their ongoing feud, she received a lot of negative publicity, which proved harmful to her brand. What are some threats that could pose a risk or problem for your venture?

---

[70] Tsioulcas, "Look What They Made Her Do: Taylor Swift to Re-Record Her Catalog," 2019.

Feel free to visit our website to access our worksheet activity to apply the SWOT analysis framework to your company!

Porter's Five Forces

Last but certainly not least, we have Porter's Five Forces. Porter's Five Forces is a very commonly used analysis method, especially when investors are evaluating a business. What makes Porter's Five Forces an interesting tool is that you can analyze *why* there is competition, specifically the main market drivers and sources for why competition exists in the market you are analyzing. It is particularly helpful for identifying the strengths and weaknesses of different industries.[71] Porter's Five Forces consist of the following forces:

- Threat of rivalry
- Barrier to entry
- Threat of substitutes
- Power of suppliers
- Power of buyers

Each of these forces is often described in terms of high, medium, and low—for instance, high threat of rivalry or low power of suppliers. Feel free to visit our website to access our worksheet activity to apply Porter's Five Forces to your own company idea. If you choose to use the worksheet, here are some key considerations to keep in mind as you analyze each force:

---

71 "Porter's 5 Forces Explained and How to Use the Model," *Investopedia*, 2022.

Threat of Rivalry

Threat of rivalry describes the intensity of competition in the current marketplace. Some key determinants you can consider include the following:

- *Number of existing competitors in the space:* If there are a lot, you have a higher threat of rivalry.
- *Size of competitors:* If you have competitors that have been around for a while and have greater market share, your threat of rivalry is high. Threat of rivalry can also be high if your competitors are similar in size and power because it will basically become a race between you and them to see who can get to the finish line faster!
- *Industry growth:* Does it take longer to become established in your market? Is it fast or slow? Why? If it is slow, you have a higher threat of rivalry.
- *Product differentiation between rivals:* Are all competitors' products pretty much the same thing or is yours actually very different from the rest? If it is fairly different, you have a lower threat of rivalry.
- *Exit barriers:* Will it be a challenge for you to exit the marketplace when the time comes? Will it be hard for you to sell your company or reap the benefits of your hard work? Are there even any benefits?

Returning to our competitive analysis of Taylor Swift, it is safe to say that she has a very *high* threat of rivalry. She has a lot of existing competitors in her space; she is competing against every other artist and record company. The size of her competitors is also massive. Record companies often have greater resources to promote artists. But as one of the top artists globally, she certainly has a fair chance. The music industry grows relatively quickly given how brands can grow virally overnight. Think of some singer influencers on TikTok! Additionally, Swift dabbles in country, pop, and even electronic remixes. This means she must compete against more artists in other styles of music. However, there are very few competitors that are able to cross those boundaries like she has, which presents an opportunity to grow her market. Lastly, artists' exit strategies can be challenging to execute because of the way they often sell to music label companies, as illustrated in the battle Swift underwent to maintain full ownership of her music to reap more profit from her own music.

Barrier to Entry

Your **barrier to entry** describes how feasible it is for your company to obtain market share to put pressure on prices, costs, and investments to compete. Some key determinants you can consider include the following:

- *Economies of scale:* Will the average cost of each product you are producing decrease as you make more products? How extreme is this? If the answer is yes, your barrier to entry is likely low.

- *Customer loyalty:* Is it easy to build customer loyalty in this space? Why? If the answer is yes, your barrier to entry is likely low.
- *Capital requirements:* How much money does it take to start your company? Is it capital intensive, like building Tesla, or more cost effective, like building Facebook? If you don't need as much capital, your barrier to entry is likely on the lower end.
- *Government policies:* Are there lots of regulations you need to navigate to produce your product (e.g., FDA approval for food)?
- *Access to distribution channels:* Do you have partners who can readily help you scale quickly? If the answer is yes, you likely have a low barrier to entry.

Overall, your barrier to entry is high if you have more players in your market; if there are fewer players, you face a lower threat, and thus, a lower barrier to entry.

Taylor Swift's barrier to entry is likely on the *lower* end of the spectrum. In the music industry nowadays, scrappy efforts can go a long way with soundproofing your bedroom and having a good microphone to record and release your first song. Platforms like TikTok and other social media platforms make it even more feasible for someone with good talent (and communication skills) to become famous and build their brand. There are also no strict government regulations for the music industry like there are for the food industry or health sector. Beyond platforms like TikTok, artists have relatively easy access to distribution channels like record label companies to help them scale even more quickly.

Threat of Substitutes

Threat of substitutes describes the availability of other products that a customer could purchase from an outside industry. An example is an energy drink versus a cup of coffee. They are two different products that exist in different markets but that serve the same purpose and thus can substitute each other to perform a similar job.

Some key determinants you can consider include the following:

- *Number of substitutes:* If there are more substitutes available, then the threat of substitutes will be higher for your space.
- *Buyers' willingness to want to substitute your solution:* If they are very willing, then your social enterprise faces a lower threat of substitutes.
- *Price performance trade-off:* Will your customer feel like they have made a sacrifice with the pricing of your product/service compared to another?

Swift's threat of substitutes is likely somewhere between medium and high. The biggest substitute for music is likely other forms of entertainment or other methods of finding solace. Swift's substitutes can also consist of other genres of music, of which there are many.

Power of Suppliers

Power of suppliers describes the power suppliers have in raising prices or reducing the quality of goods or services you are providing to your customer. For example, the airplane travel market's power of suppliers could be high because it is dependent on fuel, an external factor, which can change quickly globally.

Some key determinants you can consider include the following:

- *Number of suppliers:* If you have a lot of suppliers and options to choose from, you have a lower power of suppliers, which is good. For instance, if your supplier backs out, you can choose another.
- *Supplier concentration:* You want to make sure that there are many different types of suppliers in the same or relevant space you can choose from. If there is only one supplier in the world that can cater to your business, that will likely become a big issue.
- *Switching cost:* If you switch from one supplier to another, will that be a big trade-off in terms of cost and quality?
- *Strength of distribution channels:* Can your suppliers also help you go to market and help you get more customers?
- *Uniqueness of suppliers' product:* How your supplier creates your product will greatly affect your social enterprise. If they make something too similar to everything else that is already out there in the market, you will have little differentiation.

Suppliers in the music industry can include hosting platforms like Spotify, Apple Music, Pandora, Amazon Music, and more, especially for more independent artists. There are various platforms, so there is a more distributed supplier concentration for the music industry—this is also what allowed Swift to still be popular even though she previously lacked a presence on Spotify.

We can think of suppliers in music as record companies for more big-named artists. As we can see in Swift's fiasco with her label company, there was a great switching cost when she switched suppliers, and thus we can presume that the power of suppliers in this industry is very high.

Power of Buyers

Power of buyers describes the buyers' degree of influence on the price and quantity of products sold. This refers to the capacity of customers to put companies under pressure based on the following factors:

- *Product differentiation:* How different is your product from your competitors' products? If it is fairly differentiated, buyer power will be low and they will have a hard time putting pressure on you.
- *Customer loyalty:* Is it easy or difficult to build customer loyalty? Ideally, it should be easy!

This can be subjective for the music industry, although Taylor reported on *The Graham Norton Show* that she created the ten-minute version of her song "All Too Well" partially as a result of being pressured by her fans to do so.[72] In Swift's case, the power of buyers seems to be fairly high.

Why These Strategies Are Important & How You Can Leverage Them:

Now, you can use these tactics to help you find and leverage your "unfair" advantage. Although that doesn't exactly sound like a positive thing, it is! Your unfair advantage is your or your company's unique feature that helps other people understand why *your* skills, talents, or vantage point is something special and worth investing in.

You can allow those concepts to guide your understanding of the market and how you can add unique value to it.

Now that you've performed your analyses, you have what you need to create an actionable strategy. Here are some next steps:

1. Analyze how your strengths and available external opportunities can help you improve your current internal weaknesses. Understand how improving those weaknesses can help you avoid any of the potential threats you've identified.
2. Create a strategy for how to put those ideas for improvement into action.
3. Look at your calendar and begin setting some deadlines for yourself.

---

72 Taylor Swift's Fans Demanded a 10 Minute Version of 'All Too Well'," *The Graham Norton Show*, accessed January 10, 2023.

VI. Case Study: Taylor Swift vs. Katy Perry

As we mentioned, competition isn't necessarily always between two businesses. To carry on from earlier examples, we'll make things a little more interesting—we'll analyze two celebrities!

Welcome to the Taylor Swift and Katy Perry Feud! As you might be able to tell, we're big Swifties!

Taylor Swift and Katy Perry, two of the most original and influential female artists in the twenty-first century, have quite the infamous past.[73] The two have always been in indirect competition, but their long-lasting feud has fueled it.

It's worth mentioning that they are certainly not the only two artists to have ever engaged in indirect competition!

Any group of artists that produces a similar genre of music competes among themselves every day. Think about the popular hip-hop genre in the states. Kanye, Drake, Eminem, Lil Wayne, Lil Uzi Vert, and female artists like Cardi B, Lizzo, and Nicki Minaj all share the same audience of hip-hop and rap listeners across all platforms. Bands like BTS and BLACKPINK will compete for consumers' income and attention.

Let's take a deeper look at the ins and outs of indirect competition among musical-companies that sell *different* types of products but have the *same* type of customers.

---

73 Kinane, "Taylor Swift and Katy Perry: A Timeline of Their Feud," updated August 4, 2022.

Type of Product Sold: Different

Artists will almost never engage in *direct* competition. Why? Because they create original art! If Katy Perry were to release a song that sounded similar to "Love Story" by Taylor Swift, she would not only face huge backlash from the media that would tarnish her reputation but also face legal and copyright issues that lead to financial burdens. If Taylor were to release a music video that looked just like "Roar" by Katy Perry, she would face a multitude of problems as well. The short story is, you can't copy another artist's work, so naturally, no two entities in the music industry will sell the same exact (or even similar) products.

Artists, by nature, try to create a unique image to differentiate themselves from other artists. As listeners, we like to see something new and exciting. We don't want artists to produce the same song over and over again!

Target Market: Same

Many artists, however, do fight for the same listeners (or customers, in business terms). In this case, you can think of a listener to an artist as a customer to a company. Think about it! Listeners will give artists more views on YouTube, listens on Spotify, or purchases on iTunes. Receiving a larger portion of the listener market will lead to greater profit, yield higher billboard or leader rankings, and create more job and ad opportunities for any given artist. The more listeners there are, the more revenue artists receive.

So, what does the competition between Taylor Swift and Katy Perry, or any other pair of artists, look like exactly?

Well, to begin, unlike direct competition, Taylor doesn't create her own branding or music with the sole intention to target Katy Perry. She does not have to wake up every day thinking about what she must do to perform better than Katy Perry. When she released "Midnights," "Folklore," or "Evermore," she was not thinking about what Katy Perry or other artists were doing the entire time she was developing her own album brand and personality. Because she is still selling her own, original music, she focuses on her own reputation and writes her own music on her own time.

That being said, Taylor does not overlook the fact that another artist like Katy Perry is always a threat to her, as they share the same listeners. Just like direct competitors, artists in the music industry pay close attention to what music has already been released and what artists from the past century have already done. They do this so they can introduce something new and innovative to the world. Let's look at some other examples of how other artists from the past have differentiated themselves.

Music: Rarely is there ever an entire movie dedicated to the creation of a single song, but "Bohemian Rhapsody" by Queen might be the exception. This song has it all: a mixture of various genres, impressive layering, and a complex story that allows listeners to create their own meaning. Freddie Mercury introduced to the world what many would consider "strange," but he differentiated his music from every other artist and thus made a name for himself and his band.[74]

---

[74] Lee, "'Bohemian Rhapsody': The 6-Minute Rock Single That Changed the Face of Music," 2018.

Performance: Michael Jackson, known as the "King of Pop," created an extremely strong brand for himself as a performer. In addition to his catchy songs and powerful vocals, he was one of the first artists to brand his famous dance move, the moonwalk. This single backwards slide across the stage sent his audiences into a frenzy, making him an even more memorable performer than he already was. Since then, this move is attributed to him in remembrance, as many remember him as one of the greatest—if not, *the* greatest—performers in pop history.

Brand: Back in 2019, Billie Eilish became a trendsetter in the music industry when she caught the world's attention after refusing to let society judge her physical appearance. She recognized the pressures that many female artists faced and decided to *only* wear baggy clothing in hopes of redefining the focus toward her music, as revealed in a 2019 Calvin Klein ad where she opened up about it.[75] This attracted many of Billie's current fans, as she openly demonstrated authenticity and empowered younger audiences. This also led Billie to attain more ad and commercial success, which became a part of her artist brand.

So, why are artists so adamant about doing something "out of the box?"

One of the primary reasons is because they are all competing for mainstream recognition: Grammy awards, music awards of all kinds, Billboard Top 100 placement, followers on social media platforms, and more. There are a limited number of awards that every artist in the United States competes for, which naturally puts every artist in competition.

---

[75] "Billie Eilish #MYTRUTH #MYCALVINS," Facebook, 2019.

These examples are just a glimpse of how artists have found and used their "competitive advantages." They each recognized that they work in an industry where every musician is competing against another. They realize that if they want to attract a portion of the listener market, they need to bring something new and exciting to the table. Remember this: indirect competitors risk losing their target audience to another artist at any time. Because of this, they must make their competitive advantages significant and memorable to their audience. Let's take a look at how Taylor and Katy have risen to the top and branded themselves as indirect competitors.

Think about how these two individuals have branded themselves as artists in the music industry and what they have achieved to stand out from the millions of other aspiring artists in the world. Based on the different forms of competitive analysis, think about how indirect competitors can make optimal decisions given their circumstances. You can apply this framework to the company you are trying to build.

Below, we have listed some questions to further prompt more thoughts about competition:

- What product or service does each provide?
- Who are their customers? Are they loyal customers?
- How do they market their products to customers?
- What is their *positioning*? List some attributes and description words you would use to describe the "vibe" of each artist.
- What are their brand values?

- What devices and tools do they use to enhance customer loyalty?
- What is their approach to customer acquisition?
- Who are their employees and what caliber of employees do they attract?
- Who owns the business and what sort of person is he or she?
- How do they use technology and media?
- How actively are they using social media?
- Which specific social media platforms are they present on?
- What is their strategy for their content?
- What type of music do they produce?

Given these questions, what do you believe are the top two competitive advantages of each artist? How do they stand out from each other? How do they stand out from others in their industry? What do they offer that no other artist does? What do they do better than any other artist?

Whether you are Taylor Swift, Katy Perry, or the leaders of companies like Netflix, it is important to remember to engage with your customers. Interview them, listen to their social media conversations, and understand big trends to understand what they really want and use them to predict what they will want in the future. Customers' expectations change, so it is important for companies to be able to adapt to those changes. This echoes the concept of empathy and listening that we explored in a previous section that covered design thinking.

When you're just getting started, the competition may be intimidating and the process of differentiation may also seem like an overwhelming and confusing path to take. We won't beat around the bush—it is overwhelming and confusing! But it is also important to remember that for many companies, even the seemingly most organized and strategic ones, differentiation is a *constantly evolving* process.

As you develop an understanding of your company's unique value proposition, it is important to always plan for growth. Avoid marketing strategies that you feel are going to limit you down the road. Keep up with developments in your sector and be open to investing in new technologies and ways of doing things. Where do you want to be in one year? Three years? Five years? Try to keep that in mind. What is out of reach now can be long-term goals that play a role in your decisions today.

How can understanding competition be applicable to your own life?

This might seem like a philosophical tangent, but competition is actually a really important and applicable concept to understand as it relates to your personal pursuits outside of business and social entrepreneurship. Over the time Fulphil has existed, our students have realized just how relevant and important understanding competition can be in how we all embark on our various goals. We've included some of the invaluable takeaways we hope you can benefit from as our reader.

You will always face competition. Competition is a fact of life, not just in business. At a young age, overly competitive behavior is not encouraged in schools, as it may seem to prevent students from obtaining valuable collaborative skills. Yet knowing how to differentiate ourselves from our peers will become increasingly important as we get older. We must grow accustomed to leveraging our unique qualities to our advantage. After all, we are constantly comparing ourselves to our peers. Understanding your strengths and where you have room to grow can spur immense personal and professional success.

Nurture a growth mindset. Understanding our competition can help us develop a resilient growth mindset. It's essential that we continually learn how we can improve and become the best versions of ourselves so thar we can realize our aspirations. This way, our self-awareness and identity are stronger, which pushes us to take on bigger challenges and develop our full potential. The growth mindset also builds others' perception of your social capital and makes you competitive in the job market.

Develop keen decision-making. By mapping out your competitive landscape, you are performing an analysis to that will help you understand risks that may lie ahead as well as opportunities to seize. Life is all about the right timing and knowing when to take calculated risks.

Understanding how to analyze your competition and identify and cultivate your unique advantages is the key to success whether it's building your next social enterprise or it's for your own professional development.

VI. Cheat Code Review

1. Competitors are organizations that strive to win or gain commercial or economic success in a market by establishing superiority over others who are in a similar sector and trying to do the same.
2. Three types of competitors are direct competitors, indirect competitors, and replacement competitors.
3. There are various ways to analyze your competition: competitive landscape, competitive matrix, SWOT analysis, and Porter's Five Forces.

Chapter 11
Introduction to Marketing

Written by: Brooke McCormick and Aditya Desai

"From the store windows, the store touchpoints, the website, social media, or a magazine, it has to be one pure customer experience, not just to gain market share but to gain mind share." —Angela Ahrendts, former Burberry CEO

I. Creating Buzz About Your Biz

Get it "Out There"

Now that we have a problem defined, a unique and competitive solution ideated, and the right intrinsic motivations and have understood who can gravitate toward those, we now have to understand how to actually launch that idea—how can we take this idea that feels like nothing more than a napkin sketch and make it an actual business? How do we make it look better than competing solutions in the market? How do we get this "out there?" What would success look like if this is executed well? Like the unicorn companies out there, it all has to begin somewhere.

Instagram

Ever heard of Justin Bieber or Twitter co-founder, Jack Dorsey? Guess what! They were some of Instagram's earliest adopters and quickly spread word of the new application to their millions of followers.[76] Formally called **influencer marketing**, this strategy fueled an instant rise for Instagram, which gained 25,000 users on just its first day after launch! By definition, influencer marketing is a type of social media marketing that endorses specific products or services with the help of influencers who have a sizable following.

Airbnb

Unfortunately, Airbnb didn't have the same pop culture icons at their disposal—instead, they had emails. Hear us out: Airbnb, a revolutionary online marketplace for lodging, got its start by tapping into its target audience with rather scrappy means. Noting that Craigslist captured their prospective customers, Airbnb designed an ingenious email marketing campaign that urged homeowners who

---

76 Griggs and Kelly, "23 Key Moments from Twitter History," 2013; Gayomali, "Justin Bieber Joins Instagram, World Explodes," 2011.

listed their properties on Craigslist to do the same on Airbnb, which drove traffic and ultimately success![77] By definition, **email marketing** is the use of email campaigns within a company's marketing efforts to promote the products or services provided by that company.

These strategies used to increase the number of users sharing photos on Instagram or booking properties on Airbnb is also referred to as marketing! The **marketing strategy** of a business is their overall game plan for getting their products or services into the hands of potential leads and cultivating those relationships so that the leads become customers.[78]

II. Marketing to Your Target Audience

Oftentimes, when we think of marketing, we think of advertising; advertising is just a piece of the puzzle. Marketing is an intensive process that involves consumer research, user interviews to understand the needs of your potential customers, product design to cater to their needs, and understanding your competition across the board. Sounds a lot like our design thinking methodology, right?

Marketing involves leveraging your takeaways from those nonlinear steps in the design thinking process and to design a strategy that puts you in front of your customers, so they know about your social enterprise and your potential to add value to their lives. It's

---

77 Gobry, "Airbnb Admits It Farmed Craigslist, Blames Outside Salespeople," 2011.

78 Barone, Adam. 2022. "Marketing Strategy." Investopedia. June 13, 2022. https://www.investopedia.com/terms/m/marketing-strategy.asp.

about communicating your product-market fit to your audience. To understand how you should go about marketing for your own businesses, you can approach it using the following steps:

1. Define your target market
2. Develop your customer profile
3. Leverage user interviews
4. Define the foundations of your marketing strategy using the four P's (product, price, place, promotion)

Define Your Target Market

Your **target market** is the subgroup of people you plan to target with your marketing efforts. As a refresher, in Chapter 9, we reviewed how you can quantify the size and potential of your market through segmenting it into your total addressable market (TAM), serviceable addressable market (SAM), and serviceable obtainable market (SOM).

Beyond this, it is important to note that your target market will consist of a few different groups of people who you should categorize separately:

- **End users** are the people who will actually be using the product or service you are offering; this does NOT always mean they are paying for it. They can be the ones who pay for it, but end users also simply are those who use your product or service.
- **Customers** are the people who are actually paying for your product or service. They are NOT always the end users.

There are situations where the end users and customers can be the same people. For instance, you can be the end user *and* customer for companies like Uber, Chick-fil-A, and Amazon. You are using the service and paying for it. However, in other cases, the end user and customer can be different people, such as in cases like schools buying textbooks, where the customer is the school and the end users are the teachers *and* students.

Who your end users and customers are depends on the scenario, but it is important to remember that although end users and customers are two *separate* types of target market groups, they *can* be the same people. There's also the reality that while end users and customers are often people, they can also be entities (like a school, as mentioned earlier). Even when the customer or end user are entities, there is still some individual you have to cater your marketing strategy toward. Like in our example of schools buying textbooks, that individual could be the principal, or the head of curriculum, or the tenth-grade science teacher who teaches environmental sustainability. To execute an effective marketing strategy, you need to consider what they have to prioritize in their job at that organization.

Develop Your Customer Profile

This part should mostly be a piece of cake! You've already done most of your consumer profiling in the previous section that covered design thinking, where you practiced empathizing with potential buyers, observed them, and carefully considered their wants and needs to come up with an appropriate and effective solution. Now it's time to solidify the characteristics that you noted to define your target population with the following criteria:

- **Age/gender:** Be careful not to be too specific! It won't make a difference if your average customer is 34 or 36 years old (this is why age ranges are helpful here), but knowing their gender and their decade of life or generation is essential!
- **Location:** Yes, you need to know where on earth your customers live! Finding a set of target geographic areas (towns, counties, cities, states) can help you determine and narrow down different qualities about your customers. Perhaps people who live in urban cities tend to be more drawn to your company than people who live in suburban neighborhoods. What trends are you noticing about your customers that you should use to inform how you manage your business?
- **Interests:** What do your customers like to do for fun? What other businesses do they shop at or interact with? Learning about this can help you tailor your product/service to make it a "better fit" for your customers!
- **Income level:** Wondering whether you should charge $1 or $100 for your product? Well, that's why knowing the income of your target customers is key! Based on how much they make, you'll know how much your customers are willing and *able* to pay for your product. It's hard to know how much people make exactly, but oftentimes, even knowing their zip code can help inform you of their area's average household income

after a quick Google search, in addition to other socioeconomic metrics.

As mentioned, knowing how to define your customer profile can be useful in helping you cater to their needs, and when it comes to marketing, you can now communicate to them how exactly you plan to do so through your social enterprise.

Leverage User Interviews

We learned about user interviews in the last section. Now it's time to mobilize your knowledge! Remember that user interviews are a great way to get answers to three critical questions:

- Why is your design easy or difficult to use?
- Why would people want to use your design?
- When would people see themselves wanting to use your design?

What potential users tell you—no matter if it's before you have a design or after your product is released into the market—is foundational feedback that allows you to hone your marketing objectives! You will learn what your consumers like, and what part of your product is worth highlighting to attract even more consumers, along with what pushes consumers away from your product!

Define the Foundations of Your Marketing Strategy: The Four P's

It's time to create your marketing strategy! Are you excited yet?

As we noted earlier, a marketing strategy is any company's go-to game plan for attracting customers and communicating the benefits of their business. A great way to develop this strategy is by contextualizing the **Four P's of the marketing mix** for your social enterprise:

- Product
- Price
- Place
- Promotion

Product: What

What unique value does your product offer that others don't? Successful marketing involves being able to tactfully explain the qualities of your product or service to customers so that they understand what it is and what it does. Without proper understanding, they won't be able to understand why they need it.

This is where a customer profile and definition of the problem that customer faces can be helpful. Remember the example we used earlier, where we pitched a product to provide healthy school lunches to kids?

Meet Sydney. Sydney is nine years old and lives in the suburbs with two busy working parents who don't have the time to make her lunch every day. As a result, her only options are to eat school food, which she still barely touches, or to visit the vending machines for junk food. After surveying 50 kids across Pleansanton, I found that 79% of students face this same problem.

By stating the problem in this way, or in an even more creative way, your audience will begin to understand who exactly you are trying to sell to.

You can then proceed to tell them your solution. For instance, let's say it's the following:

Bento is a solution that creates convenient, nutritious, kid-friendly lunch meal packages for busy working families.

In this statement alone, we addressed what makes it interesting and valuable, who the end users are, and who the customers are. This is also an opportunity where you can leverage different methods of competitive analysis. Reference the four frameworks of competition analysis again if that's helpful. How much are companies similar to yours being valued? What specific, unique benefit are you providing that other companies aren't?

Being able to tactfully explain these elements to your customers is the foundation of building an effective marketing strategy.

Price: How Much

Next, you must link your price to the perceived value of the product or service you are selling. In business, **perceived value** is the idea of a customer's sense of how desirable a product or service is. Perceived value is essentially how valuable a customer believes something is. How low or high you price your product or service affects perceived value.

Here are a few common pricing strategies that businesses utilize:

- **Cost-Based Pricing:** Perhaps the simplest way to price your product, this method involves calculating the total costs it takes to make your product, then adding a percentage markup to determine the final price. Here's an example: if the total cost to produce your product is $10 and you want to make a 50% profit, you would have to make the following calculation: $10 + ($10 * 0.5). You would then price your product at $15.
- **Market-Oriented Pricing:** Sometimes referred to as a competition-based strategy, this pricing method allows you to set the price higher or lower than your competitors, depending on how well their own product matches up. Remember, pricing is not about beating your competitors—you need to price based on your own quality and specifications!

We will expand on a number of other strategies at more depth in the next chapter, but you should keep in mind that pricing should be thought about as a partner to marketing. How expensively or affordably you are pricing your business' offerings is a way of communicating your value to your customers.

Place (Location): Where and When You Get It

This is all about how your product is bought and where it is bought. This could be through a combination of intermediaries, such as distributors, wholesalers, and retailers, or maybe you're selling through online platforms and marketplaces like Amazon or Instagram.

Choosing where you sell your product is an important aspect of reaching the right target audience at the right time. If you've already defined your niche market, you're already on your way to figuring out the best placement of your product or service—so consider: what is a good place to get in front of your market? The best way to come up with the "place" is by examining your competitors. Perhaps you'll use similar locations and channels of distribution as those with comparable products, or maybe you'll market on a totally different platform with the hope of tapping into a different and unique market.

Promotion: How You Get It Out

For this component, you need to focus on communicating to customers why they *need* your product.

The first step to creating some buzz about your biz is by building awareness, or an identity, for your product. For example, Turo, a rental car company, crafted its niche benefit to be the availability of luxury and sports cars that consumers can't find anywhere else. Similarly, find what makes your product unique and generate interest! This can be as simple as providing information directly to consumers, whether it be through talk shows, articles, or some other medium, to guarantee that customers know what you're offering.

Keep in mind that promotion is not a one-time thing! You'll always have to promote to further strengthen your brand and its place in the market. Continual promotion is what turns a first-time buyer into a lifetime customer!

When we think about promotion, we often have to tie in elements of the three other P's as well to be able to properly communicate the value of what we are selling.

The Four P's ultimately capture the main factors that you need to be thinking about to inform your marketing strategy. If you need help defining your Four P's, visit our website to download our online worksheet to get started.

III. Marketing Strategies Behind Success

Types of Marketing Strategies

There are two main types of marketing strategies: **business-to-consumer (B2C) marketing** and **business-to-business (B2B) marketing**.

You can think about it this way: if you want to sell your products to customers who are *individuals*—like babysitting services, clothing lines, hair styling services, restaurants, booksellers, or consumer electronics—then you should be interested in B2C marketing. It's likely that you're much more familiar with the B2C model.

On the other hand, if you're selling to *businesses*, like a corporate party planner, then you are in the realm of B2B marketing. Basically, B2B businesses sell products to other businesses. Think management software, raw materials, human resources consulting, or office supplies (you know, like the Dunder Mifflin Paper Company from *The Office*).

For now, don't get too tripped up over the semantics; the methods of marketing, regardless of whether your enterprise is B2B or B2C, can be remarkably similar! There are some nuances, though, which we will review in a later chapter.

Here are a few common strategies you can use for your B2B or B2C business as you apply the Four P's:

Paid Advertising

Paid advertising is the model of internet marketing where you pay a fee each time one of your product ads is clicked through platforms like Google and Facebook. With paid advertising, you can also use influencers or popular industry names to encourage your target audience to choose your brand, but remember that this is often a strategy leveraged by larger, more experienced businesses.

Cause Marketing

We discussed TOMS and Warby Parker earlier because they do this kind of marketing well. Maybe it's what got you to buy their products! With this strategy, you link the services and products of your company to a social cause or issue. This will be more relevant to you given that you are seeking to start a *social* enterprise. Take a deeper look at this model: TOMS has pledged to donate one pair of shoes to a child in need for every pair its customers purchase, and Warby Parker donates a pair of glasses to an underserved individual for every transaction with their customers. Providing customers with a sense of moral satisfaction, this method is often a great way to generate empathy and popularity!

Word of Mouth

You've probably already adopted this strategy! Through word of mouth, you spread information about your social enterprise either on your own or through customers who are satisfied with your service/ product. For instance, Coke used the "Share a Coke" campaign to prompt its happy customers to buy a drink for their friends, ultimately allowing them to revive sales. With effective word-of-mouth marketing, your customers do the marketing for you!

Which strategy seems most interesting and relevant to your social enterprise? How would you apply that strategy to promote your products or services?

IV. Measure Your Marketing

Rock on! You've nailed down the fundamentals of marketing campaigns, but let's not forget that measurement is the key to optimizing any process. Marketing campaigns are no exception.

Here's the tea: when you measure performance indicators for your marketing campaigns, you can clearly see what works and what doesn't. With this data in mind, you can then direct your marketing dollars toward the most effective campaigns to achieve marketing success! Here's a brief overview of some metrics:

- **Return on Investment (ROI):** We reviewed this briefly in the beginning of this book in broader terms. In this case, the ROI is a relatively simple figure: the sales revenue a campaign brings on every dollar spent. The formula for ROI is as follows:

  ROI = Investment gain/cost of investment

Because investment gain is the difference between the current value of investment and the cost of investment, you can reframe the formula as follows:

ROI = (Current value of investment - cost of investment)/cost of investment

For example, if Kyle spent $100 on marketing to generate $1,000 in sales, Kyle's ROI is 900%!

ROI = ($100 - $10)/$10 = $90/$10 = 9 × 100 = **900%**

- **Customer Acquisition Cost (CAC):** This measures how much you spend in marketing to create that win or acquire that sale from your customer. Think about this one as cost per win! The formula for CAC is as follows:

  CAC = (Marketing costs + sales costs)/number of new customers acquired

  For example, if Kyle spent $100 on marketing to win fifty customers, Kyle's CAC is $2.

  CAC = $100/50 customers = **$2/customer**

With these two methods, you can track the efficiency of your strategies and adjust your approach to marketing accordingly. Remember, you always want as high of an ROI and as low of a CAC as possible!

As we continue exploring different topics, it is important to recognize that good marketing can have an incredible effect on your social enterprise—it can ultimately boost sales, build your reputation, and maintain your relevance among your customer base, which is everything when it comes to business!

V. Cheat Code Recap

1. Marketing is a company's overall game plan for getting its products or services into the hands of potential leads and cultivating relationships with those leads into customers.
2. Effective marketing involves defining your target market, developing your customer profile, leveraging user interviews, and defining the Four P's.
3. The Four P's are product, price, place, and promotion.
4. To optimize your marketing campaigns, you must quantify your metrics, measure your success, and keep doing what works.

Chapter 12

Pricing & Financial Statements

Written by: Aditya Desai, Tiffany Yau, Geethika Koneru, and Yunling Huang

"You can determine the strength of a business over time by the amount of agony they go through in raising prices." —Warren Buffett, American investor, entrepreneur, and businessman

I. Introduction to Pricing

We know it's been on your mind for a while, so we're here to finally address it: *How* do you price your product or service? Finding the perfect price means that customers are willing to buy it while you make some bucks for your creative genius!

We understand the tension. Charge too much and it won't sell, but charge too little and you'll not only forgo significant revenues and profits but also fix your product's market value at a low level.

There is some good news: pricing isn't a set-in-stone number like from your algebra tests! Depending on new costs or considerations, you can adjust your price as needed. So don't sweat it—we won't be calling Ms. Quadratic Formula anytime soon!

First things first, don't let your inner worries limit you from launching your social enterprise. Just like everything else in entrepreneurship, pricing is an *iterative* process, meaning it's something that can be done over and over, based on new data. In fact, the best pricing data you can get is by launching and testing with real customers—but you still need to start somewhere with a price that works!

Trust us, you'll fall into a black hole of articles, books, and advice if you team up with Google on this one. So, we've simplified the process into a few easy-to-follow steps. It's critical to understand that all products are different and thus it's expected that they'll have different prices.

Simply put: an Xbox and an ice cream cone have drastically different prices because they offer different value, technology, and more. There are tons of ways to think about pricing, but we're here to make it easy for you to start, which is why we'll first introduce you to **cost-based pricing**!

II. Cost-Based Pricing

If this rings a bell, you're onto something: we introduced this method in Chapter 11. That was just an introduction; now it's time to go deep!

At its core, cost-based pricing is about basing the price point of your product or service on the *cost* it takes to create. At a high level, you must do the following if you choose to leverage cost-based pricing:

1. Calculate the total cost of making your product.
2. Add a percentage markup to determine the final price.

Step 1: Determining your total costs

Every business needs to worry about two types of costs: variable costs and fixed costs.

Variable costs are costs that may vary—like labor, commission, or materials needed to create your product—because of factors like the market value of these elements or your volume of production.

Let's say you are Geppetto, the wood carver from the classic story of Pinocchio. Let's assume that everything you sell is made of wood *only*. Imagine you make and sell 100 wooden products per week from 10 large boards of lumber, and each board costs you $100.

The total cost of lumber is $1,000 per week (10 boards per week x $100 per lumber).

This means that each product you create has a variable cost of $10 ($1,000 total cost of lumber per week/100 wooden products per week = $10 variable cost per wooden product).

But let's say you decide to make your products smaller in size using the same amount of wood. Let's say you are able to make 200 wooden products per week from 10 boards of lumber.

This now means that your variable cost would be only $5 ($1,000 total cost of lumber per week/200 wooden products per week = $5 variable cost per wooden product).

Your volume of production doubled from 100 to 200, and as a result, your variable cost decreased from $10 to $5.

However, if you slowed down to making 50 wooden products per week from the same amount of lumbers, your variable cost would be $20 ($1,000 total cost of lumber per week/50 wooden products per week = $20 variable cost per wooden product).

Here's a rule of thumb to keep in mind while calculating your pricing:

- When volume of production increases, variable costs often decrease.
- When volume of production decreases, variable costs often increase.

Fixed costs are costs that remain the same regardless of production output, like lease, payroll taxes, employee benefits, insurance, and interest payments.

Using the same example, Geppetto (you) hires Pinocchio to help you, and you begin paying him. You would then add in his payroll taxes, employee benefits, and more.

If you're in the early stage of business development, it is likely that fixed costs aren't as relevant to you yet.

Regardless, you'll still need to calculate your total costs. Oftentimes, this is known as our **cost of goods sold (COGS).** COGS always includes your variable costs and sometimes your fixed costs, depending on how you want to structure your business from an accounting perspective.

Stepping out of our fantasy example, let's evaluate a slightly less fictional example. Let's look at the cost per product of a real-life company: Nike (pretend you're not one of those Adidas Ultraboost shoe fans momentarily). Specifically, we'll consider a Nike shoe that retails for $50.

For simplicity, we will only consider our variable costs per product. This includes the physical cost of making the product and any associated shipping and marketing expenses.

Nike: Costs

Factory Fabric	$10.00
Assembly Cost	$15.00
Sea Freight & Insurance	$1.00
Import Duty	$2.50
Total Cost	**$28.50**

This means that Nike faces a direct cost of production from factory to facility of $28.50. If they decide to price the shoe at $50, that means they'll make $21.50 per shoe, right?

Actually, not quite!

Don't forget that there are many other costs that need to be taken into account when determining the perfect price. So far, we've learned about our COGS. The other two main categories to consider are 1) your marketing and promotion costs and 2) your **selling, general, and administrative (SG&A)** costs.

When performing a **unit economics** analysis within the marketing category, we calculate our customer acquisition cost (CAC). Think about this as any marketing or publicity expenses that must be used to draw attention to your social enterprise and acquire your customers. A great example of active CACs is when a business mails out a newsletter or coupon to local residents, prompting them to use its new service.

The other category is SG&A. This primarily includes rent and salaries for your social enterprise. That's right, you can't forget that your own time is valuable! Many early-stage entrepreneurs often neglect to include this in their calculations because they just want to see their product or service get out there, and often make the excuse that they'll pay themselves later. If you can't factor in pay for yourself—the person who is most invested in the business—that is only discounting your own value and actually destabilizes your own long-term well-being and motivation.

To price your time, set an hourly rate you want to earn from your business and then divide that by how many products you can make in that time. To set a sustainable price, make sure to incorporate the cost of your time as a variable product cost.

Going back to our Nike example, their total COGS for their sneakers per unit is greater than $28.50, which means they are making less than $21.50 per shoe.

Here's a separate example:

Ryan's Apparel Store: Costs

Cost of goods sold	
Fabric	$3.25
Packaging	$1.78
Shipping	$4.50
Marketing, Advertising, Promotional	
Promotional materials (CAC)	$0.75
SG&A	
Production time (your paid time per unit)	$2.00
Total unit (per-product) cost	**$12.28**

In this example, Ryan's total unit cost is **$12.28.**

Let's keep this number in mind as we explore how to calculate a profit margin for a product or service. We'll use the total unit cost from Ryan's Apparel to illustrate.

Step 2: Add in your desired profit margin

Now that know how to calculate the true cost of your product or service, you have to ask yourself how much you want to make. **Profit margin** is a measure of how much money a company is making by selling their products or services.

If Ryan selling his products for $12.28 per unit, he's not making any money! This is why you need to add a profit margin. You can calculate this by dividing how much extra money you want to make (profit) by revenues:

Profit margin = profit/revenue

For example, if you are selling lemonade for $1 per cup and it takes you $0.50 to make each cup, your margin is 50%.

50% = ($1.00 - $0.50)/$1.00

Going back to Ryan's Apparel Store, let's say he wants to earn a 30% profit margin on his products on top of his variable costs. When choosing the percentage you want to add, it's important to remember two things:

You haven't included your fixed costs yet (costs that are always present), so you will have costs to cover beyond just your variable costs.

You need to consider the overall market and make sure that your price with this margin still falls within the overall "acceptable" price for your market. If you're charging double the price of all of your competitors, you might find it challenging to make sales.

Now, to calculate Ryan's desired price given a 30% profit margin, he should use the following formula:

Price = Total costs + profit margin

Total costs = $12.28

Profit margin = 30%

Price = $12.28 + ($12.28 × 0.3) = $12.28 + $3.68 = **$15.96**

Ryan's Apparel would charge $15.96 if he plans to use the cost-based pricing strategy.

What does a cost-based pricing model look like for your company? You can access our online worksheet to get started.

III. Market-Based Pricing Strategy

If the cost-based pricing model doesn't excite you, we don't blame you! Today, there are so many emerging ways to price your products, so let's take a look at another commonly used strategy.

Also known as competitive pricing, **market-based pricing** is a pricing strategy that evaluates the prices of similar products that are already on the market—they're a tidy reference point!

Remember to only consider products or services that are similar to the product or service that your social enterprise is offering. Of course, depending on the features of your product, you'll be able to set the price higher or lower than the competitor price.

Let's go back to our shoe example. Suppose you're about to launch a sweet pair of new kicks on the market—and the pair of $50 Nike running shoes are your competition. If both shoes offer similar materials, longevity, and benefits, you would price your product around $50 per the market-based strategy. But let's change the stakes a bit: let's say your shoe is particularly special (because of course it is). Specifically, it has foot-warming capabilities and a portable charger installed in the heel of the shoe—now that's cool! In this scenario, you wouldn't charge in the ballpark of $50 like Nike is because your shoe is offering far *more* features than the potential competition!

How would you price your product or service if you're using a market-based pricing model?

IV. Additional Product Pricing Strategies

Value-based pricing is a strategy based on what customers think a product or service is worth, rather than what it actually costs. The value is determined through market testing, based on feedback regarding the perceived value. For example, customers will sometimes pay more if a new good or innovative solution saves them a lot of time because they see it as more valuable.

Premium pricing is a pricing strategy that reflects the prestige, luxury, or exclusive value of the products or services a company provides. Typically, at a premium price, customers have high expectations of quality, performance, and service.

There are many product pricing strategies you can use, some of which we've listed as follows:

Penetration pricing

With this approach, you have the opportunity to set a low initial price on a new product or service to gain high sales or market share. Once this point is reached, the prices are increased to normal pricing levels. This tactic is often used when releasing new products or services. For instance, at the beginning of every new year, various gyms often have discounts to make themselves more approachable to potential new members.

Skimming pricing

This strategy sets a high initial price with the aim to excite audiences who desire products or services. Once the required profits are made, the price is then lowered for a wider market! Think of how Tesla has lowered its prices of its cars significantly.

Loss leader pricing

This strategy aims to attract customers by offering a product or service below what it actually costs. The strategy works on the hope that customers will also purchase other products or services that have a higher profit margin from that same company.

Even with these market-based or value-based strategies, you always need to consider *product demand*, or how many people are willing to buy your product at a given price point. With higher demand, your company will be able to offer your product at a higher price. However, if and when the demand falls, many companies offer discounts to maintain consumer interest. Yep, we're talking about all those flash sales you see in the paper and on TV—it's all a response to product demand!

Don't think that the price of your product is subject to change due to demand only—its *product life cycle,* or phases in the market, is an important regulator as well! Rest assured that this isn't a repeat of the caterpillar-to-butterfly process that you've been taught for so long; we have something new and exciting for you! When talking about products, we're looking at the introduction stage when demand is building to the end of the life cycle when demand begins to fall off. Here's the traditional pattern that you should always keep in mind: the market-based price will be higher in the beginning and lower at the end of the life cycle as the product begins to phase out and be replaced by competitors or an updated version (either yours or someone else's).

Next up, we have **price sensitivity**. Have you ever filled up on a few gallons of Slurpee at 7-Eleven on July 11th (i.e., 7.11)? July 11th is National Free Slurpee Day for a reason! Price sensitivity—a measurement of how much the price of goods and services affects customers' willingness to buy them—is a real thing and plays a role here! It determines the degree to which the price of a product affects consumers' purchasing behaviors. Let's entertain a little visual: load your potential customer on a slingshot and see how far you can stretch them back. If it's a lot, that means they have low price sensitivity, meaning your company can easily price above the competition and justify the pricing by explaining the unique value of that produce at that price. However, if that slingshot will barely budge, then you know your customers are very sensitive, thus, it's to your advantage to match the pricing of competitors or price your product just below the competition's price.

A Wicked Pricing Case Study: The Harry Potter Series

Pricing applies to everything, even outside of your traditional startup or small business. For instance, let's take a look at fantasy books to understand different pricing strategies.

If you go to Amazon, one of the largest book-selling platforms, and look up "fantasy books" in the search bar, you are going to find fantasy paperbacks with a price range from less than$10 to $50 or more.[79]

A new author may utilize cost-based pricing to start. Although the cost of a book depends on the type of paper used, the number of pages, and the presence of illustrations in the book, it is highly unlikely that the price of a book would differ so vastly based on printing costs alone. Some other things that might be accounted for in the baseline price can include the cost of distribution, cost of sales and book marketing, costs of royalty paid to the author, and costs of the cover and other elements of production. The publisher could then add their own profit margin to the book based on the projected sales, which depend on the author's popularity, the reader demographics, and the genre of the book.[80]

---

79 Wikipedia, s.v. "List of Online Booksellers," accessed December 12, 2022, https://en.wikipedia.org/wiki/List_of_online_booksellers.

80 Lavanya, "Book Pricing: How the Cover Price of a Book Is Set," 2014

New authors can also follow market-based pricing by basing the price of their book on the prices of other fantasy books.

More established authors, on the other hand, might use value-based pricing to price their books higher than market cost because they know their readers are going to buy the book for a higher cost. An extreme example of value-based pricing is the case of a single first edition of *Harry Potter and the Sorcerer's Stone*, the first book in the Harry Potter series, selling for a whopping $471,000 in 2021, two decades after it was first released.[81]

When *Harry Potter and the Deathly Hallows* was first released, it ran for an initial print of 12 million copies, with 8.3 million copies sold in the United States within the first 24 hours alone.[82] Because of the Harry Potter series popularity, the book was priced higher at the time compared to its counterparts.

Pricing also varies based on the type of product. For example, the Harry Potter paperbacks are generally priced around $10 as of today, more than a decade since the books were released, whereas the e-books and audiobooks are available for free—an interesting strategy to help more and more children discover and explore the magical world of wizardry years after the conclusion of the story.

Once people immerse themselves in the world of Harry Potter (and develop a sense of brand loyalty), they will be interested in buying

---

81 Reuters, "'Harry Potter' First Edition Sells for Smashing $471,000," 2021.

82 "Scholastic Announces Record Breaking Sales of 11.5 Million Copies of Harry Potter and the Deathly Hallows in First Ten Days," Scholastic Mediaroom, 2007.

the extensive merchandise available, such as Hogwarts' robes, Harry Potter stationary, and maybe even a visit to Universal Studios for the Harry Potter Gringotts experience!

Then there are the spin-offs like the Fantastic Beasts series that have been made into movies and are available as illustrated books, which are priced around $20 today.

Did you know that J.K. Rowling was one of the producers of the Fantastic Beasts movies? Do you see how pricing the Harry Potter audio and e-books for $0 is still an effective profit-making strategy when you look at the bigger picture?

These books may be sold at a lower price, but they pave the way for consumers to buy other, more expensive products in the future. So, a product's pricing can depend on not only the cost of the production, or even the value the marketplaces on similar products, but also where the product is in the grand scheme of things you want to achieve beyond that one product alone. Ultimately, profit can be made indirectly, depending on how loyal of a customer base you are able to build.

We have discussed the Harry Potter series a bit here. But did you know that this is not the only world the author has created? J.K. Rowling has also authored adult crime fiction books under the pen name Robert Galbraith, who is responsible for the six-book Cormoran Strike series.

These books have paperbacks priced around $11 and audio and e-books available for free. And like the Harry Potter series, these books are currently being brought to life in a live-action film.

These books may have been written under a pen name, but when you search them online, the results show that they are authored by J.K. Rowling. So, as expected, you as the consumer might be more likely to take a look at the books and pick them out from all the crime fiction books available out there (assuming you like J.K. Rowling's work already).

Beyond the wizarding world, J.K. Rowling has also written two children's books (a different genre from the Harry Potter books, which come under young adult fiction). *The Christmas Pig*, the latest children's book by J.K. Rowling, uses a different pricing strategy than the Harry Potter books. The audiobook is free only if you have select platform subscriptions, and both the paperbacks and e-books are priced around $11 and $15, respectively.

Children's books often include illustrations that tend to make them pricier than young adult novels. The pricing strategy here is more of a typical market-based pricing strategy rather than a value-based pricing strategy. And, these prices are slightly higher than the average children's books—likely due to the widely established and acknowledged storytelling skills of the author.

Ultimately, a product is often priced using a cost- or market-based strategy, and if successful, may change to a value-based model. It is important to keep the big picture in mind when projecting or planning profit margins.

The first book by a new author may not yield much of a profit margin, but if done right, others down the road may be more likely to yield much more, assuming that the author successfully scaled a loyal customer base.

Beyond the sector of publishing, the same concepts can be applied to your social enterprise's product or service. Consider pricing different versions of the product according to different pricing strategies.

VI. Communicating Your Company's Financial Potential

Since we're on the topic of money, we should talk about how to communicate your social enterprise's financial performance. This involves creating **financial statements**, which are formal written records that investors frequently use to evaluate a company's financial health and earnings potential.

Financial statements are useful because they tell you a few things:

- If your pricing is too low or too high
- If you are spending too much or too little in other areas, like production costs, marketing costs, etc.
- How to budget and set goals for increasing your net worth

There are three main types of financial statements you need to know about:

- Cash flow statements
- Balance sheets
- Income statements, or profit and loss (P&L) statements

Cash Flow Statement

Ever heard of the phrase "cash is king?" It refers to when companies or individuals have large amounts of cash on hand and/or liquid assets (i.e., assets that are easily turned into cash), which gives them more flexibility in their spending, whether that be for their business operations or personal lives. The phrase can be interpreted a variety of ways, but it ultimately means that cash is superior to other forms of payment at the end of the day.

To really understand how to build financial stability and achieve your financial goals, it is important that you fully grasp the concepts of cash inflow and outflow.

Cash inflow is the cash you are gaining. This is a term that can be used to describe the cash that a business is bringing in.

On the other hand, **cash outflow** is the opposite—it is the cash that is spent or goes "out."

You can categorize cash flow (both cash inflow and cash outflow) in the following three ways:

- **Operating cash flow:** This is the cash flow related to your business operations. Cash inflow here would be your revenue from your sales. Cash outflow would be salaries.
- **Investing cash flow:** This is less relevant to you as an entrepreneur building an enterprise, but it's still good to know that that this is the cash flow as a result of company's investment in another company.
- **Financing cash flow:** This is related to companies selling ownership for investment. Cash inflow here includes selling

bonds to make cash, whereas cash outflow would include activities like companies buying back their stock from investors.

The term cash flow, or **net cash flow**, is used to describe the difference between your cash inflows and cash outflows.

Net cash flow = cash inflow – cash outflow

Obviously, the better-case scenario is to have a positive net cash flow, which means you have more than you spend. Negative cash flow means that you spend more than you earn, which either puts you in debt or bankruptcy.

We measure cash flow with a **cash flow statement**. A cash flow statement is a type of financial statement that measures your cash inflows and outflows for a specific period of time (monthly, annually, etc.).

Feel free to use this template from our website to practice creating your own cash flow statement.

Understanding your cash flow is important because it will help you figure out your main sources of income and how you can wisely spend your money. We are here to help you learn some ways you can improve your cash flow so you can reach the financial goals you set for your new company.

The cash flow statement is useful for businesses and their investors because it tells them how to act upon certain strategies, including the following:

- Increase your income

- Cut down on your expenses
- Pay off or refinance your debt

Balance Sheet

Meanwhile, a **balance sheet** is the second type of personal financial statement. This one provides an overall snapshot of your company's **wealth**, or **net worth** (the sum of your **assets** and **liabilities**) during a specific period in time.

Net worth = assets – liabilities

Assets are anything you own that has the expectation of creating future economic value, like the embroidery and sewing machines employees use to stitch sneakers together for Ryan's Apparel Store, the pots and pans for your bakery business, or the trucks Amazon uses to deliver their packages. Liabilities are what you owe, like your outstanding payments, bills you still owe on an asset if you had an initial **down payment** (the amount of money you pay when purchasing an expensive product or service if you don't pay the full amount upfront), credit card debt, and other loans.

The difference between your assets and your liabilities is your net worth. It's important to understand and communicate your net worth because it is quantified evidence to demonstrate whether you are in good financial standing. Your net worth is an indicator of your company's overall wealth—not just how much you make but also how much you own (your assets) and how much you owe (your liabilities). In the long game, having good control over your net worth is vital for financial planning—and not just for your business but also for your personal life, like planning how you want to buy your first home or reach your retirement goals.

Feel free to use this template from our website to try creating your own balance sheet.

Income Statement, or P&L Statement

Lastly, we also have our income statement. **Income statements** represent a company's revenue, expenses, net income, and earnings per share during a particular period. These periods are most commonly segmented into a year or quarters, as in every three months—January 1 to March 31 is the first quarter of the year (Q1), April 1 to June 30 is Q2, and so on. Income statements are also commonly known as P&L statements.

Net income is different from net worth. Net income is the amount of money you have available after paying off your company's variable and fixed expenses, like operating expenses, SG&A expenses, COGS, taxes, insurance, and more.

An overly simplified formula is as follows:

Net income = (revenue + gains) - (expenses + losses)

Feel free to use the templates from our website to try creating your own income statements.

Ultimately, understanding and maintaining these three types of financial statements is essential to helping you plan effectively for your enterprise's financial future—whether it's figuring out how to price your products or services appropriately or figuring out how you want to plan out the next few years. Regular provision of these statements also demonstrates the financial health and potential of your business to your potential future investors.

VII. Cheat Code Recap

1. Cost-based pricing bases the price you're selling your product or service for on the cost it takes to create it. This involves calculating the total costs of making your product and adding a markup percentage to determine the final price.
2. Market-based pricing is a type of pricing strategy that evaluates the prices of similar products that are already on the market.
3. Cash flow statements, balance sheets, and income statements are the main types of financial statements needed to communicate your company's financial health and earning potential to stakeholders.

Part 4:
Getting It Out There!

Chapter 13
Marketing Strategies

Written by: Brooke McCormick, Aditya Desai, and Ashley Han

"You are everywhere, but you don't have to be. Strategy is a decision to take a path, to say no." – Kristina Halvorson, American author and content strategist

I. Strategy Equals Success

In Chapter 11, we introduced the foundations of what it takes to effectively market your social enterprise. Now, it's time to get your idea out there with the last of the Four P's of marketing: promotion!

Let's say you've crafted this unique, life-changing product that uses the principles of social entrepreneurship to solve real problems in your community. This is not just a hypothetical—it could totally be you by the time you finish this book!

It would be unfortunate to let that idea just sit there and never connect with customers. This is where marketing strategies step in. There are lots to choose from, but not every strategy works for every product.

For instance, if you're trying to create a home aide startup, is targeting senior citizens specific enough?

The short answer is no, it's *not* specific enough. Carefully consider everyone who could possibly benefit from your service. As you've learned in previous chapters, finding your target market is time consuming and requires that you apply an analytical perspective to find exactly who you're selling to. Remember to study your competitors to see the kinds of customers *they* target, and consider your customer's age, location, gender, lifestyles, attitudes, and behaviors. Senior citizens between 70 and 80 years old in Los Angeles who often take walks at the park could be a more appropriate target.

So, back to the example. What kind of marketing strategies would be effective for this target audience?

Word-of-mouth would be good, as would print flyers through the mail or posted to local businesses that are frequented by older people. Crafting your unique marketing strategy does require you to implement some design thinking strategies. You need to *empathize* with the end user to discover *how* they could come across your concept.

Marketing is All Around Us

Sometimes there's this notion that marketing is duplicitous, just a sneaky way to sell the customer snake oil. Although there are businesses that do use marketing to disguise the low quality of their product, there are also many companies that use marketing to connect with customers to introduce an amazing product or service to them that adds real value to their lives.

Marketing is all around us. And it can influence our day-to-day and long-term decisions more than we think. For instance, let's say you're out and about running errands on a hot summer day. You're craving a cold caffeinated beverage for a jolt of energy and refreshment. Where are you going to go to obtain this drink?

Although you might just *see* a coffee shop and stumble in, there's definitely a chance that where you go is actually influenced by marketing:

- If Starbucks has been running a campaign on social media and displaying appealing billboards throughout town highlighting the latest Frappuccino, complete with rainbow pastel colors and a mound of whipped cream, you'll likely step into the closest location for a taste of the sugary goodness.
- If you've been wanting to support local businesses and the environment, you might step into the shop that has a

handwritten sign that reads "locally roasted, ethically sourced coffee" and purchase their expensive cup of joe. This coffee shop also has a few locations around the city and never fails to mention its pride for, let's say, Philadelphia, which resonates with your high value for civic pride.

- If you're in a hurry, the bright orange and pink branding of Dunkin' Donuts might catch your eye and convince you somehow that it's the fastest, cheapest option. After all, the slogan "America runs on Dunkin," complete with the image of a running stick figure, surely sounds like it's a speedy operation that's perfectly fitting for your day running errands, right? Or maybe you enter Dunkin' Donuts because your favorite TikTok star, Charli D'Amelio, has spotlighted the company many times on her platform.

If you look at it from a businessperson's perspective, marketing can make you see the world differently. The field requires a deep understanding of human psychology to match the product or service with the right customer.

Here's a simple "formula":

good marketing = well-communicated product-market fit = customer satisfaction = customer loyalty = competitive advantage

When a company finds unique ways to brand their product and leverage effective marketing strategies (also known as your **go-to-market strategy**), customers will naturally develop trust and appreciation for the company, leading to a loyal customer base.

Before we go any further, we should recall the steps of finding the right marketing strategy. These should feel familiar, but feel free to reference past chapters if you're fuzzy on any concept:

1. Define your target market
2. Develop your customer profile
3. Leverage your user interviews
4. Define the foundational Four P's of your marketing strategy

Let's also recall whether you'll use a business-to-consumer (B2C) marketing strategy, or a business-to-business (B2B) marketing strategy.

Overall, there are a lot of similarities—you need to consider the average customer, the branding of your product or service, and the advertising channels, just to name a few factors.

However, B2B marketing has to get even more specific. This is because, in B2C marketing, you can theoretically reach any potential customer—word spreads easily. For example, if you know that one of your friends is trying to redecorate their house, and if you happened to have seen an advertisement for a sale from a homeware brand, you could easily send it to them. Thus, the final customer (your friend) is not necessarily the person who was exposed to the marketing (you).

But in B2B, there's not a lot of room for customer conversion. Only a small portion of the company will make the decision to buy a product or service. For instance, in a huge retail company, it's not up to the salespeople on the floor to buy the signage, but rather a group among the upper tiers of corporate management.

B2B customers aren't as easily swayed by impulse compared to, say, a hungry B2C customer eyeing a Snickers bar in the grocery store checkout line. So, if you're marketing to B2B customers, you need to be exact and provide a lot of information to sway their purchasing decisions.

II. Marketing Strategies Crash Course

Some of the most successful brands employ a number of marketing models and approaches—they don't stick to just one. We reviewed a few in Chapter 11, but we also wanted to give you a crash course on some more strategies you might consider for your business.

Paid Advertising

Pay-per-click is a model of internet marketing in which advertisers pay a fee each time one of their ads is clicked. Here, you set a budget for your ads on a given platform, such as Google or Facebook, and then pay when someone clicks on your ad. It is also known as pay-per-impression or pay-per-view. Some commonly used channels where you can see pay-per-click advertising also include Facebook paid ads, Twitter ad campaigns, and sponsored messages on LinkedIn.

Social Media Ads

We'll be expanding on this more on this in Chapter 14, but it's exactly what it sounds like: an ad displayed on social media personalized to your preferences, depending on how you engage with the platform. For instance, Facebook's "audience insights" feature makes it easy for marketers to home in on target demographics, learn about users' preferences, and create compelling ad content.

Social media ads can expose a much larger demographic to a company's product or service offering and reposition their branding.

Banner Ads

Banner ads are a type of image-based internet marketing that stretches across the top, bottom, or sides of a website in order to bring traffic to the product or service's website. These can create brand awareness and pivot customers to a newsletter, promotion, website, etc. When you think of Adobe, you probably think about photography, creativity, and images. They embed these very words into their banner ads.

Influencer Marketing

Influencer marketing is a type of marketing where you work with a well-known industry name to encourage your target audience to choose your brand. You're probably familiar with influencers on Instagram. #Ad, anyone?

Think of those times you saw the White House bring in celebrities like Olivia Rodrigo to advocate for vaccination during the peak of the COVID-19 pandemic or BTS to bring awareness to the rise in hate crimes against Asian Americans.

Cause Marketing

Cause marketing links the services and products of a company to a social cause or issue. It is also known as "cause-related marketing."

For instance, Pampers and UNICEF engaged in a partnership where the purchase of every pack of diapers equated to the distribution of one vaccine.[83] UNICEF's brand name added substantially to the campaign's power to build a new business for Pampers and was beneficial to the recruitment and retention of staff at Pampers' parent company. Meanwhile, other brands, such as clothing brands Patagonia and The North Face have consistently supported causes that work to protect the environment.

Relationship Marketing

This type of marketing is basically focused on building customer relationships. It is all about enhancing existing relationships with customers and improving customer loyalty. Tesla famously spends very little on marketing. Think about the last time you saw a Tesla ad—never! Instead, they rely on word-of-mouth referrals to their fleet of electric cars and the occasional shoutouts from Elon Musk's tweets.[84]

Undercover Marketing

No, not like the TV show *Undercover Boss*! Rather, this type of marketing strategy focuses on marketing the product while customers remain unaware of the marketing strategy. It is also known as "stealth marketing."

---

83 "Pampers '1 Pack = 1 Vaccine' Campaign: 'Happy Birthday' Ad," YouTube, October 30, 2016, https://www.youtube.com/watch?v=Ca3gOvpoJHU.

84 Loveday, "Tesla Spends Least on Ads, Most on R&D: Report," 2022.

Product placement is an example of this incredibly effective type of marketing! Companies gain exposure for their products by paying for them to be featured in the media. For example, Eggo waffles were featured prominently in the hit Netflix original show *Stranger Things*.[85] This led to a 14% increase in Eggo purchases in 2017 Q4 sales.[86] I mean, who *wouldn't* want to emulate Eleven?

But it's not so easy to get your product or service featured in a hit TV show or movie; such a fear requires complex legal negotiations. You've probably seen "The Pear Company" computers instead of Apple computers featured in shows like *iCarly, Sam & Cat, Henry Danger,* and *Victorious*.[87] Apple was not able to sue these shows because The Pear Company is a creation of parody rather than an actual company.

Word of Mouth

Have you ever tried a product because your friend recommended it? This marketing strategy is called **word of mouth**. This strategy totally relies on the impression a company's products or services leaves on people. It is traditionally the most important marketing strategy. When you give quality services to customers, it is likely that they will promote you to their colleagues, friends, and family.

---

85 Beer, "Netflix's 'Stranger Things' Is Dangerously close to Becoming 'Sponsored Things'," 2019.

86 Wittmer, "Netflix's 'Stranger Things' Boosted Eggo Waffle Sales Because One of the Main Characters Is Obsessed with Them," 2018.

87 "Pear Company," ICarly Wiki, accessed November 29, 2022. https://icarly.fandom.com/wiki/Pear_Company#:~:text=Pear%20Company%20is%20an%20obvious.

For instance, Coca-Cola used the "Share a Coke" campaign to revive sales across 70 countries. Coke printed bottles with common names on them so people would be inspired to buy them for a friend or relative.[88]

Dropbox offered 500 megabytes of extra storage space to new customers and the people who referred them.[89] Customers can continue to earn more space by referring more people, which increases loyalty.

Transactional Marketing

Transactional marketing is a type of marketing where companies, particularly retailers, encourage customers to buy with coupons, discounts, and huge events. It grows their likelihood of increasing their number of sales and motivates the target audience to buy the promoted products.

This can include limited-time deals at a reduced rate or providing coupons for certain purchases. The purpose of transactional marketing is to focus on driving sales not building long-term customer relationships.

For example, let's say you need a pair of headphones and you decide on the product that's on sale and fits your requirements. Perhaps it is wireless and has a long battery life. However, you may

---

88 Tan, "9 Brilliant Coca Cola Advertising Examples of Referral Marketing," 2022.

89 "How to Refer Friends to Dropbox and Get More Storage Space," Dropbox, accessed February 14, 2023, https://help.dropbox.com/storage-space/earn-space-referring-friends.

never purchase a product from the company again because they have low brand awareness.

Diversity Marketing

Diversity marketing caters to diverse audiences by customizing and integrating different marketing strategies toward a particular group. This strategy considers aspects of the customer like their culture, beliefs, attitudes, and specific needs. Some examples include the following:

- Coca-Cola's "America the Beautiful" Superbowl commercial featured a cast of diverse individuals singing various lines of the song.[90] The song, which began in English and included portions sung in Hindi and Arabic, also featured imagery of a gay couple, a Latino family, a group of women in traditional Middle Eastern attire, and a group of Jewish men wearing yarmulkes.
- Harley Davidson marketed to women by creating classes to teach women how to ride motorcycles.[91]
- Cheerios addressed diversity by advertising with an interracial family.[92]

---

90 Cause Marketing, "Coca-Cola #AmericaIsBeautiful 2014 Super Bowl Commercial," YouTube, https://www.youtube.com/watch?v=4-KxPRptu_Y.

91 Barrett, "In Quest to Expand Market, Harley-Davidson Reaches out to Women," 2013.

92 Elliott, "Vitriol Online for Cheerios Ad With Interracial Family," 2013, https://www.nytimes.com/2013/06/01/business/media/cheerios-ad-with-interracial-family-brings-out-internet-hate.html.

- McDonald's tailors its message in advertising based on its geographic location.[93]

III: Digital Marketing & Spotify

When was the last time you touched your smartphone? What was the last app you used on your smartphone? Next, grab your phone and check your screen time. What is your daily average? What about your weekly average? Which app did you use the most? How does this data compare with what other people's average screen time is? Here's a fascinating fact: according to a blog post on TechJury, Americans spend an average of 5.4 hours on their mobile phones daily.[94] What do you think about 5.4 hours of screen time? Is it too high or too low?

The rise in smartphone usage has changed the way people view, buy, and connect online. Whether it is booking flights, buying groceries, ordering food, online banking, or finding answers on search engines, people expect everything to happen and be delivered quickly. There are apps for almost anything and everything! And because of that, the marketing trend has been shifting lately. Today, marketers must rely on the most reliable source of information: the customer data. Data is now one of the most valuable resources on the planet.

When data is turned into insights, companies can offer greater relevance and personalization to enhance the marketing content,

---

93 Vignali, "McDonald's: 'Think Global, Act Local' - the Marketing Mix," 97–111.

94 Georgiev, "How Much Time Do Americans Spend on Their Phones in 2020?" 2020.

message, and experience to put out. Have you ever gotten a chill down your spine because of an ad that was too accurately relevant or targeted?

In this chapter, we are going to dive deeper to understand the main factors that drive digital marketing today. You will be able to understand what data-driven marketing and user experience is, why it is important, and how you can apply it in real life.

Data-Driven Marketing: Turning Data into Insights

Do you ever get surprised at how well Netflix chooses the right movie or show to add to recommendation list? You were into comedy recently and BOOM. The stand-up comedy show you've been meaning to watch is recommended right there. Or maybe you binge-watched Squid Game over a weekend and suddenly you have an endless list of recommended Korean dramas popping up on your screen. How convenient! It's like they read your mind and predicted your interest for you.

Personalized marketing can be defined as the implementation of a strategy by which companies deliver individualized content, informed by data collection, analysis, and the use of automation technology and real-time consumer insights. By using personalized marketing, companies can deliver more customized, personalized content to the end user. What are some other examples of personalized marketing you've noticed?

Personalized marketing is an outcome of data-driven marketing. **Data-driven marketing** is the process of creating marketing and advertising campaigns based on real consumer insights rather than intuition or assumptions alone. Basically, it is an approach that optimizes brand communications based on customer information. The data can be collected and used to predict consumer needs, desires, and behaviors.

For example, Spotify knows what kind of music genre you have been into recently and might recommend similar songs on your "recommended radio" list. This allows marketers to connect and form bonds with their customers at the right time, with the right products. Not only does it improve communication with the consumers but it also does the following:

- Personalizes the user experience
- Targets well-defined market segments
- Collects new data to help inform future strategies
- Brings in new customers
- Improves their strategies in real time

After learning about the benefits of data-driven marketing, you might wonder, what is the difference between data-driven marketing and traditional marketing? To understand the difference, we need to go back and review what traditional marketing is.

To make it simple, marketing has always focused on two objectives:

1. Discovering customers' needs and desires
2. Using those insights to deliver what customers wanted to buy

Marketing as a whole has come a long way from traditional marketing. Traditional marketing teams used a combination of two aspects to reach those objectives:

- Market studies available *at the time*
- Their *assumptions* about the target audience

However, this meant companies had to go through a lot of trial and error. They had to try many different strategies to find one or two that would work. In contrast, data-driven marketing allows marketers to connect with customers with the right offering at the right time thanks to the data customers provide simply by living their lives. Technology and the internet have made data-driven marketing possible. What a luxury it is to be able to validate our assumptions about our target audience!

There are four main steps to creating a personalized marketing strategy: identify, differentiate, interact, and customize.[95] They might seem similar to the design thinking steps, but they are different—don't get them confused!

- **Identify**. This is when data collection happens. Markers such as gender, age, and location are gathered.
- **Differentiate**. This is when the analysis happens, allowing companies to segment users into the specific niches they want to target.

---

[95] Peppers, Rogers, and Dorf, "Is Your Company Ready for One-To-One Marketing?," 151–160.

- **Interact**. This is when the collected data is used to contact a prospective or a current customer. It is important to reach out via a specific, preferred medium and through the methods they are most likely to respond to.
- **Customize**. This is where the personalization happens, and it's where a company can close the deal.

Why is personalized marketing so important nowadays? Why does it matter? The main benefits of personalized marketing are that it can

- improve customer experience,
- drive revenue,
- increase brand loyalty, and
- create consistency across channels.

This is everything for a business and its success.

IV. What Is User Experience and Why Does It Matter?

In the past, businesses had to build themselves using a one-way communication model where they broadcasted their message. This is where the term "**broadcast media**" originated. However, today's consumers are digitally native and tech-savvy, to the point they were practically born with phones in their hands. Phones and tablets are getting smaller and faster yet they hold more data than ever before. Everything—literally, everything, from streaming services to groceries—can be bought with just a click on the screen. Thanks to Amazon, consumers nowadays tend to have very high expectations for getting their needs delivered instantly. This is why a deep understanding of user experience is key to digital marketing success.

User experience, as we mentioned earlier on, can be defined as understanding user needs well enough to create products and services that provide a meaningful experience to the customers. A critical factor of that experience depends on one question: How easily can consumers find, access, review, and buy products or services? Businesses want to convert consumer interest into revenue, so user experience is crucial to business success and, in other cases, survival.

Now that you understand what user experience is, let's look at how user experience can fit into five tiers of content marketing:

- **Search engine optimization (SEO)**: SEO is the process of improving the quality and quantity of your content to attract website traffic from search engines. When you Google something and one website pops up higher on the results than another, there's a high chance that website leveraged SEO marketing. SEO marketing is the process of reorganizing the structure and content of a website to appear higher on the search results page. If your website is not optimized for search engines, your target audience or consumers in general will hardly ever find your product in the first place. It's important to know how to leverage SEO.
- **User experience**: By now, you are probably familiar with the importance of user experience but let's put it into perspective. According to a study by Adobe, when given fifteen minutes to consume content, two-thirds of people would rather read

something beautifully designed than something plain.[96] It is important to make your users' experiences enjoyable!

- **Content strategy**: You can now use the metrics you've gathered, such as **visitor numbers** (number of total visitors who visit your site) or **bounce rate** (the percentage of visitors who leave a web page without taking an action), to figure out how to curate your content most effectively to reach your audience. The goal of your creating an effective strategy is to get your target market's eyes onto what you're trying to put in front of them.
- **Content creation**: With a strategy in place, it is now time to do the fun part: creating convincing content! Now is the time to refresh any existing content, create new blog articles with your strategy in mind, and make sure each piece is formatted for digital consumption. The goal is to ensure all your content appeals to your buyer persona. If your content is appealing enough, potential customers will read the blogs, which leads them to your website and to all the awesome products and services you offer.
- **Content distribution**: Strategy done. Creating done. Now all you need to do is distribute and share the content all over social media. Share it with the right audience by using different social media channels and any other connections you've got. Get noticed. The content you create isn't meant to only be interesting, entertaining, or helpful—you created

96 "The State of Content: Expectations on the Rise," Adobe, 2015.

this content to *convert* website visitors into customers who will buy your product or service, hopefully more than once. The number of converted customers out of your total traffic is your **conversion rate**. The higher this is, the better!

V. Case Study: Spotify Secrets

Do you like to listen to music and podcasts? Who are your favorite artists? Most importantly, what is your favorite streaming platform? Let's talk about Spotify. Spotify is a Swedish audio streaming and media services provider that Daniel Ek and Martin Lorentzon co-founded in 2006.

Spotify is a relatively new company but one of the world's largest music streaming service providers, with over 356 million active users per *month*, including 158 million paying subscribers, as of March 2021. With an estimated 286 million monthly active users at the beginning of 2020, the Swedish company controls 36% of the global streaming industry.[97] Evidently, that's no small number of people! Spotify certainly must have had an effective marketing strategy.

What was their marketing strategy? What was the key to their users' hearts? Let's use the knowledge we have gained to take a critical look at this case study!

---

97 Schnoor, "Understanding Spotify's Marketing Mastery," 2020.

The Audience

Spotify's target audience is undoubtedly millennials. As of 2016, 72% of Spotify's user base consisted of millennials—this percentage has only grown since then to include more Gen Zers. In addition, Statista reports that 26% of Spotify users are between the ages of 18 and 24.[98] Spotify even created a marketing guide that companies can use to learn how to more effectively target millennials using Spotify![99] One reason Spotify has been so successful among millennials is because of the social media elements incorporated into the platform. For example, you can add friends on Spotify, create playlists, share playlists with friends, and follow other peoples' playlists. As Facebook and Twitter lose favor with millennials and Gen Zers, they will increasingly be seeking new social platforms that they can use to connect with their friends in unique ways.

Spotify's Content Creation

We can confidently say that Spotify has always been the front runner when it comes to following popular social media trends. Because its user base predominantly consists of millennials as of 2016, Spotify focused heavily on social media trends. That is why, unlike other companies that have a set platform and stick with their consistent marketing strategy, Spotify likes to change their marketing strategies from year to year. It is the era of fluidity; they do not settle on only one thing.

---

98 Cummings, "Infographic: 72% of Spotify Listeners Are Millennials. Here's How They Use the Service," 2016; Götting, "Spotify Users n the U.S. 2018, By Age," 2018.

99 "Marketing to Millennials on Spotify: Key Streaming Moments," Spotify Advertising, accessing February 14, 2023.

Their marketing strategy constantly evolves to become more *customer-centric.* Not only do they know and embrace the trend but also put a little spin of their own to make it unique to enhance the UX.

Let's look at Spotify's "Thanks 2016, it's been weird" campaign.

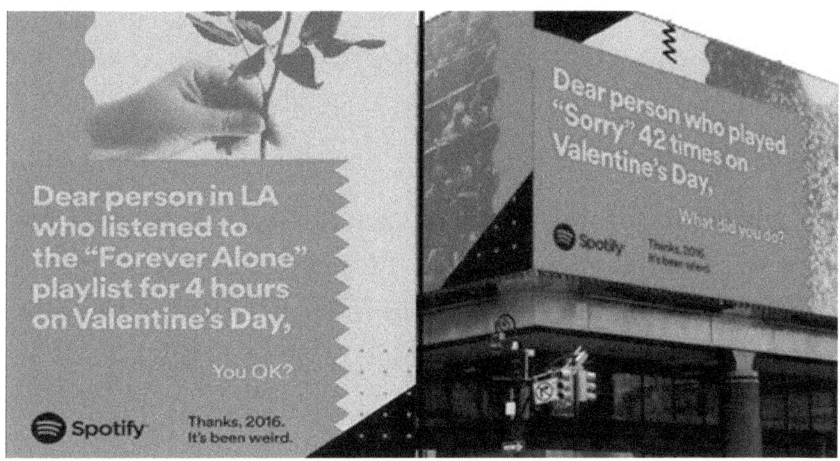

In 2016, the marketing team captured the oddity of the year and printed fun, spirited billboards with small black letters: "Thanks, 2016. It's been weird." This was their biggest campaign yet.[100]

Spotify's goal of launching this personal campaign was to interact with its audience. Thus, Spotify chose to launch a campaign that would reflect on music culture through its listener behavior. The campaign was specifically launched toward the very end of the year, as that tends to be a common time for people to reflect. This campaign was successful because it was primed to generate a human

100 Roberts, "Spotify Says: 'Thanks 2016, It's Been Weird,' in Its Largest Ad Campaign Yet," 2016.

connection with audiences around the globe by displaying relatable and humorous quotes.

Spotify's content strategy

Spotify went through four strategies to officially launch the "Thanks 2016, it's been weird" campaign.

Print Ads

The first step was to launch print ads across the world that displayed slogans that represent the music culture of 2016. These ads were splattered all around the world on the sides of buildings, billboards, and posters. The launch was global but highly localized.

Social Media

The second step was to release more exclusive data to be advertised on social media platforms. These ads didn't showcase just the kind of music people were listening to but also the trends of the music that were more popular among users. On social media, Spotify also presented quirky data-driven insights to its viewers based on the music listened to, creating humorous charts like "How many dances did Drake create in 2016?" and the documentation of Justin Bieber's hairstyle changes.

Personalized Lists

The next step was for Spotify to truly personalize their relationship with their users. Every Spotify user received an email that served as their own personal recap of 2016. Each email listed and ranked a consumer's favorite artists and songs of 2016. Over 30 million emails were opened. The personalized content from their emails remarked about how their unique preferences in music symbolized something about them as individuals and their year as a whole. This was an especially effective strategy because Spotify's content stood for some part of listeners' identities. If done well, effective brands have the unique power to help users express and communicate their individualism to those around them in a subtle way that they otherwise would not be able to.

Rewarding Committed Users

The final step was to reward the users who listened to a selection of artists and songs the most. Users that ranked number one in certain categories, like top listener of Migos's *Culture* album and Sia's *This Is Acting* album were rewarded with gifts. The winners of specific sections were mailed Christmas-themed presents. For example, winners who listened to the most trap music were sent wrapping paper with pictures of their favorite rappers on it, which they called "rapping paper." The winners of these gifts were announced through a series of live videos produced by Spotify that resulted in 10 million views.

Across these four strategies, creativity was the major driving force behind this campaign to make it a success. The utilization of witty messages written with bolded words and bright colors captured individuals' attention, and Spotify's noticeable and unique advertising has statically proven to be more eye-catching in comparison to other companies. The campaign was shared on social media over 669,000 times and resulted in about 1.2 million earned views.

Spotify's Personalized Marketing: Spotify Wrapped

Beyond using engaging marketing billboards, Spotify has completely re-imagined the way we listen to music. With instant access to favorite artists and songs under one roof, it's easier than ever to connect with the music that resonates with you the most, not just locally but also globally.

And by collecting and repurposing data around its users' listening behaviors, Spotify can recommend new artists, genres, or even the right music for your mood, which creates a resonating user experience that keeps its listeners engaged and curious.

To really take advantage of this data and create an even more personalized experience for listeners, Spotify introduced its "Spotify Wrapped" campaign in 2016. Because of the positive response, they officially launched Spotify Wrapped in 2017. If you've never received one of these reports, you can think of it as a personalized review of the kind of music, genre, and artists you have listened to throughout the year. Other information included covers how many minutes a user has spent on the app and how many times they listened to specific songs.

Spotify Wrapped is now a recurring annual campaign with its own distinctive, timely content. At the end of every year, users can view and share their Spotify Wrapped. It boosts the company's exposure to new, potential users because the visual content can be shared outside of the Spotify platform (think Instagram and Facebook). This annual event is a win-win for both sides since the users are able to make more connections through the content they share, and the company is able to drive new user adoption. Every year, the format changes and the data collected only gets more accurate.

In 2019, the campaign was shared 1.2 million times, according to Twitter, in December alone.[101] In 2021, Spotify even created a data-driven game based on users' results called "Playing Cards," which challenged users to identify two truths and a lie from statements given about their results. As a result, the 2021 Spotify Wrapped was shared over 60 million times just 48 hours after its release, according to the numbers from their 2021 Q4 report. This is fifty times more than two years before. That is a *lot* of shares.[102]

Spotify Wrapped is an interesting case study that relates to what we talked about earlier.

First, Spotify uses data to empower its users to storytell *for* them. Spotify used in-depth analyses to gain insight into the trends of its users' preferences and transforms the data into a visually appealing graphic to tell a story that entertains their users. From this, Spotify interacts with its users by posting the result on users' Spotify main page and social media such as Instagram for their social networks to see. Strengthening the engaging user experience reinforces a bond among the users and the company. Consequently, its valuable streaming experience built more customer and brand loyalty.

Second, beyond the data, the company focuses on making its overall user experience feel authentic. Doing so makes the app and

---

101 Fidaul, "Data-Driven Marketing Campaigns: How Spotify #2020Wrapped Nailed the Human Desire for Reflection," 2021.

102 Spotify. 2022. "Spotify: Shareholder Letter 2021 Q4." Spotify. February 2, 2022.

their experiences on it feel familiar to users. By injecting its own unique blend of data, style, and storytelling, Spotify is delivering a true brand experience—and that's what gets people talking. A good brand is what helps companies get users interested, drive adoption, and even keep users coming back.

For example, nostalgia sometimes plays a huge role in user experience. Through Spotify Wrapped, users are able to rediscover old favorites, which brings to a realm of nostalgia. They are reminded of the old days and strongly identify with the song they have listened to or are listening to. Spotify Wrapped also doesn't include albums that were not listened to within that specific year. This creates a sense of timeliness that helps the users appreciate the campaign album even more and feel more inclined to listen to it now while they can. Spotify Wrapped is especially unique because it's not just a one-time thing. It's timely content that its users wait for until the end of the year. It also does not feel repetitive since their users' tastes could have changed over the years. They can compare the similarities and contrast the differences from last year's Spotify Wrapped. The users have something to look forward to! The fleeting nature of Spotify Wrapped feeds into itself, building momentum and excitement for the campaign while it is occurring but also leading up to the next one.

Third, it leverages the design thinking methodology of the SCAMPER technique! Do you remember it? Substitute, combine, adapt, modify, put to another use, eliminate, or reverse.

If you think about it, Spotify Wrapped isn't *really* original. Like we mentioned, no idea is *really* a new idea. Spotify Wrapped might seem familiar to people because it imitates the framework of Snapchat and

Instagram Stories, where users can toggle between different frames to get updates. Even though it is such a simple adaptation, the campaign's success has effectively promoted the company.

Great job to the creators of Spotify Wrapped!

VI. Digital Marketing Deep Dive

When you think of digital marketing, social media is likely the first thing that comes to mind. Although SEO marketing and content creation are strategies that fall under this category, we'll start with understanding how our beloved Instagram, Facebook, and Twitter feeds are prime places to boost your brand's presence and sales.

The first thing to note is that there is a real need for organizations to execute social media as a marketing strategy in an official capacity. Marketing teams typically create detailed social media calendars to map out future posts and study the best days and times to receive engagement on their content. Hootsuite and Sprout Social are two examples of programs that facilitate such calendars.

Additionally, every social media platform will differ based on the times their users are most active. Every user base is different as well, depending on how their lives operate—if your audience consists of teens, they might be more active after school ends, but if your audience consists of more working professionals, they might be more active after they get off work. With this, every platform might still have different popular times for user engagement.

For instance, if Instagram users visit your account most frequently on Tuesdays, you could create a special post series called "Testimonial Tuesdays" that highlights positive customer experiences every week. On the other hand, your Twitter followers might be more engaged on the weekends, making them more interested in funny, colorful tweets.

Next, we'll read more about the four most popular platforms in social media marketing, plus we'll throw in a bonus lesson on few other popular channels.

Instagram

Instagram leverages eye-catching visuals and can be intensely creative. Approximately 63% of users are between 18 and 34 years old, and there is an even split between male and female users.[103] It's one of the biggest platforms for influencer marketing, which means widespread promotion of products from companies *and* users. Sponsored ads, both photos and videos, are pushed into the feeds of users who fit a target market.

Instagram includes an online shopping feature and business profile option, which is perfect for product-based companies. Instagram even gives business profiles free analytics tools so they can track followers' demographics and engagement.

Companies also have the option to buy just one ad or multiple ads (called a "carousel"). Additionally, 24-hour-long Instagram Story can

---

103 Dixon, "Instagram: Age Distribution of Global Audiences 2018," Statista, 2022. https://www.statista.com/statistics/325587/instagram-global-age-group/.

also be purchased for advertisement, in which users swipe through the ad like a slideshow at the top of their screen (this is especially helpful for behind-the-scenes and informal posts).

With the more traditional Instagram features, companies can post user-submitted photos on their accounts, which creates a more personal feel to the brand. Hashtags can be used to promote a campaign (such as #shareacoke)

TikTok

TikTok is a short-form video hosting service that is home to wide range of entertaining content—everything from pranks, stunts, and tricks to dances, jokes, and storytelling. TikTok has completely disrupted the social media industry and has over 1 billion active users as of 2022 and an average of 755 million monthly users.[104]

TikTok is a platform that is meant to entertain users above all else, which is why you probably would feel more comfortable following users you don't know. Engaging content is engaging content. What makes TikTok so *sticky*—meaning, the user experience *sticks* and users can feel a sense of connection—is the fact that almost anyone can go viral. Everyone's post starts off with 0 views, but as more people like, comment, and share, a post gains momentum.

Over the past few years, TikTok has also been known more for its authenticity compared to other platforms like Instagram. Instagram has received some mental health–related backlash in terms of causing

---

104 Geyser, "50 TikTok Stats That Will Blow Your Mind in 2020 [Updated]," March 31, 2022, https://influencermarketinghub.com/tiktok-stats/.

users to compare themselves too much to their peers with their "picture perfect" posts. TikTok, on the other hand, is most popularly used amongst the Gen Z demographic, which has been shown to appreciate more "raw" types of content as opposed to the "picture perfect" filtered posts.

When it comes to TikTok advertising, it is all about creating organic content to increase brand awareness. One of the easier ways to do this is by leveraging trending hashtags (e.g., #moneytok), tapping into influencer marketing, or collaborating and "duetting" with other users and their posts.

Twitter

Twitter is a microblogging and social networking service that relies on primarily text-based content (basically, nonstop conversation!). It's also worth noting that select, eye-catching images and videos can lead to posts with a high number of retweets and likes.

You can truly craft your brand's voice by posting, replying, and interacting with users. Certain businesses thrive on Twitter, including media, entertainment, sports, politics, and marketing. Twitter also has ad features, including promoted tweets and conversational posts. Brands can create polls, which is fun for followers and an informal way of gathering customer information.

Like TikTok, hashtags are huge on Twitter, but short and clever hashtags garner the most success. Similar to TikTok, Twitter is known to also be a more authentic platform where users can share their "live" thoughts and are encouraged to tweet multiple times a day to really gain momentum in their accounts.

In 2022, Elon Musk bought the platform for $44 billion and has added different features, including a monthly paid subscription for official verification, views per tweet count, and more.

Facebook

As the world's most popular, original, tried-and-true social media platform, Facebook is a major player for nearly every industry, as the user gender ratio is even and there are users of all ages.[105]

Like Instagram and Twitter, Facebook allows businesses to target specific markets through paid advertisements that appear on users' profiles. Facebook collects a lot of demographic data from users' profiles so your ad can reach specific audiences. It is worth noting, however, that this feature has generated controversy in recent years in regard to the issue of data usage.

Users can also like and share Facebook Pages (your business profile), allowing for greater visibility. Facebook Pages serve as hubs for businesses to display useful information and the basic ethos of the brand.

But businesses can use their timelines to their advantage, too, and post new product announcements, links to blog posts, media coverage, promotions, and videos. E-commerce businesses can

---

105 Statista. 2022. "Facebook Users Worldwide 2020." Statista. February 14, 2022. https://www.statista.com/statistics/264810/number-of-monthly-active-facebook-users-worldwide/.

especially benefit from the Facebook Marketplace feature, which is similar to Craigslist. Harness the power of Facebook!

Below, we will briefly review a few more social media platforms that allow users to post content:

- **LinkedIn** is known as the social media platform for professionals. Users can display their career paths and positions, post about accomplishments, and network with other users. Companies can also recruit new employees and promote their products and services on the platform. LinkedIn has even been leveraged to facilitate business partnerships.
- **YouTube** is the world's premier video platform and carries a huge and diverse audience. Companies can create channels to post relevant videos or purchase advertisements. Think of YouTube videos like a blog post: users who live in your niche are likely to encounter your channel; the emphasis on this site is viewing the content, not discussing and sharing; users expect informative, interesting content, unlike comparatively mindless Facebook and Instagram scrolling.
- **Pinterest** allows users to "pin" images, links, and videos to their "boards," self-grouped by category. It is perfect for anything that displays high-quality visuals, such as fashion, food, travel, and DIY ideas. Approximately 76% of users are female but more men are gradually joining.[106]

---

[106] Sehl, Katie. 2019. "23 Pinterest Statistics That Matter to Marketers in 2019." Hootsuite Social Media Management. February 27, 2019. https://blog.hootsuite.com/pinterest-statistics-for-business/.

Social Media Metrics and Tools to Consider

When working across different social media platforms, it is important to define your metrics. After all, understanding how you are performing over time is the only way you can measure your success and figure out how to continue to improve your presence and grow! We have listed some of the main metrics you will need to measure to be fluent in your social media management lingo.

- **Follower growth** is a metric that refers to the total number of new followers on your social media account over a specific period. Facebook, Instagram, and Twitter all have detailed summaries of your account's data on follower growth over time. Other metrics from these platforms can inform you of what your existing followers respond well to (or not) on your account. Your follower growth metric is often a number or percentage, either an increase or decline in your number of followers or the percentage of growth or decline of followers for a set period of time, such as a week or a month.
- **Click rate/click-through rate (CTR)** is the number of clicks that a post receives divided by the number of times the post is shown. This metric tracks your conversions, that is, when the recipient of a marketing message performs a desired action (though not necessarily a sale). CTR can help you understand how user engagement occurs and why users are engaging. You can also try different types of services like Buffer for CTR reports on your accounts.

- **Reach** is the number of people your post has reached inside and outside your network; more specifically, reach is the number of impressions on your content, *not* the number of people engaging with the content through likes and comments. Again, social media platforms offer this information, or you can access it through a social media data analysis service like Buffer.
- **Referrals** are how users get to your content through another platform, whether that's within the same media service (i.e., a customer clicking on your social enterprise's Instagram profile when they see it tagged or spotlighted on another profile) or a different media service (i.e., a YouTube ad prompting a customer to check out your website). Most platforms will show you this data.
- **Replies and comments** are a handy way to get feedback on how interested your current followers and potential followers are in your posts. All platforms should show you the number of replies and comments your post receives. **Mentions** are another form of engagement where different users can tag and mention you in their comments, in addition to their posts and stories. Mentions can be a good indicator of your posts' relevance because users are tagging their friends that they think of when they see your post.
- **Sharing content** can be very underrated. The more your content is shared, the greater your brand's reach! Your sharing performance can suggest that users have a meaningful and

psychologically strong connection with your content. Different social media platforms may have their own term for this. For instance, Facebook uses "shares" and Twitter uses "retweets."

- **Likes and reactions to your posts** are a good indication of which posts are successful and which are not. For those that don't perform, take notes on what they are so you can cut that content out.

If you can harness these tools to your advantage, your idea can really take off!

Gabriel Weinberg, author of the book *Traction: How Any Startup Can Achieve Explosive Customer Growth,* outlines how trying as many ideas as you can will lead you to explore unusual, innovative marketing strategies and give you the ability to pivot when the market changes.[107]

In a nutshell, as Paul Graham, founder of the premier startup accelerator Y Combinator, puts it, "A startup is a company designed to grow fast. Being newly founded does not in itself make a company a startup. Nor is it necessary for a startup to work on technology.... The only essential thing is growth. Everything else we associate with startups follows from growth."

VII. Case Study: Starbucks and the Iconic Green Mermaid

Starbucks is a great example when teaching about the power and application of specific marketing strategies because they nail nearly

---

[107] Weinberg and Mares, *Traction*, 2015.

every marker of a successful modern brand: a distinctive product, high-quality ingredients, and above all, a consistent feel between packaging, store design, and customer experience across their 33,833 stores as of 2021!

Starbucks' brand statement has shifted over the years. While in its humble beginnings in 1970s Seattle, Washington, the company's leadership aimed to "establish Starbucks as the premier purveyor of the finest coffee in the world while maintaining our uncompromising principles while we grow."[108] As they rapidly expanded, led by new CEO Howard Schulz, this mission shifted to "to inspire and nurture the human spirit—one person, one cup and one neighborhood at a time."

Pretty nice, right? If you want your budding startup to enjoy some of the same growth as Starbucks, you'll also need to come up with a fitting statement that will underpin all your operations—from company culture and design to philanthropic efforts.

We also can't gloss over brand statements too quickly. Their modern mission manifests itself in the concept of a "third space," establishing a neutral place to work, relax, and connect in between home and work. This genius concept actually sparked coffee shop culture as we know it.

How do they convince customers to enter this mythical-sounding "third space"? First, Starbucks knows their demographic well—primarily men and women with some disposable income. So how

---

108 "Timeline," Starbucks, accessed February 14, 2023; "Our Mission," Starbucks archive, accessed February 14, 2023.

does the marketing team convince these people to drop extra money on a beverage? First, premium ingredients, tantalizing new flavors, and a commitment to ethical and sustainable sourcing.

The store design is a huge factor too. The company designs its stores with an earthy feel to emphasize their ethical and sustainable sourcing. With its dark wood, signature green hue spread throughout, fast Wi-Fi, and beautiful packaging and ads, Starbucks stores transcend the customer experience from just a place to drink a coffee or tea.

Regarding design, Starbucks often positions its seats strategically to be by the windows or outside to make the space look more crowded. This idea of using their customers as human marketing props is something that other food and beverage retailers have done.

Starbucks has proven to be dynamic with their marketing efforts, especially through word of mouth and leveraging their customers to do their marketing for them.

For instance, whenever baristas write your name on your cup by hand, they are instructed to misspell your name. Seems strange, right? It's actually a lot more genius than strange. The misspelling becomes a conversation-starter, and customers often take pictures of their misspelled cups and share them on social media. The interesting thing is, this strategy was put in place even before the emerging popularity of social media!

Beyond this, Starbucks' branding is very subtle yet distinct. You just *know* when someone's coffee is from Starbucks. The green emblem of their iconic mermaid is a small, subtle but bold symbol for their brand. And it's everywhere—on the cups, on the cupholders, on the kraft brown paper bags. You even know if someone is drinking something from Starbucks just by the color of their straw if they're using one! The company's intentional design of their merchandise and their systems has certainly been a unique way of silently and effectively leveraging word of mouth.

Consistency is Key!

You might be thinking, this is a good example and all, but how can I directly improve *my* marketing strategy? We got you.

Here are ideas you can apply to your company that directly emulate Starbucks' strategies:

- **Create a brand loyalty program**. The Starbucks Rewards program offers freebies, such as free beverages, in-store refills, and special offers, to consumers for buying products. Customers can track their points and find locations on an app with a great user experience design. Your program doesn't have to be Starbucks-elaborate, but think about how you can reward and retain customers, whether that's through punch cards, tiered discounts, or something else! This will ultimately help build your customer loyalty.
- **Try a limited-edition product to boost sales**. The Pumpkin Spice Latte, released during the fall, *is* a meme, but it's worth copying. Can you create a special or seasonally themed edition that will pique your customer's interest?
- **Create beautiful content that is consistent across platforms**, but be sure to tailor the message to the right audience. For

instance, Twitter users might be more responsive to certain types of content than a person walking by some signage in the city.

- **Maintain friendly, helpful customer service on social media and traditional channels**. Today, customer service actually happens frequently on social media, as opposed to purely over a phone line. This strategy requires effective delegation. Make sure a few of your most responsive, knowledgeable, and cheerful team members check all the platforms regularly.
- **Be supremely organized in your marketing strategy**. This isn't unique to Starbucks, but we recommend creating a detailed calendar that outlines how and when *exactly* various campaigns will be launched. Make sure nonmarketing team members are well-versed in these plans, too.

VIII. Cheat Code Recap

1. Good marketing = well-communicated product-market fit = customer satisfaction = customer loyalty = competitive advantage
2. There are different types of marketing strategies you can leverage, including paid advertising, social media ads, banner ads, influencer marketing, cause marketing, relationship marketing, undercover marketing, word of mouth, transactional marketing, diversity marketing, and more.

3. Data-driven marketing is a powerful process that personalizes a user's marketing experience based on real consumer insights as opposed to intuition and assumptions alone.
4. Five tiers of content marketing are SEO, user experience, content strategy, content creation, and content distribution.
5. Some of the most popular platforms in social media marketing include Instagram, TikTok, Twitter, Facebook, LinkedIn, YouTube, and Pinterest.

Chapter 14
Branding

Written by: Brooke McCormick, Tiffany Yau, and Grace Coughlan

"Your brand is what other people say about you when you're not in the room." — Jeff Bezos, founder of Amazon.com

I. What Do People Say About You?

That's advice from one of the wealthiest people in the world. You don't want him saying you're nothing but bologna when you leave the room!

How can we ensure that consumers, including Jeff Bezos, value our company and believe in its path moving forward? It's all about the power of branding!

But what is branding?

Branding is the marketing process by which a company creates a name and symbol that is easily identifiable as belonging to itself.

Simply put, your brand is your company's identity. It's a representation of who you are as a business and how you wish to be seen by consumers.

Let's be clear though. Branding is NOT the same thing as marketing. Branding is a *type* of marketing process that takes place for every company. Every company has its own brand. Marketing is the process that develops and establishes a brand.

Take a moment to think about the company Nike. What comes to mind? The Nike swoosh? Just Do It? Athletic apparel? Michael Jordan taking flight from the free throw line?

We bet all four of those and more rushed into your thoughts as soon as you read the word Nike. Behold, the power of branding!

Don't worry, we'll break it down: if branding for Nike were as simple as slapping on a logo and calling itself a company, you would've just thought of the Nike swoosh. But you thought of *so much more*—its products and, more importantly, its *identity*. Nike has mastered the process of branding themselves as a durable, outdoorsy, and exciting company that empowers athletes. Nike shows us that a brand is the combination of its customers' perceptions, notions, and experience. A brand is the face and the values espoused by a business—along with everything in between.

Trust us, it's important!

Every facet of a business—whether it is its media profile, the tone of voicemails, or the way it markets and delivers a service—captures the essence of its brand and sends an implicit message about how much the company respects its own business. Just to make sure you got it down, we'll repeat that one more time: Your company's brand should be *personal*! It represents who *you* are, what *you* believe in, and how your audience will look at *you*!

II. A Good Brand is a Superpower

Now that you know what branding is, let's go over the statistically proven positive impact that great branding can have on your social enterprise.

Having a good brand can be underrated, but there are many positive benefits that come with having built a good one for your business, a few of which we will discuss next.

Signifies Intent

Your branding—inclusive of your logo, website, products, and mission—should all eagerly reflect and represent what you stand for. Furthermore, your branding will allow you to show your values and virtually everything you stand for as a company to consumers. For example, does your social enterprise support nonconforming genders? Does it advocate for disabled athletes? Does it have a purpose to serve besides earning a profit? When you focus on establishing your brand, it reflects what your business stands for!

Creates a Competitive Edge

Good branding can help you stand out from thousands of similar companies that claim to be just as good as you.

With the growing merit of the internet, many companies are realizing that they are no longer only competing at a local level. Advancements in online and offline technologies have catapulted them into a global marketplace.

While this may seem good at the onset (a larger customer base, right?, don't be fooled! This means that there are thousands of other competitors that you'll be pitted against. How do you differentiate your business from so many others?

When you get your brand well-established, customers have a valid reason to consider you as their first choice. People prefer to associate with credible organizations with reputable brands over those that don't!

Transforms Your Company into an Experience

Let's envision two companies: American Girl Doll and the Dollar Store. Both sell plastic dolls. Why in the world would someone pay $100 or more for an American Girl Doll when they could buy a similar version at the Dollar Store!? Quality? Well… plastic can only get so much better.

The real reason lies in the experience that American Girl Doll provides! People value a brand not just for its beauty or price but for the experience it provides to consumers. For example, even after you walk out of a store with a product, the quality of your experience is defined by:

- whether the product was as good as you had been promised,
- whether the product served the purpose you thought it would, and
- whether customer service was positive or beneficial.

If a company properly embeds the answers to these questions in their brand, they drastically increase the chance of developing a loyal follower base that can trust them. We can almost immediately predict an experience by looking at American Girl Doll's offerings versus those of the Dollar Store. So, simply put, consumers purchase from brands like American Girl Doll because of their service and commitment to the product, in addition to the quality.

They ultimately buy into the *value* of the brand and the *experience* it provides!

Builds Trust

Customer loyalty is everything. Something you should value is creating and maintaining a loyal customer base, which means that you must retain their trust first! This is where customer service, social media, and a great experience from start to finish comes in!

Relay an underlying message that every single initiative you take is to delight your customers and encourage them to keep coming back. Your brand's consistency will build trust, and with that trust, the chance that a consumer opts for a competitor's product is drastically reduced. After all, your reliability as a company becomes a part of your brand identity—consumers will remember you based on your ability to swiftly deliver and provide your product.

Take Amazon, for example. One of the main features that consumers know them by is Amazon Prime. Amazon Prime comes with various perks, including same-day delivery or two-day shipping that effortlessly sends consumer products directly to their doorstep. Using this method, Amazon has built a reputation of being a fast distributor, and trust along with it—so it's no surprise why they have a widespread consumer base!

Branding ultimately becomes the credible face that engages a potential audience, delights them at every touch point of their journey, and eventually earns their trust.

This translates into making sure everything you do and put out into the world is spot-on. That includes, but is not limited to, having a great logo, social media, communication, and customer service. Working on these will help you build your reputation to be in line with your brand and what it represents.

If you have a trustable brand, you're more likely to convince your audience to become your success partners, which will open up new and sustainable revenue outlets when your brand is strong and appealing!

Leverages Emotions

Branding allows you to forge a personal connection with your customers.

Humans are fond of ideas, stories, concepts, and even products that touch the tender emotional nerve in them. When brands create a sentimental connection, customer retention can often improve. People associate with brands because brands communicate something about us that we want others to know but can't put into words. Furthermore, when customers like you enough, they can become your greatest advocates. Having a good brand often can be helpful when tapping into marketing strategies like word of mouth to promote your social enterprise to others in the network. That is essentially free marketing.

III. Creating Your Brand

We know what you're thinking: we've gone over the benefits of branding, but how do you create a brand in the first place?

Let's get to it. Feel free to access our online worksheet as you continue this section.

Research your target audience and your competitors

The first step is two-fold: first, be sure you understand what your target audience likes, and second, know what other competitors are doing well when it comes to their branding. There's lots of ways to do this, including:

- Looking up your product or service category and analyzing the direct and indirect competitors that come up
- Talking to people who are part of your target market and asking them what brands they buy from in your space
- Analyzing the relevant social media accounts or pages your target audience follows and are receptive to

As you go about these searches, be sure to keep the following questions in mind:

- Who are the easiest customers to reach?
- Who are your biggest competitors? The brands that are most established and well-known?
- What are your target customers' main interests?

Once you gather this information, you can use it to determine what your brand should focus on and how you can evolve it.

Choose a Brand Focus & Personality

A big mistake that many startups make is trying to orient their brand to appeal to everyone.

But let's face it: you can't be everything to *everyone*. After all, people have very diverse interests!

So, be sure to find a focus and let that one ideal inform the other parts of your brand as you build it. Here are some steps on how you can approach this:

1. **Recall your value proposition.** Fill in this sentence based on your company: We offer [product/service idea] for [target customer] to [what you're bringing to the game!]

   When you write this out, you'll get a better idea of your mission statement as a social enterprise, or the clear promise that your social enterprise is making to your customers and to the world. What do you stand for? What are your values? After all, your values shape everything you do!

2. **Think of words that come to mind when you think about your business.** When you're building your brand, it may be helpful to imagine that you're building a person! What will

he or she look like? What type of personality will he or she have? Coming up with these factors in the context of your social enterprise will help inform its voice on social media and the tone of all other creative work (i.e., blog posts, email blasts etc.).

3. **Think of metaphors or other concepts that describe your business.** Don't be too picky here! It can be anything—an animal, a sports team, or even a celebrity. Just ensure that whatever you pick has the same reputation and vibe as the brand that you're on the path to creating. While this information won't go directly into your brand, it'll help you *visualize* how you want your company to present itself.

Check out the graphic below for some examples of brand personalities!

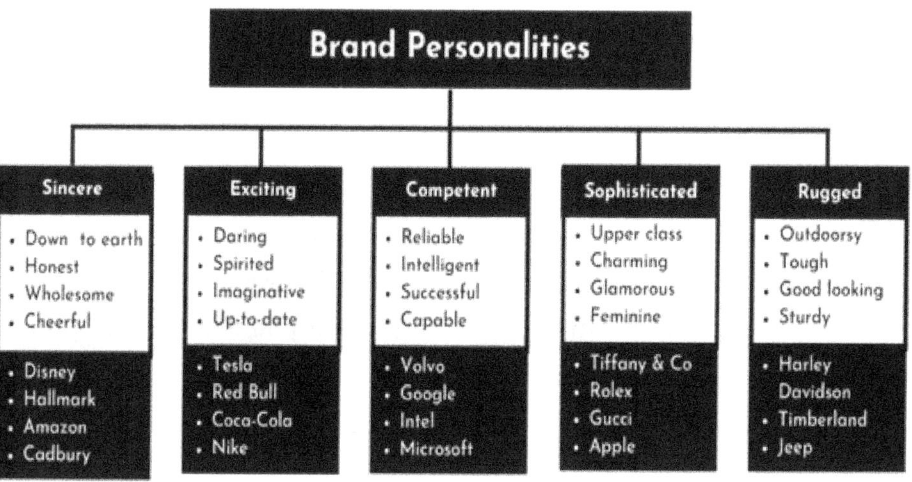

Your **brand personality** is what determines your brand identity as a whole. Our brand personalities are shaped by our values and what we want our businesses to stand for. Our brand personalities also define and affect our brand voice.

Brand voice is how you communicate your brand personality. For instance, Disney has an overall happy and friendly personality, so the words they use in their campaigns are words that communicate that personality. Meanwhile, companies like Nike are more confident and assertive, so their brand voices will likely use language that is more to the point.[109]

Your brand voice then impacts your brand tone. Your **brand tone** is basically how your brand voice translates to your audience and how they perceive it. If we were to back-track and think of voice and tone outside of branding, your normal everyday voice encapsulates more of what you want to say, and your tone is essentially how you say it. You might change your tone when speaking, depending on your context, like whom you are talking to, where you are speaking, and what the environment is like.

This is analogous to the role voice and tone play in branding. Your brand voice is all about what you say, and your brand tone is how you say it. Brand voice is affected by your audience (to whom you are speaking), your platform or medium (where you are speaking, like which social media platform or maybe a specific in-person location), and the focus and reason for your engagement (what the context is).

---

109 Tinoco, "Discover the Brand Voice Examples that Bring Success to Businesses," 2022.

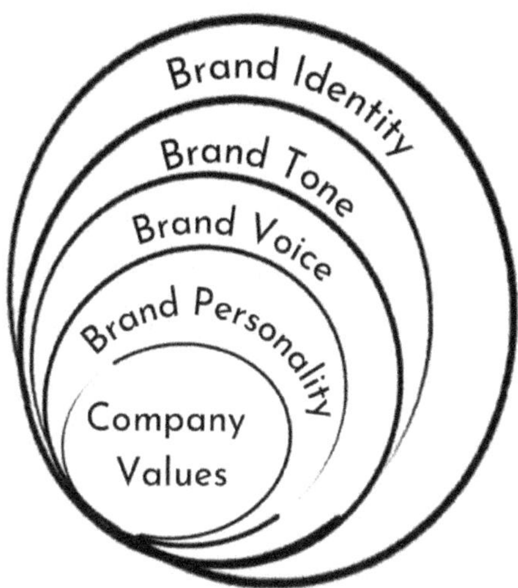

How would you define your brand values? What does your brand care about? Think about the following:

- What is your brand personality? What are three words you can use to describe your brand personality?
- What is your brand voice? How does your brand voice show up in your content? How does that brand personality speak?
- What is your brand tone? How does your audience perceive your brand? How does that brand personality make others feel?

Create a Slogan

Don't lie, we all love those brands that have catchy slogans—so definitely make sure your enterprise has one too! Your slogan will feed directly into your brand and how a customer perceives your business.

Even if it's something brief and descriptive, adding a slogan to your social media, website header, or business card can go a long way. Of course, don't think that you're gluing this slogan onto your company. In case you do use the glue, remember that it's not super glue! You can always change your slogan as you find new channels and angles for marketing.

In fact, Pepsi has gone through about 40 slogans since 1903.[110] Imagine that! Their slogan changed from "Exhilarating, Invigorating, Aids Digestion" when they were trying to be a healthy cola and "Twice as Much for a Nickel" when even movie tickets were a mere twenty-five cents to "Change the Game" as the company began to cater more to a sports-centered approach to advertising with soccer, basketball, football, and more!

In 2020, even Kentucky Fried Chicken (KFC) changed their slogan (after using "It's Finger Lickin' Good" since the 1950s) because of the controversy surrounding the COVID-19 pandemic.[111] Their Global Chief Marketing Officer Catherine Tan-Gillespie mentioned in a press release, "We find ourselves in a unique situation—having an iconic slogan that doesn't quite fit in the current environment. While we are pausing the use of It's Finger Lickin' Good, rest assured the food craved by so many people around the world isn't changing one bit."

---

110 "Pepsi Slogans and Logos throughout the Years," G&M Distributors, 2012; Sarosh, "How Pepsi Slogans Connect with Generations over the Years," 2017.

111 Kentucky Fried Chicken, "And the Winner of the Award for the Most Inappropriate Slogan for 2020 Goes to...KFC," 2020.

Companies like Pepsi and KFC are great examples of companies that are not afraid to embrace change and that have a design thinking mindset!

When creating your slogan, think *catchy*! Think *short*! Think about something that will resonate deeply with your consumers. Let's review a few examples:

- Red Bull: "Red Bull gives you wings." A metaphor!
- Folgers: "The best part of wakin' up is Folgers in your cup." A rhyme!
- Subway: "Eat fresh." A lifestyle!
- Panasonic: "Live Your Best." An inspiration!
- Target: "Expect More. Pay Less." A results-driven statement, and something to look forward to!
- Kit Kat: "Have a Break, Have a Kit Kat." An example of when you can consider purchasing and consuming their product.

There are a lot of different options to choose from when it comes to your slogan, and there is no limit on how often you can change it. Whether you brainstorm some ideas, play off the positioning statement, or come up with some one-liners, we're confident that your slogan will be one to remember! Based on the brand you hope to create, how would you phrase your slogan?

Create a "Look" for Your Brand

Your presentation and aesthetics matter so much when it comes to branding! Once you have a slogan and name, it's time to move on to the art: the colors, typography, and overall visual look of your brand.

First, choose your colors. We bet you never guessed it, but the magic of that Crayola set you got when you were younger has a substantial impact on the feeling your brand conveys. Color psychology is the idea behind how different colors convey certain feelings within us, and when it comes to business, it can be a useful tool to create a more appealing brand for your audience to gravitate toward. For instance, yellow stimulates feelings of optimism, clarity, and warmth. It is used by companies like Ferrari, McDonalds, and Best Buy. Orange suggests friendliness and confidence (think Nickelodeon, Fanta, or the Baltimore Orioles). Green suggests peace, growth, and health, which companies like Starbucks or Whole Foods go for. Oftentimes, fast food companies use red because the color has been found to create a sense of appetite and hunger, and overall, attracts attention.

Next, choose your fonts. Yes, it's time to browse that seemingly endless column of fonts. But don't worry, it's not too bad. You just need to pick out two basic fonts to begin with. One will be used for all headings on your creative media and the other will be used for body or long-form text.

Finally, design your logo. We know you've been waiting for this! A brand is most easily recognized by its logo—it is the face of your company and will be everywhere once you've established yourself!

The three cornerstones of a good logo are its uniqueness, identifiability, and scalability. These principles are similar to how you would choose your company's name—it should be easy to read, easy to say, easy to remember. Your logo, along with your profile picture, will be the centerpiece of your website and can be used on various social media platforms. So, make sure it's versatile, simple, and neat!

Here is a brief breakdown of some options below:

- Mascot (think Wendy's): Use the face of a character to represent your brand
- Emblem (think Starbucks): Circular, a combination of text and symbol to showcase your brand's personality
- Lettermark (think IBM): Turning the initials of your business into its logo (initialism can be catchy!)
- Icon (think Twitter): A visual metaphor that represents your brand's unique value

We recommend you draw out or describe the aesthetic of your brand/logo. Explain the purpose behind each element you've added.

Storytelling

Storytelling is everything. The story you tell is a great way to set the stage for customers who will interact with your social enterprise. Think about these things when you decide what behind-the-scenes story you want to tell:

- What motivates me day in and day out to run my social enterprise?

- How does my social enterprise make a positive impact on the world?
- What is the story behind my social enterprise that I want my customers to know?

It can be easy to forget the important role that an appealing brand plays in a successful business. What is the story that has helped build the brand of a business you like? What is the story of your *personal* brand? As the founder, your company's audience will naturally be drawn to the story and motivations behind why you started your company. What's your story?

IV. Case Study: Nike, Just Do It!

"Have faith in yourself, but also have faith in faith. Not faith as others define it. Faith as you define it. Faith as faith defines itself in your heart." — Phil Knight, *Shoe Dog*[112]

Nike is an international corporation with multiple product lines, like Air Jordans after the famous basketball player Michael Jordan, and subsidiaries, like Converse. Although Nike is a very well-known company that most people are aware of, it didn't start out as an international powerhouse. It started from a small, specific business. Yet, because of excellent execution of effective branding strategies and because its founders embraced the entrepreneurial mindset, the company was able to continue evolving its goals and values.

---

112 Knight, *Shoe Dog*, 2016.

Building a brand entails 1) researching your target audience and competitors, 2) choosing a brand focus and personality, 3) creating a slogan, and 4) creating a "look" for your brand.

Don't be intimidated by these steps! Let's review each of these components and how they play a role in Nike's business to give you more depth on their branding.

Nike's Target Audience & Competitors

Remember, we are all about user-centered design! The first step is to identify who your target audience is, what they are interested in, and what your competitors are doing with their brands.

Nike's target audience has evolved over time and has grown with the brand. Nike's first target audience was specifically tailored to runners, selling sneakers to those who ran track. Over time, Nike broadened its target audience to athletes in general, selling different sneakers and apparel for each sport. From athletes, Nike then expanded its brand even more to those who just like to be active and have fun doing so. With the growing popularity of athleisure and streetwear, Nike can now target average consumers interested in those niches.

However, being a huge force in the athletic apparel world means having competition. Nike competes with other international corporations like Adidas, New Balance, Reebok, and Under Armour. While we don't have insight on all of Nike's trade secrets or their exact process, it is safe to assume that they are keeping a close eye on the product design, product quality, pricing, marketing, and branding strategies of their competitors to maintain their edge and connection with their customers.

A company like Nike may be asking themselves questions like:

- What types of shoes are our competitors thinking of producing next?
- Who are these shoes for?
- What type of material will we use for our next line production?
- How have our shoes been received by customers? And how do they compare to other companies' shoes?
- How are other companies advertising their shoes? Do they have celebrity or influencer endorsements? Who is the celebrity or influencer?

All these questions are great for you to consider for your company's brand. For example, in Nike's case, asking these questions helps the company compare its products and marketing strategies to those of its competitors. This reflection allows for the evolution of its brand and how it connects with its target audience.

Nike has evolved its brand by opening its target audience to a more generalized audience. The use of celebrity endorsement is fairly common with a lot of different professional sports teams. Nike produces team uniforms featuring their signature swoosh and also provides fan apparel for all different teams.

Nike's Brand Focus & Personality

It's important to focus your brand on specifics. Your brand can't be for everyone right from the start because your audience may be too large to try to include a variety of interests. Start with a specific focus to gain a following. Starting small and more detailed can allow your brand room to growth and expand in the future.

Where Nike Was Way Back Then

Nike originally started in Oregon and the Pacific Northwest area in 1964 as Blue Ribbon Sports, a company that manufactured track sneakers that catered specifically to track athletes. CEO Phil Knight and Oregon track head coach Bill Bowerman decided that they wanted to break away and start their own company.

Nike's household name originated from hours of brainstorming between many different groups of people within the company.[113] When starting out, employees discussed the names of other companies, like Puma. They liked the idea of naming their company after an animal.

One of the very first employees of Blue Ribbon Sports, who was helping create the new company name, came across an article talking about exotic brand names like Xerox and Kleenex. Not only did he notice the unique sounds of each name but also the fact that the brand names were less than three syllables.

---

113 Levinson, "How Nike Almost Ended up with a Very Different Name," 2016.

This employee volunteered the name Nike, after the Greek goddess of victory.[114] The name had a unique sound and was also less than two syllables, just like Xerox and Kleenex.

Like your own social enterprise, Nike started with humble beginnings and a narrow focus. They expanded this vision by renaming the company, which ultimately led to an entire rebrand.

The company focused on making sure its brand would appeal to a specific region of the country first, then continued to expand across the world. By naming the company after the Greek goddess of victory, Nike is signaling their values as a company. They value the idea of victory and want to associate that attribute with their products.

Where Nike is Now

Nike has gone from catering to runners, to catering to athletes, and now to those who participate in physical activity in general. In 2018, Nike released a commercial titled "Dream Crazy" featuring former San Francisco 49er's quarterback Colin Kaepernick, who is known for choosing not to stand during the national anthem before games back in 2016.[115] Through the creation of this commercial, Nike has actively pushed their brand to focus on individuality through the idea of victory—very on-brand with the origins of their company's name. The company often also communicates the importance of resilience and pushing forward in its advertised content. With this, when your favorite sports player is wearing Nike's jersey, it organically

---

114 *Encyclopaedia Britannica Online*, s.v., "Nike," accessed February 14, 2023, https://www.britannica.com/topic/Nike-Greek-goddess.

115 "Colin Kaepernick Nike Commercial FULL VIDEO," YouTube, 2018.

motivates the player's viewers to not only want to win the race but also to be the toughest ever.

From their "Dream Crazy" marketing campaign, Nike empathized with its viewers through emphasizing the idea of chasing our dreams, even if they feel out of reach or crazy. The commercial ends with a very satisfying and on-brand statement, "It's only crazy until you do it. Just do it."

A few years later, on May 6, 2021, Nike released a one-minute commercial titled "Play New."[116] This commercial showcases all different types of people practicing and actively trying to play their sports but not doing well.

Let's compare the two commercials. Notice how the music from the "Play New" commercial is more upbeat, featuring athletes smiling and laughing at the mistakes they've made. Here, Nike is expanding on its brand identity of victory by showcasing determination while also just having fun by depicting a different kind of "failure"—though in this case, it's not failure at all!

Nike's Entrepreneurial Mindset and Storytelling

Recall the concept of the entrepreneurial mindset that we discussed in earlier chapters. If you thought about any of the attributes of the entrepreneurial mindset while learning about Nike's brand and seeing their commercials, you are onto something! Both commercials showcase grit, resilience, persistence, passion, and accountability through the act of chasing your dreams and working hard toward

---

[116] "Play New | Nike," YouTube, 2021.

something you've never done before. They reflect the value of Nike's own work ethic into the branding of the company, inspiring others to work hard to reach their goals.

Nike also highlights the company's entrepreneurial mindset through CEO Phil Knight's memoir, *Shoe Dog*. Remember how we mentioned the importance of storytelling? Well, this is a great example that shows just how effective it can be to reinforce your company's brand. The memoir highlights the struggles that Nike faced as a company when first starting out. The CEO's personal connection to the struggle of starting the company further represents Nike's brand of achieving victory and the hard work that it took to overcome those struggles. The personal branding of a CEO and how they've made it to where they are in life can have a big influence on the way the target audience views their own actions.

A Sticky Brand

Consumers often associate themselves with brands that they can identify parts of themselves in. When consumers are able to really connect with a brand, they are more likely to become loyal customers, which is great for brand loyalty! Brands that are easily relatable can be called "sticky" because it is easy for people to stick to the morals and the products of that brand.

Nike can be considered a "sticky" brand because of how relatable its values are. Think about some of Nike's values: resilience and persistence to chase dreams and work toward success. Everyone in the world has dreams, and Nike's company values motivates people to follow theirs.

Nike's partnerships with other companies, like Apple, and athlete endorsements, like from Serena Williams, Naomi Osaka, LeBron James, and more of the greats, set Nike apart from its competitors. These stars' partnerships and endorsements make Nike more *sticky* because its partners are also well known.

Ultimately, people consume brands that showcase aligned values that amplify something inside of themselves that they want to show. Most people would love to follow their dreams: starting a business, winning a race, or getting their dream job. By purchasing Nike products, people are aligning themselves with the idea of perseverance in following their dreams.

Nike's Slogan

Creating a slogan directly ties a message to your brand and your values. This means that it is going to influence the way your audience views your business. A slogan can be something simple or catchy that will help people remember your brand. Remember that just because you have a slogan, doesn't mean that it's the only slogan you can ever have! Remember Pepsi's and KFC's slogan evolutions? Just as brands evolve, so can your slogan.

Nike's famous slogan is "Just Do It." It's attached to its athletic apparel and its advertisements. It's only three words, very simple but memorable, and it packs a lot of meaning. Nike's slogan first aired in a 1988 commercial that focused on 80-year-old Walt Stack, who talks about how he runs 17 miles every day.

This commercial highlights Stack's ability to display persistence and resilience in his physical activity to achieve success. The essence of Nike's commercial insinuates that if 80-year-old Walt Stack can do it, you can do it too, hence "Just Do It." While Nike still associates itself with its "Just Do It" slogan, they have shifted its emphasis to following its values and morals.

Nike adjusted its "Just Do It" slogan to "For once, Don't Do It" in an advertisement in relation to stopping racism and the violence associated with it in America.[117] By changing their slogan for this advertisement, Nike aligned their brand with their morals in support of a specific social issue.

In effect, Nike's stock value saw a 5% increase after the release of this commercial, which contributed to a $6 billion market value. They appealed to their target audience by aligning themselves with a prominent social issue, allowing their consumers to identify with their morals.

Nike's Overall Look as a Brand

When you think of Nike's overall look as a brand, what comes to mind first? Are there certain colors that you associate with them? What about typography? What kind of fonts do they use? Are there specific people you associate with Nike's brand? Who are these people? What other things stand out about Nike's brand?

One of Nike's well-known looks is its use of the swoosh, which represents the Greek goddess Nike's wing. The swoosh is on almost every Nike product, including sneakers, shirts, shorts, headbands,

---

117 Cohen, "'For Once, Don't Do It': The Powerful Idea behind Nike's New Anti-Racism Ad," 2020.

and more. You name it, Nike's swoosh is most likely on it. It serves as a focal point on some of Nike's products.

Think about Nike sneakers. What do Nike's sneakers usually display on their sides?

Nike's typography and fonts are pretty recognizable. They stick to boxy lettering and usually use all caps for any wording. On Nike shoe boxes, the company name is capitalized in white or black writing, and it sits right above the signature swoosh.

Nike has partnered with many different celebrities for endorsements, but the one of most prominent is Michael Jordan. His partnership with Nike led to the creation of an entirely separate line called Nike Air Jordan's, which feature an outline of Jordan in a soaring free-throw stance—yet another prominent logo associated with Nike's brand.

Nike's Presence on Social Media

Social media is a platform that can affect the branding of a company, positively or negatively. Many companies use social media to not only promote their products but also highlight their values and morals. Think of social media as your platform for showcasing the "*why's*" that move your company. Branding on social media can include posting stories, motivational content, and highlighting personal connections to your *why*.

Nike started the empire that is its business and its branding way before social media became popularized, but that doesn't mean Nike doesn't use social media now to promote their values. On June 8, 2021, Nike's main Instagram account shared a post featuring Yukai

Shimizu, a Buddhist monk and community leader who runs in the Nagano mountains in Japan. They included facts about his runs as well as a personal anecdote from Shimizu himself.[118]

According to Nike's caption, Shimizu's runs help him find "reflection, focus, and clarity" while also establishing a deeper connection with nature.[119] Take a moment to reflect and compare Shimizu's values to Nike's as a company. Are there similarities between their values? What are they?

By featuring an everyday person and his journey through activity, Nike is aligning its values and sense of purpose with real people, which connects back to Simon Sinek's message of doing business with people who believe in what you believe in (and *why* you do it). In Nike's case, this is the idea of personal perseverance and passion through physical activity.

Diversified Branding and the Flywheel Effect

It's important to diversify your branding strategies. If you just post product-related content, your platform serves as a product catalog and doesn't really say much about your "*why*." People are drawn to what is familiar to them, and if they aren't familiar with your products, they often have a harder time connecting to a social media page only showcasing products.

Don't be afraid to alternate the content you post! A picture of your product alongside a quote can really emphasize your beliefs and tie

---

118 Nike, "A spiritual practice…"

119 Sugai, "On the Mountain Trails of Japan, a Buddhist Monk Runs Toward Clarity," 2022.

that into the products you sell. You never know who might stumble across your brand and really connect with that quote you used, leading to a loyal customer.

That brings us to the power of word of mouth. Loyal customers are powerful customers, and they can have a positive influence by speaking about your brand to the people around them. Another term for loyal customers is **brand loyalty**, which is the positive connection that consumers have with a brand, making them more likely to buy your products or service.

Let's say a regular customer purchases a gift for her friend. After giving the gift to her friend, your customer talks about how much she loves what your brand stands for and how your products really show your values. The friend who received the gift is more likely to be interested in checking out your brand because of how connected it is to a person they know. This customer-to-potential-customer interaction is a small win to boost the brand and familiarity of your social enterprise, which can lead you to achieve the **flywheel effect**.

The flywheel effect reminds us that there isn't one specific moment that makes our businesses become the best; rather, there are a number of small, collective moments that happen over time that build your business and brand to have a more powerful, self-sustained growth. You build momentum—you guessed it—just like a flywheel!

What might be some of the small moments Nike's experienced that have generated a flywheel effect for them? One could say that the jump from Blue Ribbon Sports to Nike was one moment, or the expansion from sneakers to athletic apparel, or the beginning of the partnership with Michael Jordan—these are all moments in the company's journey that helped it achieve its self-sustained growth!

The Power of Influencers

Nike's branding continues to reach its audience outside the realm of its own marketing. How has Nike been able to achieve that?

Well, it's partly from the generated momentum from their flywheel effect and partly because of the strong branding tactics they've implemented. Nike's branding and products have become so popular that the company's branding strategies can be carried out through its customers' personal social media pages.

Take the example of the Nike Air Force 1. These shoes are part of Nike's athleisure brand, serving the purpose of an everyday, simple shoe; however, they've become a fashion trend within the past year or two. Like any fashion trend, it seems to grow within the context of social media platforms like Instagram and TikTok. Social media influencers are a few of the people who have spread the trend of wearing Nike Air Force 1's.

Let's say an influencer posts a TikTok showcasing her outfit of the day, which shows what she is wearing and who she is wearing. In her TikTok video, she's wearing a pair of Nike Air Force 1's. The influencer has roughly 10,000 followers, so that's a potential of 10,000 people viewing Nike's product and feeling the need to buy the product because an influencer they like is wearing them.

Continuing to share your brand through social media can lead to eventual growth owing to the customers posting your products on their own social media pages. We can easily see the trail of Nike's progress: from the very bottom with a specialized and focused brand and product to now, over time, how the brand was able to expand and grow by showcasing its values and morals through its products, commercials, and social media.

Now that you've seen an inside perspective on how a company like Nike brands itself, what are some of the ways you can take this information and spread your brand's influence?

V. How Does Nike Compare?

Although Nike is a great example of what effective branding can do, they are an older corporation that started before the 2000s—that's a pretty long time ago. Let's take a look at some more modern companies, like Uber and Airbnb, and the way they have specialized their brands.

Uber

The idea of Uber came from two entrepreneurs, Travis Kalanick and Garrett Camp, who were stuck in Paris in a snowstorm without a ride. Uber was born a year later, in 2009, with the design of a smartphone app that allows people to find a ride with just a click of a button.

Uber's company timeline shows us the unique inclusivity of its brand.[120] At the very beginning, Uber's brand was about providing accessible transportation to get people to and from the places they

120 "The History of Uber," Uber Newsroom, accessed February 14, 2023.

visit. As the business has grown, Uber has dedicated their brand to embrace more corporate social responsibility initiatives to support various social justice and community issues by donating to various organizations, as well as creating partnerships.

For example, in 2013 UberKITTENS launched a partnership with different animal shelters across the country to raise money for them by allowing Uber riders to request a 15-minute cuddle with a kitten—assuming riders are not allergic to cats, of course.[121] This not only appealed to riders who may love to snuggle with cute pets but it also aided a larger cause, namely finding homes for the kittens.

Throughout its years of business, Uber has participated in numerous food drives and food donation events. In 2014, Uber set up on-location donation spots for riders to donate clothing, which all went to Goodwill.[122] Uber's partnerships demonstrate their brand's value in helping communities around the country, even though Uber has now reached an international platform. People can connect with Uber's brand through its emphasis on helping others.

Let's zoom out for a moment. How do Uber's and Airbnb's brand values compare to Nike's brand values?

Airbnb, originally called AirBed and Breakfast, was founded in 2008. The company's service started out as room rentals, but a year later, their leadership changed the company's name to Airbnb in

---

121 Lindsey, "The Cat's out of the Bag, UberKITTENS is Here!," 2015.

122 "Uber and Goodwill® Make Spring Cleaning Easy." 2015. Goodwill Industries International, accessed February 14, 2023.

efforts to demonstrate its expansion of services to encompass bigger rental spaces like apartments, homes, and vacation spots.

Just as we mentioned slogan changes with Nike, Airbnb changed its slogan as they continued expanding to refine its brand. As a startup, Airbnb was providing accessible travel services to those traveling across the country. They originally used the slogan, "travel like a human."[123]

Airbnb's brand focused specifically on the aspects of travel. Traveling can be difficult to navigate, but Airbnb's brand focuses on making traveling less of a hassle. As its brand has expanded, Airbnb has moved its focus from the concept of travel accommodation and more on the idea of "home."

Given this shift, Airbnb decided to change its slogan to represent the change. Since the company was focusing its values on the sentiment of home, its slogan became: "Belong anywhere."

Take a minute or two to think about Airbnb's second slogan. What attributes or ideas do you think consumers can identify themselves with? Do you think this slogan helped Airbnb's brand become "sticky"?

Lots of people experience homesickness while traveling or being away from where they reside all of the time. Airbnb's emphasis on finding a home wherever you go provides its target audience with a sense of comfort when using its services, knowing that they can find a place where they feel just at home.

---

[123] "A Message from Co-Founder and CEO Brian Chesky," Airbnb Newsroom, 2020.

Airbnb updated its logo around the same time they changed their slogan in 2014, and it turns out that the company wanted its logo to encompass four different principles: people, places, love, and its name, Airbnb.[124]

Take a look at how each principle was illustrated in its logo.

Airbnb's logo embodies its values as a brand. The idea of home includes people and the places they love and feel comfortable. Tying that concept into Airbnb's logo gives them a great way to show the company's values!

Company Names As a Verb

Another great aspect of Uber and Airbnb's branding is the fact that both companies' names have been used as actual verbs. Let's say you and your friends are deciding to go out to eat at a restaurant that's a 30-minute walk from where you live. Some of your friends don't want to walk that far, so someone suggests that you "Uber it."

Almost everyone is going to understand that the use of Uber as a verb means that someone is going to order an Uber for you guys to go to the restaurant. Not a lot of people will talk about calling a taxi or catching a ride. They're just going to "Uber it."

---

124 "What Airbnb Teaches Us about Having a Strong Brand Identity," SOCi, accessed February 14, 2023.

The use of company names as verbs solidifies the specificity of the product and its brand. It has become a well-known entity between consumers. Unlike Nike, both the company names Uber and Airbnb have the potential to be used as a verb, which further pushes their product out to their target audiences. It becomes memorable, useful, and concise while also helping the companies brand the identity of their businesses.

What are some ways you can connect with your target audience through your own brand?

VI. Cheat Code Recap

1. Branding is the marketing process by which a company creates a name and symbol that is easily identifiable as belonging to itself.
2. Branding is NOT the same thing as marketing. Branding is a *type* of marketing process that every company utilizes at some point. Every company has its own brand. Marketing is the process that develops and establishes a brand.
3. Building a good brand can help your company signify intent, create a competitive edge, transform itself into an experience, build trust, and leverage emotions.
4. Creating your brand involves researching your target audience and competitors, choosing a brand focus and personality, creating a slogan, creating a "look" for your brand, and storytelling.

Part 5:
Manifesting Your Impact

Chapter 15
Measuring Your Success

Written by: Tiffany Yau and Aditya Desai

"Progress is made where progress is measured." – Jack LaLanne, American exercise instructor

I. What Are Key Performance Indicators?

Don't worry, we know what you're thinking—and NO, we're not just throwing around some more snazzy three-letter business acronyms again for the sake of it! **Key performance indicators (KPIs)** are much simpler than the calculus-based double derivative that you're probably envisioning, so let's get straight to it!

KPIs are metrics you need to determine and explain how your company will progress to meet its business goals and marketing goals.

Remember that metaphorical airplane you were building earlier while free-falling into your entrepreneurial journey? When you began to build the plane, you probably had some key goals in mind. Perhaps a pointy head with even wings? Maybe a larger wingspan to extend the lateral distance you could travel? Either way, you had a vision! And, to execute that vision, you internally set milestones for small tasks and additions to the plan. KPIs are no different! As quantifiable measures that a company uses to determine how well it is meeting its operational and strategic goals, KPIs will help your social enterprise stay on track to fly to success!

We cannot overemphasize the importance of KPIs. They are essential to help you do all of the following:

Measure Progress Over Time

You need to be able to assign a measurement to something to be able to confidently determine and quantify its growth. Examples of KPIs that help show growth in your business include revenue, number of physical locations, number of employees, and more (we'll be diving into more detail with these shortly)! Setting targets at the beginning of each quarter or year and evaluating your KPIs on a weekly or monthly basis allows you to measure progress toward your end goals. Measuring progress is so important, especially when you have investors who care about your growth and their return on investment.

Analyze Patterns and Make Adjustments

Here's where we introduce you to the tricks up our sleeves! There's a simple but wholly useful one: when you measure a set of KPIs quarter-over-quarter without changing them, you can detect patterns in your numbers.

Don't underestimate the power of patterns – they can be remarkably helpful in the long-term growth of your social enterprise. KPIs are things you must always measure. After all, the patterns emerge from the numbers. Remember our discussion of A/B testing in Chapter 8? Perhaps you can predict, through KPIs, when your slowest quarter will be and launch a team-building initiative (whatever that may be!) during the same period. Or maybe you'll be able to tell when a quarter will produce extra profits and allow you to set the stage for a nice vacation to the Bahamas – the possibilities are endless!

Your KPIs are invaluable when you keep them front and center because they will tell you when it's time to change your strategy. Numbers don't lie. If your website or social media receives less engagement when you post at 5 p.m. instead of 7 p.m., that might be a signal to make some adjustments. Same goes for if you make 25% less in revenue this month compared with last month.

Remember, you'll always need indicators that will tell you when you're in danger of missing your targets and goals, especially before it's too late! KPIs will give you quantifiable metrics for your vision for of the future (our secret way of time traveling)! KPIs will keep you iterative and help you stay on the path you need to be on!

Monitor Company Health

Simply put, KPIs are a go-to when gauging how healthy your business is. Think about it like a good ol' visit to the doctor's office. What do they do? Check your blood pressure, heart rate, body mass index, etc. and compare the new numbers against the old. That's right—they confirm that your vital signs are on point before saying goodbye and scheduling your next check-up. Similarly, KPIs are your company's vital signs. When you monitor them, you can ensure that every part of your company—from human resources to business strategy—are going with the flow!

As mentioned earlier, KPIs include any key measures that are normally quantified, or translated into numbers to determine how well a company is doing. All KPIs share three main characteristics:

- **Practical and Measurable**: The KPIs you use should allow you to measure what you need to inform better decisions for your social enterprise. They need to be aligned with your strategy and relevant to your social enterprise's goals.
- **Actionable**: KPIs can help you track efficiency, quality, timeliness, governance, compliance, behaviors, economics, project performance, personnel performance, and more. In other words, they provide you with a plethora of insights that you can directly act upon to improve your sales or your social enterprise's impact.
- **Directional**: KPIs are normally divided into two categories—**leading indicators** and **lagging indicators**. Let's say someone wanted to use KPIs to help shed some pounds. In this case,

their actual weight over time would be a lagging indicator because it indicates past success. On the other hand, the number of calories they eat per day is a leading indicator because it predicts future success. Most successful companies balance their KPIs between leading and lagging indicators.

II. The Types of KPIs

KPIs might just sound like some complex business term, and we don't blame you for thinking this. But consider this: how did you ultimately learn to ride a bike? It might sound rudimentary, but it was all about setting goals! First, you aimed to keep your balance in a seated posture on the bike. Next, you sought to ride with training wheels. And, finally, you set the goal of taking off the training wheels and venturing into the open on two wheels. KPIs are no different! No matter how complex they sound, at the end of the day they are merely methods of setting goals. The goals are what matter most! Here are some real-life examples of KPIs within different categories that you can reference and leverage for your social enterprise. Depending on your needs, they can be measured weekly, monthly, quarterly, or annually.

Sales KPIs

- The number of new orders or purchases per period
- The dollar value of new orders or purchases per period
- The number of hours spent following up on sales

- The percentage growth in net sales per period

Financial KPIs

- The growth in business revenue, or the total value of all sales
- The change in net profit margin, or the amount of money you make after all expenses are deducted
- The inventory turnover rate, or how fast your business can sell its products

Customer KPIs

- The number of customers retained, or customers that order from you more than once
- The percentage of market share, or the proportion of your industry that you're in control of
- The average ticket resolution time, or how long it takes to solve a customer problem

Operational KPIs

- The average order fulfillment time, or how long it takes to package and deliver a customer's order
- The average employee satisfaction rating

Marketing KPIs

- The website traffic per period
- The number of keywords or search terms that trigger your website, in the top ten of search engine (primarily Google) results
- Number of blog articles published per period

Yeah, that is a lot of KPIs—and it's only the tip of the iceberg! The tricky part is that there are no definite guidelines on which KPIs you should use. In fact, the KPIs that you use to keep your social enterprise on track are bound to be different than those your fellow entrepreneurs select. So, how should you pick?

First, choose the KPIs that are directly related to your business goals. For example, if you're most concerned about generating sales immediately, you might choose to monitor the growth in sales and revenue on a monthly or quarterly basis. On the other hand, if you're interested in growing your brand recognition and loyalty to start off with, you might measure your percentage of market share and customer retention rate (the percentage of customers you can retain over a period of time).

Next, be sure to focus on a few key metrics instead of a slew of data points. Nowadays, marketing has become so advanced that you can easily determine views, clicks, conversions, opens, and so much more. Here's a simple rule though: *less* is always *more*. Rather than choosing dozens of metrics to report on, you should just focus on the most important ones.

Finally, consider your company's stage of growth. If you are reading this book, you are likely in the early stages of your social entrepreneurial journey, which means that some metrics are far more important than others. As an early-stage entrepreneur, you should be most concerned about the data related to whether your business model is working, like simple conversion rates, whereas seasoned businesses should focus on other metrics, like **customer lifetime value** (which is the average net profit from your entire relationship with one customer).

As you move along your entrepreneurial journey, be sure to set your goals and use metrics to spur growth. It's important to acknowledge that goals and metrics refer to different things – a goal is an end result, whereas a metric tracks progress toward that goal. KPIs are metrics. With that in mind, we'll teach you how to get out there to kickstart some effective goal-setting.

III. Goal Setting: OKRs and SMART Goals

Setting your Objectives

Now that you are more informed on KPIs and their many kinds, it is important that you also know how to use your KPIs to define your **OKRs (i.e., objectives and key results)**. Don't worry, we don't have many more three-letter acronyms to throw at you!

OKRs are an effective goal-setting tool you can use to communicate and accomplish different milestones you set for yourself.

- **Objectives** are *goals* that inspire and set the direction for what your social enterprise wants to do. This should answer the question, "Where do I need to go?"
- **Key results** are the *steps* that measure your progress toward your objectives. This should answer the question, "How do I know I'm getting there?"
- **Initiatives/actions** are the *tasks* required to drive progress to the key results. This should answer the question, "What will I do to get there?

In a more real-world, nonbusinessy context, you can understand the importance of OKRs through the example of New Year's resolutions and why most of us have a hard time achieving them.

Over 30% of New Year's resolutions tend to be health-related. Let's say your resolution for the new year is "to be healthier." In this case, that is your *objective*. It sets the general direction for your new year.

Your *key results* are a bit more specific. Let's say it is to "lose/gain X pounds by the end of the year." It is quantifiable, allowing you to measure your progress toward your objective of being healthier, and it answers the question of "how do I know I'm getting there?" You can set a variety of key results to further break down your objective, such as:

- Lose/gain X pounds by the end of March.
- Lose/gain X pounds by the end of June.
- Lose/gain X pounds by the end of September.
- Lose/gain X pounds by the end of December.

In this case, your KPI is also the number of pounds you lose or gain, depending on what your goal is.

These are all associated with a deadline (time-bound), so you can keep track of your progress as time passes.

Lastly, you must define some initiatives and actions. Here are some examples:

- Work out 15+ minutes per day
- Do 10 sit-ups every morning as soon as I wake up
- Drink 60+ oz of water per day
- Eat 1+ cups of veggies per day

Here, your KPIs can include:

- Total pounds lost every 3 months and by the end of the year
- Number of minutes working out per day
- Number of sit-ups per day
- Ounces of water consumed per day
- Cups of veggies consumed per day

Your initiatives and actions should make your key results even more tangible. They define the steps you need to take to make those results come true.

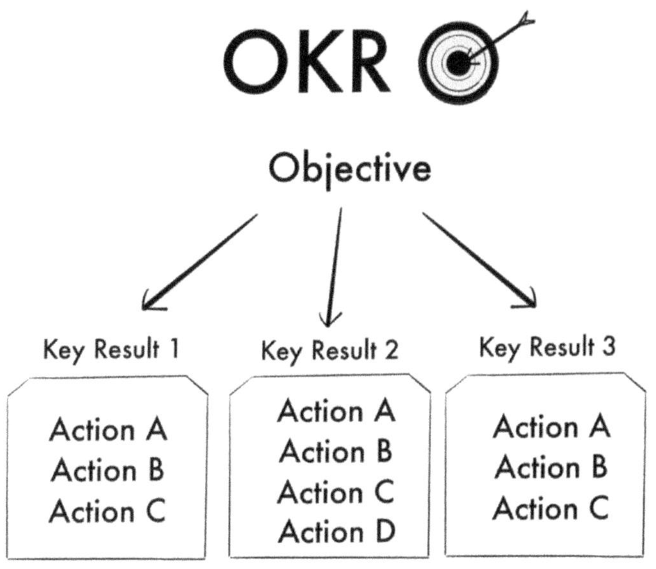

Creating OKRs: Setting up S.M.A.R.T. Goals

An effective way to define your OKRs so that you set yourself up for success is to make them into S.M.A.R.T. format. A well-defined goal is one that checks off each box of S.M.A.R.T., a goal-setting acronym for being:

- **S (Specific)**
- **M (Measurable)**
- **A (Achievable)**
- **R (Realistic or relevant)**
- **T (Timely)**

Specific goals must be:

- Well-defined, clear, and unambiguous
- Simple, sensible, and significant
- Able to answer what, why, who, where, and which resources or limits are involved

Measurable goals must be:

- Quantifiable and must utilize criteria that measure your progress
- Meaningful and motivating
- Able to address how much, how many, and how will I know when it is accomplished

Achievable goals must:

- Be attainable and not impossible to achieve
- Answer how can I accomplish this goal
- Address how realistic the goal is based on recognized constraints

Realistic or relevant goals must be:

- Within reach and relevant to your life purpose
- Reasonable, resourced, and results-based
- Able to answer whether or not this goal seems worthwhile. Is this the right time? Does this match other efforts/needs? Am I the right person on my team to help the company reach

this goal? Or is it applicable in the current socioeconomic environment?

Timely goals must:

- Define a clear timeline that creates urgency and drive
- Be time-bound, time-limited, and time-sensitive
- Give a sense of "*when*": what can I do six months from now, what can I do six weeks from now, and what can I do today?

Defining your goals in a S.M.A.R.T. format will help you maintain attainable progress and enable you to grow your social enterprise. With a very relatable example, here is a summary of Fulphil's OKRs that follow the S.M.A.R.T. criteria for the first quarter of 2020:

Fulphil Q1 Objectives & Key Results (January 1–March 31, 2020)

- *Objective*: Expand school presence.

  Key Result 1: Solidify 2 more school partnerships. Have a total of 10 partners by March 31, 2020.

  Key Result 2: Implement marketing strategy developed with Philadelphia partners to increase unique clicks by 15% by March 31, 2020.

- *Objective*: Increase funding.

  Key Result 1: Gain $20,00 in funding from grants by March 31, 2020.

  Key Result 2: Gain $5,00 in funding from donors/funders by March 31, 2020.

- *Objective*: Create good experience for existing school partners.

  Key Result 1: Successfully deliver curriculum to 2 confirmed partner schools by March 31, 2020.

  Key Result 2: Hire a developer to enhance our website and to complement our curriculum by March 31, 2020.

These were S.M.A.R.T.—but they sure were easier said than done! OKRs are big, ambitious goals but should be within reach. They should be just close enough to motivate and inspire you to do everything you can to achieve them.

If you take a few minutes to thoroughly think about and plan your OKRs in S.M.A.R.T. format for the next quarter, we promise you'll have a clearer picture of your company's future! Feel free to download our online worksheet as you plan out your OKRs.

IV. Measuring Impact

So, now we know a bit more about how we should measure and quantify our goals for our business. But how do we measure our *impact*?

This is different from how much money we are making. This is measuring how effective we are at our mission and the difference we are making in the world. But let's get a few things straight first.

The Importance of Measuring Impact

Measuring impact is so important. It keeps organizations accountable for the work they do to show that it is actually effective and bringing value into the world. When it comes to entrepreneurship, it is so important to be accountable—but even more so for social entrepreneurship. This is also what makes social enterprises stand out as they create more brand loyalty and better funding opportunities! You can't build with impact until you know how to define and measure it.

However, both people and businesses often perceive it as one of the hardest things to measure. Because it is *perceived* as hard to measure, it is even more useful that you know how to measure it! Don't worry—you may not know how to measure it right now, but we've got the cheat code for you right here.

Quantifying the "Unquantifiable"

The thing about measuring impact is that it is never straightforward. It isn't like measuring how much revenue you earned this past month or how many new visitors you attracted to your website. Those metrics can be evaluated quickly for almost any company, and that is one thing that makes measuring impact seem so tricky—it is a nonlinear process. Some of the most challenging aspects of measuring impact can include:

- **Defining your impact:** What does success look like if we are effective? What does "impact" even mean to our organization?

- **Creating a process to feasibly measure impact:** How do we create a process to measure that impact that makes sense and tells us if it is working?

Before even measuring your impact, you will need to understand how to define your impact.

Defining Your Impact: Long Term and Short Term

When we need to measure impact, we first need to understand what impact actually means to us—what does success look like? It's time to reverse engineer! For every company and organization, impact can mean something different.

When you define your impact, you must consider two types of impact: long-term and short-term impact.

- **Long-term impact** is the type of impact that describes the difference your company or organization has made over a long period, like 5 or more years.
- **Short-term impact** is often the type of impact that describes the difference your company or organization has made within the span of a short period, like a year or less.

Here is an example of Fulphil's short-term vs. long-term impact metrics defined:

- Long-term impact:
    - By 2030, 8,000 Fulphil alumni believe they are pursuing impactful careers.
- Short-term impact (1-year period):

- Students develop a social entrepreneurial mindset and be career-ready by the time they complete the curriculum.
- Students enjoy their learning experience by the time they complete the curriculum.

Notice how these follow the same S.M.A.R.T. format—they are specific, measurable, attainable, realistic, and timely!

Given that the mission of Fulphil is to make education fun and effective to help all students develop the skill sets they need to be career-ready, the short-term impact objectives make sense:

- Students develop a social entrepreneurial mindset and be career-ready by the time they complete the curriculum.
    - Context: Fulphil's philosophy revolves around inspiring students to make a difference and be problem-solvers. Fulphil's curriculum also educates students on meaningful skills they will need to know and build beyond their time in school.
- Students enjoy their learning experience by the time they complete the curriculum.
    - Context: Fulphil's curriculum design and philosophy is that learning and education should be fun! Students renew and rewrite the content every year to reflect more modern trends in the world, and it is designed to convey a spunky tone, as opposed to the same tone your stale textbook might have for your usual classes.

Your short-term goals should add up over time to help you achieve a big, somewhat lofty and exciting long-term goal.

Assigning a Measurement

You're probably wondering how can you know that students are "developing a social entrepreneurial mindset and are career-ready" after going through your courses? Or how do you know students are actually enjoying their learning experiences?

Of course, we can't just assume! To measure these short-term goals, Fulphil issues pre- and post-school-year surveys to students and teachers to get their overall feedback, which are measured based on our KPIs. The answers in those survey results determine and validate how Fulphil quantifies these short-term impact metrics.

Some examples of the survey questions include some of the following, where students will submit their own 1 to 10 ranking. Each of these questions represents a KPI:

- Survey question example 1: After completing this curriculum, how much more or less confident do you feel in your own ability to make a positive impact on your community and the world?
    - The KPI for this is our students' perceptions of their confidence levels to make a positive impact on their community and the world.
- Survey question example 2: After completing this curriculum, how much more or less confident do you feel in your ability to overcome obstacles?

    - The KPI for this is our students' perceptions of their confidence levels in their resilience and overall ability to overcome obstacles.
- Survey question example 3: After completing this curriculum, how much more or less engaging was this entrepreneurship course compared to your other subjects in school?
    - The KPI for this is our students' perceptions of their general levels of engagement in our entrepreneurship course compared with that of other subjects they are learning in school.

Based on various questions that align with answers of whether we met our short-term impact goals, we can state something like "82% of students felt more confident in their ability to make a positive impact on the world by the end of the school year. This increased by 30% since the beginning of the year." These quantified results are known as **outcomes**. Outcomes are basically the verifiable pieces of evidence and data defined by the KPIs you need to prove your impact exists.

With this stated outcome example, we bridged our survey results and showed our progress over a period of one year. Thus, overall as an organization, Fulphil students (and readers like you!) can expect to experience the following outcomes:

- An increase in confidence to make a positive impact on the community and the world
- An increase in confidence in resilience and overall ability to overcome obstacles

- An increase in engagement in our entrepreneurship course compared with that of other subject areas learned more traditionally

When stating your desired outcomes, it is okay to say an overall "increase" in whatever KPI you define. However, quantifying your impact more specifically with numbers will serve as a pivotal role in not only proving your impact but also helping you rally more interest, support, and respect from your customers and funders.

Let's recap. To define your impact, you must:

1. Look back to your mission. What does your company stand for?
2. Define your long-term impact. What does impact look like to you at least a few years from now?
3. Define your short-term impact. What needs to happen so that your long-term goal is achieved? What will you need to achieve to keep yourself accountable for reaching that goal?
4. Define how you want to measure your short-term impact.

As we alluded, these measurements are a lot like KPIs and OKRs in a normal nonimpact business context! Let's draw some comparisons:

1. In both cases of defining your normal business metrics and impact metrics, you must look back to your *mission* and what your company stands for. Defining your mission is analogous to defining your *objectives*. Remember, objectives are goals that inspire and set the direction for what your business wants to do. This should answer the question, "Where do I need to go?"

2. Defining your *long-term impact* and *short-term impact* is like defining your *key results*. As mentioned, key results are the steps that measure your progress toward your objectives. This should answer the question, "How do I know I'm getting there?" The same can be said for defining your short-term impact.
3. Defining your *outcomes* is like defining the quantified measures of your *KPIs*. When defining outcomes, you are defining the *measurements* of your short- and long-term impact. KPIs are your metrics for measuring success.
4. In both cases, defining your *initiatives/actions* is necessary, and ultimately, they take on the same role. Your initiatives/actions

Normal Business Metrics (the metrics you need to show your business is growing)	**Impact Metrics** (the metrics you are making the impact you say you are)
Objectives	Mission/Purpose
Key Results	Long term impact Short term impact
KPIs	Outcomes
Initiatives/Actions	Initiatives/Actions

are the tasks required to drive progress to the key results, which also answers the question, "What will I do to get there?"

Based on all of this, how would you define your company's mission, long-term impact, short-term impact? How do you want to measure your impact?

Visually Showcasing Impact Measures: Logic Model

Keeping track of every component of measuring your impact can be a lot.

Logic models are incredibly helpful in showcasing how you intend to measure your impact. The **logic model** is a framework that allows you to visually map the cause-effect relationship behind everything you do in your business. Logic models rely on, well, a lot of logic!

On the other page is an example of the logic model we used in the process of defining Fulphil's impact.

Some things might look more familiar to you. The main components of a logic model are:

- **Purpose**, which is the equivalent of your objective or mission
- **Impact (long- and short-term impact)**, which is analogous to our key results
- **Outcomes**, which are essentially our KPIs
- **Activities,** which are the *initiatives/actions* we need to actually do to be able to reach those key results in our measurable KPIs
- **Inputs**, which are the resources we have at our disposal to be able to do the activities to achieve our key results

Fulphil Logic Model

Purpose: To make education fun and impactful to empower our next generation to build compassion and succeed in their careers

Inputs

- **Fulphil curriculum**
  - Social entrepreneurship
  - 21st century skills
  - Sustainability
  - Diversity, equity, & inclusion
  - Financial Literacy
  - Mental Health and Wellness

Activities

Students

- Students identify pressing problems of their local communities
- Students understand how to problem-solve for their local communities
- Students learn key concepts of entrepreneurship (marketing, budgeting, pitching, stakeholder analysis, fundraising).
- Students learn soft skills needed to succeed in the workplace.
- Students learn about key social issues of our time and how it applies to the world around them

Teachers/Feedback Loop

- Monthly teacher check-in/professional development sessions
- Teachers iterating content/providing feedback

Outcomes

Perception of curriculum (Students/Schools)

- Accessibility
- Fun
- Human-Centered (how well we meet users where they are)

Student outcomes (increase in...)

- Confidence
- Grit & resilience
- Creativity
- Leadership
- Compassion & Empathy
- 21st century soft skills
- Financial literacy
- Understanding of social impact concepts & ways to implement them in their own lives

Impact

SHORT-TERM

- Students develop a social entrepreneurial mindset and be career-ready
- Students enjoy their learning experience

LONG-TERM

- By 2030, 8,000 Fulphil alumni believe they are pursuing impactful careers

Each one of these factors feeds into another, which is why it is *logical*! Try creating a logic model for your company idea with the help of our online worksheet.

V. Balanced Scorecards

We have just one more framework to show you—a method to keep track of indicators that was developed by the Harvard Business Review (HBR).[125]

Known as the **balanced scorecard**, HBR's method consists of a set of measures that gives top managers a high-level but comprehensive view of their business. At its core, the balanced scorecard illustrates a company's financial goals and measures but also reflects operational goals and measures like customer satisfaction and the organization's innovation. Keeping these operational drivers in check can help you stay accountable to achieving your future financial performance goals.

The indicators on a balanced scorecard are no different than the indicators that you would find in the cockpit of a plane. When a pilot is tasked with navigating the skies and flying the plane, they must know all the information relating to the flight—fuel, airspeed, turbulence, altitude, and other measures that summarize the environment that the pilot has to navigate. On the other hand, if the pilot was to rely on only one metric, it could end fatally for the passengers. Similarly, the balanced scorecard allows managers to take several parts of

---

125 Kaplan and Norton, "The Balanced Scorecard—Measures That Drive Performance," 1992.

an organization into consideration simultaneously to make well-informed decisions.

The Balanced Scorecard Links Performance Measures

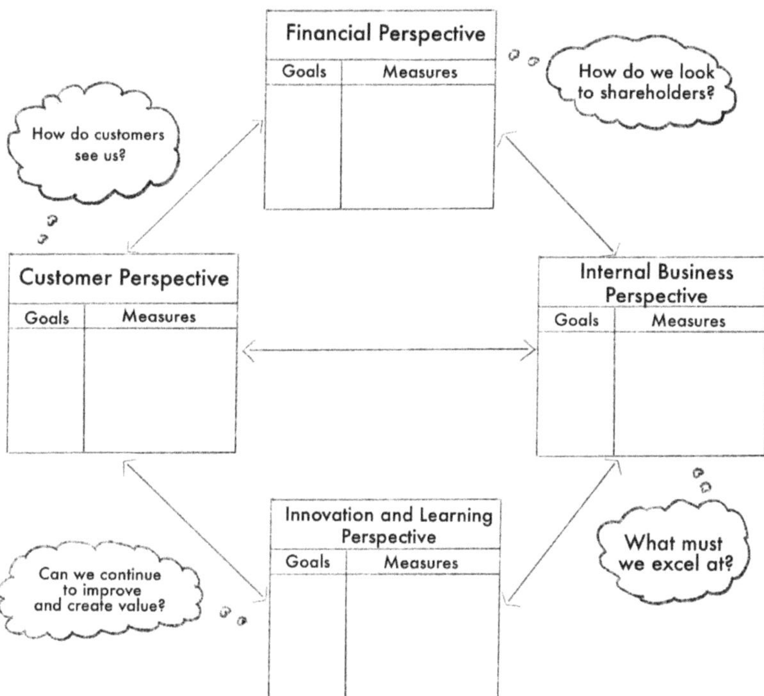

As a result, the balanced scorecard allows us to understand:

- **Customer perspective:** How do customers see us?
- **Internal business perspective:** What must we excel at?
- **Innovation and learning perspective:** Can we continue to improve and create value?
- **Financial perspective:** How do we look to shareholders?

The balanced scorecard can be an incredibly helpful tool—don't underestimate it. Even senior managers at large companies get overwhelmed with the vast array of KPIs that they have to choose from to determine their company's success. The balanced scorecard conveniently minimizes this information overload by limiting the measures that you can and should be using.

You can create your own balanced scorecard using the online worksheet from our website.

So, to sum it up, we learned about the power of measuring your company's indicators and setting S.M.A.R.T. goals. Going forward, if you live by these practices, we guarantee that leveraging your KPIs effectively will help you become a *key* player in your industry in no time!

VI. Cheat Code Recap

1. KPIs are metrics required to determine and explain how a company will progress to meet its business.
2. KPIs can help companies measure progress over time, make adjustments, analyze patterns, and monitor company health.
3. OKRs are effective goal-setting tools used to communicate and accomplish different milestones you set for yourself.
4. S.M.A.R.T. is a goal-setting format; the components are specific, measurable, actionable, realistic or relevant, and timely.
5. Measuring impact is important because it demonstrates the value a company brings to the world. Measuring impact follows a similar structure to how we set and measure OKRs.

6. The logic model is a framework that allows you to visually map the cause-effect relationship behind everything you do in your business.
7. The balanced scorecard is a framework that both shows a company's financial goals and also measures and reflects operational goals and measures like customer satisfaction and the organization's innovation.

Chapter 16

Bringing It All Together: Making Sense of Business Models, Executive Summaries, and Pitching

Written by: Tiffany Yau, Brooke McCormick, and Emma O'Neil

"Presentations rise or fall on the quality of the idea, the narrative, and the passion of the speaker. It's about substance, not speaking style or multimedia pyrotechnics." — Harvard Business Review[126]

You can have a great idea, but it won't go anywhere if it isn't shared properly. It's not *what* you say, it's *how* you say it.

---

126 Anderson, "How to Give a Killer Presentation," 2013.

Frankly, there are a lot of ways you can say what you want to say! And in entrepreneurship, there are *lots* of different ways to present your ideas. The main ones we will review in this final chapter are the following:

- Executive summaries
- Pitch decks
- Business canvas models

In addition to your financial statements, you will inevitably be asked to submit these three types of documents in consideration for any investment opportunity. Each of these formats communicates similar ideas regarding your social enterprise but in different ways. In each of these, you must remember that you are not writing *everything* about your social enterprise. You are telling your audience (whoever is reading the documents) the "TL; DR" of your social enterprise. Your goal with each of these is to write *enough* to pique their interest and get to the *next* meeting.

We might watch TV shows like *Shark Tank* and have this whole idea about what it is like for an entrepreneur to secure an investment. We are kindly asking you to scratch almost everything you have learned from TV. It might *seem* like first-time entrepreneurs are pitching their products and services in front of investors. But the fact is these entrepreneurs on *Shark Tank* have been vetted. They had to apply to pitch on the show, submit more materials, have an interview and audition, and if lucky enough, they pitch on the show in front of a panel of investors.[127] That is the final meeting out of so many that already took place. We need to focus on *how* they got there. Beyond building tons of momentum in their businesses, one of the most important things these entrepreneurs had to do was submit good materials.

The documents and written verbal communication you submit to your audience essentially builds the foundation for your first impression. If it is interesting and captivating enough, they will follow up with another meeting and be more likely to give you their attention—no pressure, right?

You *must* devote time to creating respectable materials that demonstrate that your social enterprise is worthy and deserving of attention.

As you continue reading this chapter, feel free to access our online resources to help you build each one of these forms of presentation.

I. The Essentials: Executive Summary & Pitch Deck

When funders evaluate your social enterprise, they will analyze the following:

1. The problem and opportunity
2. The solution and value proposition
3. The business model

---

[127] Crouse, "How to Get on Shark Tank," accessed February 14, 2023.

4. The market and the go-to-market strategy
5. The competition
6. The financials
7. The achievements/progress/traction/measured success
8. The future plans
9. The team
10. The current status and the ask

Each of these components must have some presence in your executive summary and your pitch deck.

Executive Summaries versus Pitch Decks

Your **executive summary** outlines all of these points in a few pages at most. It is industry standard to send this together with your pitch deck when you are seeking funding. In your executive summary, you want to have a section on each of the ten points mentioned, dedicating a short paragraph to each, approximately—maybe two paragraphs max. The goal with your executive summary is to be thorough but concise enough to get the point across.

Meanwhile, your **pitch deck** is not really a written document but rather a visual presentation with slides. You don't have to write nearly as much for your pitch deck, but it should be neat, organized, and aesthetic. If you are on the less creative side of the spectrum, use websites like Canva to create your pitch deck rather Google Slides or a Microsoft PowerPoint template—trust us, it will look so much more professional!

With pitch decks, *less* is often *more*. The rule of thumb for pitch decks is to follow Guy Kawasaki's 10/20/30 Rule of PowerPoint[128]:

- **10 slides:** According to Kawasaki, you don't need any more than ten slides in a PowerPoint to get the point across. If you think about it, a business should be simple and straightforward to explain—at least, a good business should be. Kawasaki even says, "If you must use more than ten slides to explain your social enterprise, you probably don't have a business." We recommend making one slide for each of the bulleted essentials we listed above.
- **20 minutes:** If you were to speak through your slides, it should comfortably take you 20 minutes. Sure, the setting and context of your presentation will vary. Maybe you only have five minutes to pitch for a competition—that's different, and for such a case, you'll probably need fewer than ten slides. But maybe your investor meeting is set for one hour. Even if you have one hour allotted, there are bound to be different elements of such a meeting that will eat some time, including a question-and-answer session.
- **30-point font:** Use a bigger font. Not only is it easier to read but Kawasaki cites that he often sees tiny fonts jammed into a presentation and it's never good when your audience reads your text while you are speaking because they might read ahead of you. Being "out of synch" with your audience

128 Kawasaki, "The Only 10 Slides You Need in a Pitch," 2015.

is not ideal and makes the conversation choppy and harder to follow. Unlike what you write for each section of your executive summary, you do not need to cram a paragraph or two onto each of your pitch deck slides. Each slide should remain minimal in terms of content.

II. The Business Model Canvas

Meanwhile, the **business model canvas** is a type of template that is used in business and entrepreneurship to visually show the building blocks of your company's plan to deliver *value* and earn revenue. The idea of this structure was created by Alexander Osterwalder and Yves Pigneur.[129] The business model canvas is usually less often requested than executive summaries and pitch decks, but creating one is still a great exercise to do for yourself as you continue to think through the nuts and bolts of your business. Your audience will likely have questions on what you will flesh out in your business model canvas, so it is helpful to prepare one or work through one on your own regardless! Within the business model canvas, there are nine sections you will need to address:

1. Key partners
2. Key activities
3. Key resources
4. Value propositions

---

129 Osterwalder and Pigneur, *Business Model Generation*, 2010.

5. Customer relationships
6. Channels
7. Customer segments
8. Cost structure (financial and social costs)
9. Revenue streams (financial and social benefits)

You'll insert your description for each of these categories. Your descriptions can vary from a few written sentences to a few bulleted points—however you display your answers, they should be as concise as possible.

Key Partners

This section is used to describe who your partners are among your stakeholders. Are there any types of partnerships you can form as strategic alliances to help get your product to market? Is there any partner that can help you achieve economies of scale? Any partner that can help you reduce the chances of risk and uncertainty that your social enterprise will have to face? Any partner that can lend you their services in exchange for your own or for some other type of value you can deliver? When we think about identifying our key partners, we want to think about how a stakeholder can really drive value to our business.

Whether you have confirmed partners or not, you can simply state what ideal partners look like. What types of specific value can they provide to you? Perhaps you are creating a product for moms, and your ideal partner would be any organization that interacts with children, like a daycare or afterschool program. As you get further along in the process of developing your social enterprise, you should be able to name specific businesses you are already partnered with.

Key Activities

This is where you talk about what your social enterprise does. Beyond what your solution is and how it works, what do you need to do to get there? Some examples of key activities include *how* you are getting it out there or producing your product. Does it involve use of a manufacturer? Does it involve you teaching classes? Will you need a platform like Amazon to sell your product on? Will you need Instagram or TikTok for marketing? What needs to be done to make your solution and value proposition possible?

Key Resources

This is somewhat similar to the inputs you used for the logic model framework. What key assets will you be leveraging to make sure your social enterprise can exist and deliver value? Your assets can be anything from materials that help you operate as a business to the types of human capital you need—remember asset-based community development?

Value Propositions

What value are you delivering to your customer? For this category you should state the value proposition that you defined earlier in this book. Remember our format?

For [who] are [effect/problem] in [where], [Your Company] provides [rephrased root cause of the problem] through [solution].

This is your time to concisely define the problem your customers are facing and how your solution has the potential to add value. Beyond this statement alone, you can add a sentence or two that clarifies how severe the problem you're addressing is. Are there any studies or statistics you can leverage? Beyond what your solution is, *what* is it doing to actually solve the problem they are facing?

Customer Relationships

What type of relationship are you trying to build with your customers? Is it more transactional in a one-and-done purchasing approach or are you trying to build loyalty with them over time to make them into repeat customers? Does your product or service require a lot of human touch points where you have to speak with your customer a lot or do the customers mostly help themselves? Do you plan to build an online community where users can interact with each other?

Channels

Think back to our marketing chapters. This category description outlines your go-to-market strategy and how you are hoping to reach your customers. What go-to-market channels will you be leveraging? Why are you picking those specific channels? Are more of your potential customers on that channel? Is it more cost-effective? Are you partnering with organizations as a channel to better distribute your product? How will these channels help bring value into the world?

Customer Segments

Here, you are spelling out exactly who your customers are. Define who your market consists of. You can find how to do this in our Chapter 8 on product-market fit and also Chapters 9 and 11 on marketing strategies. In this section, you want to identify key characteristics of your customer. By doing so, you will be able to demonstrate why you listed the channels you did in the Channels category of the business model canvas.

Cost Structure

In this section, you will list out the key costs that determine your business model and pricing strategy. This section should list out the most expensive line items that you need to run your social enterprise. You can refer to our chapter on pricing to determine your overall costs.

Revenue Streams

In this section, you will list out exactly how you plan to make money. How much are your customers willing to pay for the product or service you are offering? If there are multiple products and services, list them out! How much are you trying to earn? How much do you need to sell to get to that goal? What products and services drive your revenue the most? You can also return to Chapter 12 on pricing to get more ideas as you continue to build out this description.

III. About Public Speaking and Pitching

Okay, so now you've learned the basics of an executive summary, a pitch deck, and a business model canvas. You've got all your content down in writing, so now it's show time and you're up to give your pitch!

If thinking about public speaking makes you think "OH MY GRACIOUS NO," you're not alone. As it turns out, research shows that 77% of people fear public speaking—which is also known as glossophobia (because of course, there is a phobia for everything).[130] It is very natural to feel anxious when it comes to speaking! Often, we think that it has to do with being scared of messing up or perhaps even having a low sense of self-esteem. But let us dispel that myth for you.

Being scared of public speaking is very *human*. Anthropologically speaking, resistance to public speaking has been programmed into us since the very beginning of human existence! Since prehistoric times, people have been terrified of being killed and eaten alive (very logical, right?).[131] If we are prey, then we know predators are watching for us. This is the mechanics of fear about public speaking. As humans, we have a fear of being watched because historically it has the potential to lead to our demise. There is a part in our brain that is responsible for managing our fear known as the amygdala. Our amygdalae have

---

130 Heeren et al. "Assessing Public Speaking Fear," 2013.

131 Gershman, "To Overcome Your Fear of Public Speaking, Stop Thinking about Yourself," 2019.

worked overtime to keep us alive, so whether it's being eaten alive by our predators or our audience, evolution has programmed our amygdalae to make us fearful.

It's absolutely *okay* to be scared of public speaking—technically, we're all still here today because that part of our brains works! We *know* public speaking is challenging! Public speaking is *not* a soft skill; it is a *hard skill* (such as coding) that demands practice and iteration—much like entrepreneurship.

Developing your public speaking skills as an entrepreneur can take you a long way. Pitching your ideas and articulating your thoughts in front of an array of audiences can boost your confidence and self-esteem.

Practicing this skill can give you comfort speaking to more unfamiliar groups of people. When you are challenged to present your business plan in front of investors for instance, you will be ready to deliver the strategy, vision, and finances with ease. Such preparedness can set you apart from your competition, even.

There are three things we'd like you to keep in mind:

1) **Know your audience**. That is always the first step. When you know your audience, you can understand how to effectively get your message across. Why do you think salespeople can be so convincing? They regularly analyze their audience and tailor their pitches to particular needs and desires. Whether you're selling to your customers to get them to buy your product or service or you're pitching to investors to get some funding, you need to cater your message to your audience.

2) **Know your stuff.** You've done all the hard work and research to get to the point where you have the chance to share. Whether or not the audience asks question, it is important to know what you're talking about. If they do ask questions, it will absolutely be helpful to be prepared! When you are confident about the material you are speaking about, you will also *sound* more confident and *feel* more confident! Being a subject matter expert for what you'll be speaking about is a great way to decrease the chances of you "messing up."

3) **Build trust.** Well-versed communication can *increase* trustworthiness. People will know they can rely on you to deliver the facts and engage in purposeful communication. Public speaking enhances your research and deductive reasoning skills.

It requires you to work from a premise and draw a conclusion based on research you have gathered. This research can be based on observation, it can be based on experience communicating with experts, or it can be information gathered from the internet.

Why Public Speaking/Pitching is Important for Your Business

As a burgeoning entrepreneur, learning to perfect your **elevator pitch** (a brief speech, typically well under a minute-long, about your business) is critical to success.

Maybe you need funding and have to address a group of investors. Maybe you have the opportunity to appear on a panel of experts. Maybe you are asked to explain your vision in a TV interview. Perhaps, as your company grows, you must host customer seminars. Perhaps in the future, you will need to represent your company at industry association events.

You need to be able to capture how innovative and necessary your venture is and the unique value it offers to the world in a very short communication. With consistent public speaking practice, you can develop that persuasive capacity, fine-tune your verbal skills, and expand your leadership potential.

What Makes an Effective Presentation?

Alright, let's dive into the critical aspects of an effective presentation. Don't worry—you've got this. One of our aims at Fulphil is to take away the anxiety of presentations and make sure you can tell your story with ease and excitement.

1) Know your audience (yes, we're emphasizing this again!)

Try asking yourself "Who is my audience? What do they need to hear from me?" They are the ones in the spotlight here. Feel free to create a list of questions to serve as prompts for what you intend to say.

For instance, you could hypothesize that an audience might want to know how your product stacks up against a rival. In your presentation, all you'd need to do is literally pose the question "How is my product different from X?" and proceed to answer your own question. This makes you look prepared and convincing.

Give your audience a reason to care. Be relevant and authentic, and always personally relate what you are talking about to them. If you are speaking to a group of elementary school students, for example, they might love hearing about YOUR experience in elementary school. Rather than a first step, this is more a point to keep in mind throughout the preparation and delivery.

You should *always* be thinking about your audience!

2) Frame your story: purpose and narrative

What is it that you want to say? While this question may seem obvious, many presenters do not contemplate this question enough before delivery. You have a purpose. Know what that purpose is and envision how you can take your audience on a journey. Don't just deliver a presentation—craft a full narrative. Your goal is to inspire your audience to see the world a little differently as they hear you speak. Here are a few tenets you can follow to achieve this:

- Limit the scope of your presentation to that which can be explained and enlivened with specific, engaging examples
- Keep it simple, concentrating on your core message
- Remember that ideas and stories are what interest us
- Identify your strengths to effectively build up your story

3) Structure: know where you're going

Develop the direction of your presentation by highlighting your main points. Try to limit this to three concise points at most. What is critical for you to get across? You want to have a clear (and limited) sense of purpose throughout the presentation.

It is also important to intimately know your product or service offering. What are the details of how it works and why it is unique? What numerical figures can you weave into your story to enhance your credibility?

According to a study that examined data from two television shows built around entrepreneurs in search of venture capital (*Shark Tank* and *Dragon's Den*), entrepreneurs who demonstrate evident signs of preparedness and a clear grasp of their material created credibility among investors and received greater funding regardless of the venture.[132]

4) Consider the format and your presence

Remember to make eye contact. We are all human, and communication is all the more powerful when you are really connecting with the people in front of you. Acknowledge them and make it clear that your purpose is to connect with them.

Try to use variation in sight, sound, and evidence to better connect. Vary your speed and emphasize changes in pitch and tone. Be aware of your posture and use gestures with purpose. When considering your evidence, pull from data, testimonials, and anecdotes.

In planning the multimedia aspect of your presentation, if you have photographs or illustrations that make the topic come alive, absolutely present them. These are not always required or permitted, and if they do not enhance the delivery of your message, then doing without them can be more effective.

However, if you are presenting an investor-style business pitch, you should *always* have slides. Visit our online resources for more insights on how to create a presentation using multimedia.

---

[132] Pollack, Rutherford, and Nagy, "Preparedness and Cognitive Legitimacy as Antecedents of New Venture Funding in Televised Business Pitches," 2012.

5) Stay flexible

Even if you nail down your structure and key points, try to stay flexible and open to spontaneity. As you talk, watch and listen to your audience, then adjust your pitch or presentation based on the **clues** you are receiving.

Also: try to relax and breathe! Public speaking will often induce a jolt of **adrenaline**, but it shouldn't be an overly stressful activity if you're confident with the material.

Practice Makes Perfect

These days, there are innovative ways to practice without having to give a spiel to your friends and family countless times. Record yourself! Set down your phone or any device with a camera and record your presentation over and over.

We are our own worst enemies, as the saying goes, and watching yourself can really clarify where your presentation can improve. Although digital recordings are useful, you can supplement this practice by giving your speech to a trusted mentor or peer. Just make sure it is someone who will offer encouraging yet constructive feedback.

Get your presentation down but do not memorize it! This can create a disconnect with the audience. According to a study where 760 volunteers rated hundreds of hours of TED Talks looking for patterns, memorized lines and scripts are not memorable, and there is power in the first seven seconds of a talk.[133] Make a grand entrance.

---

[133] Van Edwards, "5 Secrets of a Successful TED Talk," accessed February 15, 2023.

Something else to think about: look and feel your best when you're giving an especially daunting presentation.

Consider how your appearance can strengthen your connection to a group of people and boost the growth of your endeavor.

When you are putting it all together, do not forget that there is no one good way to do a talk. There is no one good way to effectively communicate to your audience. There's not even one type of occasion to give a speech – video messages are becoming increasingly powerful.

So, let your talk be *yours* and be confident in your unique delivery!

Here are some more exercises you can consider as you prepare for your big event:

- **One-minute impromptu speeches.** Set a timer on your phone for one minute and record yourself giving an impromptu speech on any topic that interests you. Do not prepare for it. Inject some variation by giving yourself one minute to prepare your message delivery and structure.
- **Tell a photo story.** To practice developing a narrative, find an interesting photo online and record yourself presenting a story about it. Discuss what you think the backstory is, who the subjects are, their dreams, their motivations, and anything else that will tell a compelling story about them.
- **Make up a definition.** You should always seem like you have authority over the topic of your presentation. Choose a word you do not know the definition of and record yourself saying,

with authority, what you think it means. Pay attention to how you use your *voice and intonation* to assert more command.

- **Make a commercial.** Choose an item in your home and create a one-minute commercial about it. Record yourself saying what makes it special, how it can enhance lives, and why everyone must have it.

IV. Cheat Code Recap

1. Three common forms of presentation that communicate your business model include executive summaries, pitch decks, and business canvas models.
2. The executive summary and pitch deck are two different methods of communicating the problem you're hoping to solve, your solution and value proposition, your business model, your market overview, your go-to-market strategy, your competition, your financials, your achievements, your progress and traction, your measurement of success, your future plans, your future team, and your current status and ask.
3. The business model canvas is a template used in business and entrepreneurship to visually show the building blocks of your company's plan to deliver value and earn revenue. This is a framework that communicates details on your key partners, key activities, key resources, value propositions, customer relationships, channels, customer segments, cost structure, and revenue streams.

Conclusion

"You are never too small to make a difference." – Greta Thunberg, climate activist & Nobel Peace Prize nominee

Making a meaningful, positive difference in the world is no small feat, but we hope that we've inspired and encouraged you to believe that you can make an impact, no matter how big or small. This is at the core of what it means to be a social entrepreneur and to have a social entrepreneurial mindset.

Having a social entrepreneurial mindset means making impact the priority in everything we want to do. It is something we can't afford to leave as an afterthought if we genuinely care about living in and creating a better future. The funny thing with impact is that the bigger the impact we seek to have, the more work and time it will take to achieve. But that's where the entrepreneurial part comes in.

Social entrepreneurship is about being an effective problem-solver, which requires constant iteration. You'll find yourself back at the drawing board more than once, and perhaps more than you would like. But that is okay! That is what it is all about, and the best social entrepreneurs, innovators, and changemakers find themselves questioning *everything*. They see opportunities in problems and know that for every problem there is a solution—and surely, there are lots of problems that need solutions. And above all, it is about keeping our hearts full of empathy and compassion so that we may seek an intimate understanding of the problems surrounding us but also stoking the desire to do something about them in a thoughtful and intentional way.

We hope that everything in this book continues to serve as a useful and meaningful resource to empower you to become an impactful problem-solving leader. Thank you for going on this journey with us. *Build With Impact* is meant to be a guide that you can return to whenever you need to revisit certain topics or need inspiration as you embark on your social entrepreneurial adventure to hack away at your own metaphorical plane and build it with *impact.*

For additional resources and online worksheets, visit: https://fulphil.org/class-projects

The Build with Impact Cheat Code

PART 1: Redefining Impact, Entrepreneurship, & Yourself

Chapter 1: Making Sense of Impact & Entrepreneurship

1. Impact can look different, depending on the context.
2. The people closest to the problems are closest to the solutions.
3. Entrepreneurship can create social and economic value.
4. There is a fine balance between maximizing profit and value creation in entrepreneurship.

Chapter 2: Defining Social Entrepreneurship

1. Social impact takes on different forms in business.
2. A social enterprise is a self-sustaining for-profit or nonprofit business entity that intends to make a positive impact on humanity or the planet.
3. Social entrepreneurship revolves around ways we can disrupt issues in society that the market economy has failed to address.
4. Social entrepreneurship can happen at different scales, depending on its scope of work (community, nonprofit, transformational, global).

5. The promises of social entrepreneurship in the world include prosperity, empathy and citizenship, and the future.

Chapter 3: Build with Impact: Aligning Your Values and Purpose

1. The entrepreneurial mindset is an established set of attitudes that includes grit, resiliency, accountability, passion, and persistence to overcome obstacles and achieve results, and can be applied outside of the scope of entrepreneurship.
2. Social entrepreneurial mindset = being impact-driven + being a problem-solver.
3. Your North Star provides your sense of direction and purpose.
4. Your core values define your moral compass, which will guide your actions and decisions along your journey.

PART 2: Designing Your Impact

Chapter 4: Introduction to Design Thinking

1. Effective problem-solving requires design thinking.
2. Design thinking, according to the International Design Foundation, is defined as a "non-linear, iterative process that teams use to understand users, challenge assumptions, redefine problems and create innovative solutions.
3. The five nonlinear steps of design thinking are empathize, define, ideate, prototype, and test.

4. Iterative design is powerful because it identifies unmet needs, reduces risk, builds entrepreneurial skills, and redefines/refines your value proposition.

Chapter 5: Problem-Finding: Digging Into Our Roots

Effective problem-solving begins with effective problem-finding.

1. Problems have root causes and effects (or "symptoms").
2. Root cause analysis is a formal process of effective problem-solving in which we can understand how to solve the root cause rather than the "root effect."
3. Validation is an essential step in the problem-finding process to ensure you save yourself time and money by trying to solve the wrong problem.

Chapter 6: Innovating & Designing Great Solutions

1. Good solutions tackle the problem, are feasible, scalable, and aligned with our values.
2. Ideation is the creative act of generating innovative ideas. Quantity > Quality
3. A value proposition is a single statement that explains why your customers would go to you over another.
4. SCAMPER is an effective problem-solving/ideation method.

Chapter 7: Prototyping

1. Prototyping is an iterative process that allows you to troubleshoot and build in a low-stakes situation before you fully scale a product or service to market.
2. Prototypes will fail and help us troubleshoot and pivot.
3. Empathy is important in prototyping because we are creating solutions that meet the needs of people. Effective prototyping involves listening, building, getting feedback, and listening more, and building again.

Chapter 8: Testing for Product-Market Fit

1. Product-market fit is when a product generates high demand from the market because it addresses a specific customer or user need within that market. This begins with an in-depth understanding of the customer.
2. Assumptions are statements that you presume to be true without concrete evidence to support them. It's important to identify the assumptions you're making for planning and decisions-making purposes, despite the inevitable uncertainty, but these assumptions must be tested and validated to proceed successfully with your social enterprise.
3. User interviews can help you understand if your product will be successful based on how your target market perceives it.

PART 3: Getting Down To Business

Chapter 9: Defining Your Market

1. "The market" is the ecosystem around the transaction process between businesses and consumers.
2. Defining your market involves segmenting it into your TAM, SAM, and SOM.
3. You can analyze your market with either a top-down or bottom-up method.
4. Every market has unique standards and needs.

Chapter 10: Competition

1. Competitors are organizations that strive to win or gain commercial or economic success in a market by establishing superiority over others who are in a similar sector and trying to do the same.
2. Three types of competitors are direct competitors, indirect competitors, and replacement competitors.
3. There are various ways to analyze competition: competitive landscape, competitive matrix, SWOT analysis, and Porter's Five Forces.

Chapter 11: Introduction to Marketing

1. Marketing is a company's overall game plan for getting its products or services into the hands of potential leads and cultivating relationships with those leads into customers.

2. Effective marketing involves defining your target market, developing your customer profile, leveraging user interviews, and defining the Four P's.
3. The Four P's are product, price, place, and promotion.
4. To optimize your marketing campaigns, you must quantify your metrics, measure your success, and keep doing what works.

Chapter 12: Pricing & Financial Statements

1. Cost-based pricing bases the price you're selling your product or service for on the cost it takes to create it. This involves calculating the total costs of making your product and adding a markup percentage to determine the final price.
2. Market-based pricing is a type of pricing strategy that evaluates the prices of similar products that are already on the market.
3. Cash flow statements, balance sheets, and income statements are the main types of financial statements needed to communicate your company's financial health and earning potential to stakeholders.

PART 4: Getting It Out There

Chapter 13: Marketing Strategies

1. Good marketing = well-communicated product-market fit = customer satisfaction = customer loyalty = competitive advantage

2. There are different types of marketing strategies you can leverage, including paid advertising, social media ads, banner ads, influencer marketing, cause marketing, relationship marketing, undercover marketing, word of mouth, transactional marketing, diversity marketing, and more.
3. Data-driven marketing is a powerful process that personalizes a user's marketing experience to be based on real consumer insights as opposed to intuition and assumptions alone.
4. Five tiers of content marketing are SEO, user experience, content strategy, content creation, and content distribution.
5. Some of the most popular platforms in social media marketing include Instagram, TikTok, Twitter, Facebook, LinkedIn, YouTube, and Pinterest.

Chapter 14: Branding

1. Branding is the marketing process by which a company creates a name and symbol that is easily identifiable as belonging to itself.
2. Branding is NOT the same thing as marketing. Branding is a *type* of marketing process that every company utilizes at some point. Every company has its own brand. Marketing is the process that develops and establishes a brand.
3. Building a good brand can help your company signify intent, create a competitive edge, transform itself into an experience, build trust, and leverage emotions.

4. Creating your brand involves researching your target audience and competitors, choosing a brand focus and personality, creating a slogan, creating a "look" for your brand, and storytelling.

PART 5: Manifesting Your Impact

Chapter 15: Measuring Your Success

1. KPIs are metrics required to determine and explain how a company will progress to meet its business.
2. KPIs can help companies measure progress over time, make adjustments, analyze patterns, and monitor company health.
3. OKRs are effective goal-setting tools used to communicate and accomplish different milestones you set for yourself.
4. S.M.A.R.T. is a goal-setting format; the components are specific, measurable, actionable, realistic or relevant, and timely.
5. Measuring impact is important because it demonstrates the value a company brings to the world. Measuring impact follows a similar structure to how we set and measure OKRs.
6. The logic model is a framework that allows you to visually map the cause-effect relationship behind everything you do in your business.
7. The balanced scorecard is a framework that both shows a company's financial goals and also measures and reflects operational goals and measures like customer satisfaction and the organization's innovation.

Chapter 16: Bringing It All Together: Making Sense of Business Models, Executive Summaries, and Pitching

1. Three common forms of presentation that communicate your business model include executive summaries, pitch decks, and business canvas models.
2. The executive summary and pitch deck are two different methods of communicating the problem you're hoping to solve, your solution and value proposition, your business model, your market overview, your go-to-market strategy, your competition, your financials, your achievements, your progress and traction, your measurement of success, your future plans, your future team, and your current status and ask.

The business model canvas is a template used in business and entrepreneurship to visually show the building blocks of your company's plan to deliver value and earn revenue. This is a framework that communicates details on your key partners, key activities, key resources, value propositions, customer relationships, channels, customer segments, cost structure, and revenue streams.

Glossary

Chapter 1: Making Sense of Impact & Entrepreneurship

social impact: the net effect of actions on a community and the well-being of individuals, families, and society.

entrepreneurship: the act of creating one or more business entities with the hope of creating value and making a profit while taking on financial risk.

globalization: is the process by which businesses or other organizations develop international influence or start operating on an international scale.

status quo: the current situation or the way things are.

value creation: the process of turning hard work and resources into something that meets the needs of others; really, value creation is about creating value for Others.

stakeholder: any individual or entity that has an interest or concern in something.

return on investment (ROI): the metric investors use to determine how effective their investments are.

Chapter 2: Defining Social Entrepreneurship

social entrepreneurship: the process of creating and running a for-profit or non-profit business entity that intends to make a positive impact on humanity or the planet; a business that makes a positive impact and also makes money to employ conscious capitalism.

social enterprise: a for-profit or nonprofit business entity that intends to make a positive impact on humanity or the planet; a business that has a positive impact and also makes money to employ conscious capitalism.

net profit: how much money a business gets to keep after it deduct all costs and expenses from what they earned.

bottom line: another term for net Profit.

double bottom line: a company's measure of its social impact in terms of both its commitment to society and its efforts to make a positive difference for people.

triple bottom line: in addition to the two factors used to measure the double bottom lines, a company also must measure its efficacy on the planet by how it practices sustainability.

corporate philanthropy: the efforts and initiatives companies undertake to voluntarily make an impact on society with their available resources as a form of corporate social responsibility.

corporate social responsibility: the practices and policies undertaken by corporations that are intended to have a positive influence on the world.

the market economy: the overall ecosystem where businesses interact with consumers; the ecosystem that surrounds that transaction process between businesses and consumers, which includes investment, production, and distribution—all of which are affected by forces like supply and demand; also known as "the market."

Fulphil Profit-Impact Matrix: a matrix created by Fulphil used to define organizations based on their self-sustainability and intention of making an Impact.

community social entrepreneur: a type of social entrepreneur who creates an organization to serve the niche needs of a very specific geographic area.

nonprofit social entrepreneur: a type of social entrepreneur who prioritizes their social well-being over traditional business Needs.

transformational social entrepreneurship: a type of social entrepreneur who is focused on creating businesses that can meet the social needs that governments and other businesses aren't currently meeting.

global social entrepreneur: a type of social entrepreneur who bases their success on their work around transforming an entire social system worldwide.

Asset-based community development: a bottom-up methodology that communities follow to develop sustainably; they community development process is executed by those who are directly affected. This methodology largely focuses on the assets and strengths of a community rather than on the deficits and problems.

empathy: the ability to understand and share feelings and experiences with other People.

global citizenship: the idea that we as individuals do not identify as a member of a state, nation, or tribe but rather as a member of humanity.

global citizen: is an individual who is aware of the world and his or her role in it.

UNESCO: United Nations Educational, Scientific and Cultural Organization; a special agency of the United Nations aimed at promoting world peace and security through international cooperation in education, arts, sciences, and culture; the entity that ranks global citizenship as one of the top three priorities in education.

United Nations Sustainable Development Goals: universal goals for all people created by the UN to accomplish the 2030 Agenda for Sustainable Development

Chapter 3: Build with Impact: Aligning Your Values and Purpose

entrepreneurial mindset: an entrepreneur's way of thinking; specifically, it is an established set of attitudes that includes grit, resilience, accountability, passion, and persistence to overcome obstacles and achieve results.

social entrepreneurial mindset: a term coined at Fulphil to describe the characteristic of being not only an effective problem-solver but more importantly one who does so with the intention of making a positive impact.

symbolic interactionism: a theory in sociology that explains the phenomenon of how we as individuals embody and symbolize meaning from our interactions with things, people, and experiences.

core values: a set of beliefs that guide you in your decision-making.

moral compass: what guides your journey and decisions based on your judgment of right and wrong.

Chapter 4: Introduction to Design Thinking

design thinking: "a non-linear, iterative process that teams use to understand users, challenge assumptions, redefine problems and create innovative solutions"; the concept and process of solving complex problems by thinking like a designer.

wicked problems: a design thinking term for complex situations without an obvious fix

iterative: a term that describes how a process can repeat itself various times after taking in and implementing continuous feedback to improve; in design thinking, you are using an iterative process to best serve your users' needs

minimum viable product: a version of a product or service with just enough features to be usable by early customers who can then provide feedback for future product development.

test/validate: one stage of the design thinking process where you implement your solution on a small scale to see how effective or wanted it actually is.

hypothesis-driven entrepreneurship/lean startup: a startup methodology where entrepreneurs translate their vision into falsifiable business model hypotheses then test those hypotheses using a series of minimum viable products.

lean startup method: an iterative approach to entrepreneurship that reflects the design thinking methodology; a methodology for developing business models that allows you to flush out design flaws rapidly through prototyping and innovating to see if a product will make it to market and be viable.

Chapter 5: Problem-Finding: Digging Into Our Roots

root cause: the main problem that gives rise to other effects or symptoms.

cause: a change that gives rise to other effects.

effect: the consequence of a change that is due to a deeper cause.

gravity problem: problems that exist based on something you cannot change, like gravity.

symptom: a design thinking term that is indicative of being an effect of a greater cause or problem; a sign of the existence of something.

root cause analysis: a formal process of effective problem-solving that can be used to understand how to solve the root cause.

validation: one stage of the design thinking process where you implement your solution on some scale to the problem to see how effective or wanted it actually is.

Chapter 6: Innovating & Designing Great Solutions

ideation: the creative act of generating innovative ideas.

divergent thinking: the process of ideation where one creates as many different choices to choose from as possible.

convergent thinking: the process of ideation where one narrows down their options after successfully completing the process of divergent thinking.

value proposition: a single statement that explains why your customers should come to you over another company.

SCAMPER: a design thinking methodology that maps out different thinking techniques a person can use to figure out ways how to improve their product or service; Substitute, Combine, Adapt, Modify, Put to another use, Eliminate, or Reverse.

Chapter 7: Prototyping

prototype: an early sample, model, or preliminary release of a product or service that is built to test a concept or process.

prototyping: the process of building an early sample, model, or release of a product built to test a concept or process

pivoting: the act of changing strategies in entrepreneurship to meet your goals, especially if something isn't working.

low-resolution prototyping: the first step of prototyping where you create a rough model or sketch of your idea.

storyboarding: the process of detailing every step of the user journey by visualizing and drawing out a sequence of steps.

customer journey: the customer's experience and step-by-step movement through the use of your product or service.

high-resolution prototyping: a more refined version of prototyping in the medium of delivery, or how your product/project will look in real life.

Chapter 8: Testing for Product-Market Fit

product-market fit: a product that generates high demand from the market because it addresses a specific customer need within that market.

customer profiling: the process of defining who exactly your customer is, and what they care about (also known as customer discovery).

assumption: a statement that you presume to be true without concrete evidence to support it; assumptions are used to allow companies to plan and make decisions despite inevitable uncertainty.

customer discovery: the process of defining who exactly your customer is, and what they care about (also known as customer profiling).

idea stage: a term entrepreneurs use vaguely to tell others that they have an idea but have not done much about it.

user experience design: the process used to create products that provide meaningful and relevant experiences for users.

human-centered design: a method of design that focuses on putting the individual's wants and needs first, keeping in mind their pain points and frustrations from prior experiences!

user interviews: a type of UX research model to test out the assumptions you've made about your customers and to inform how you build your product or service.

A/B testing: the process of comparing two or more variations of something and statistically comparing which variation performs better.

Chapter 9: Defining Your Market

market size: the total number of customers you can expect to have over a given time Period.

due diligence: the formal process that investors and funders go through when they are in the process of deciding whether or not to fund a company.

total addressable market: the total overall market that your business can potentially serve.

serviceable attainable market: the portion of your total addressable market that you can realistically and logistically serve based on your business model.

serviceable obtainable market: a portion of your serviceable attainable market (and a smaller portion of your total addressable market) that you can realistically win in the short term.

Chapter 10: Competition

crowded market: a scenario when there are a lot of competitors selling similar products or services.

competitors: organizations that strive to win or gain commercial or economic success in a market by establishing superiority over others who are in a similar sector and trying to do the same.

competition: the process and act of organizations striving to win or gain commercial or economic success by establishing superiority over others who are in a similar sector and trying to do the same.

direct competitor: a type of competitor that targets the same audience you are trying to Target.

indirect competitor: a type of competitor that does not compete by selling the same product but can still take away potential customers.

replacement competitors: a type of competitor who can replace your product or service by providing a new solution.

customer retention: a company's ability to keep a customer for a certain amount of time.

freemium model: a type of business model that offers a certain set of features for free but will charge for additional features.

competitive landscape: a type of business analysis method that identifies direct or indirect competitors; at the same time, it helps you understand those competitors' missions, visions, core values, niche markets, strengths, and weaknesses.

competitive matrix: a type of analysis model that helps you map out your company's competitive advantage using a four-quadrant analysis with two axes, which represent two main lenses of comparison.

SWOT analysis: an analysis tool that allows you to build on **S**TRENGTHS, minimize **W**EAKNESSES, seize **O**PPORTUNITIES, and counteract THREATS concerning your venture.

Porter's Five Forces: an analysis tool that you can use to identify the main sources of competition in your industry or Sector.

threat of rivalry: a way to describe the intensity of the current competition in the marketplace.

barrier to entry: describes how feasible it is for your company to obtain market share to put pressure on prices, costs, and investment to compete.

threat of substitutes: describes the availability of other products that a customer could purchase from an outside industry.

power of suppliers: describes the power suppliers have in raising prices or reducing the quality of goods or services you are providing to your customer.

power of buyers: describes the buyers' degree of influence on the price and quantity of products sold.

Chapter 11: Introduction to Marketing

influencer marketing: a type of social media marketing that endorses specific products or services with the help of influencers who have a sizable following.

email marketing: the use of email within a company's marketing efforts to promote the products or services provided by that company.

marketing strategy: a company's overall game plan for getting their products or services into the hands of potential leads and cultivating those relationships so that the leads become customers.

target market: a subgroup of people you plan to target with your marketing efforts.

end user: those who will be using, but not necessarily paying for, the product or service you are offering.

customer: those who are paying, though not necessarily using, for your product or service.

Four P's of marketing: a framework that outlines the foundations of effective marketing (product, price, place, promotion).

perceived value is the idea of a customer's sense of how desirable a product or service is.

business-to-business marketing: a business model that sells products to customers who are entities, or individuals who control the budgets of those entities.

business-to-consumer marketing: a business model that sells products to customers who are individuals.

customer acquisition cost: the measure of how much you spend in marketing to create a win or acquire a sale from your customer; the total for marketing or publicity expenses that must be used to draw attention to your business and acquire your customers.

Chapter 12: Pricing & Financial Statements

cost-based pricing: a pricing strategy that involves calculating the total costs it takes to make your product, then adding a percentage markup to determine the final price.

variable costs: costs that may vary, like labor, commission, and materials needed to create your product, etc.

fixed costs: costs that remain the same regardless of production output, like lease, payroll taxes, insurance, and interest payments

cost of goods sold: your total costs, which include variable costs and sometimes fixed costs, depending on how you want to structure it from an accounting perspective.

selling, general, and administrative expenses: total of all overhead costs of doing business.

unit economics: a specific business model's revenues and costs in relation to an individual unit.

profit margin: a measure of how much money a company is making by selling their products or services.

market-based pricing: a pricing strategy that evaluates the prices of similar products that are already on the market.

value-based pricing: a pricing strategy based on what customers think a product or service is worth rather than actual costs.

premium pricing: a pricing strategy that reflects the prestige, luxury, or exclusive value of the products or services a company provides.

penetration pricing: a pricing strategy that sets a low initial price on a new product or service to gain high sales or market share, then increases prices after enough momentum

skimming pricing: a pricing strategy that sets a high initial price with the aim to excite audiences who desire products or services, then lowers it later on to reach a wider

loss leader pricing: a pricing strategy that attracts customers by offering a product or service below what it actually costs, assuming that customers will also purchase other products or services that have a higher profit margin from that same company

price sensitivity: a measurement of how much the price of goods and services affects customers' willingness to buy them.

financial statements: formal written records that investors use to evaluate a company's financial health and earnings potential; statement types include cash flow statements, balance sheets, and profit and loss statements.

cash inflow: a term used to describe the cash that a business is bringing in.

cash outflow: a term used to describe the cash that a business spends.

operating cash flow: the cash outflow related to your business operations.

financing cash flow: the cash outflow related to selling ownership for investment.

net cash flow: a term to describe the difference between your cash inflows and cash outflows.

cash flow: a term to describe the difference how your cash flows, both in and out.

cash flow statement: a type of financial statement that measures your cash inflows and outflows for a specified period of time (monthly, annually, etc.).

balance sheet: a type of personal financial statement that provides an overall snapshot of your company's net worth at a specific period in time.

net worth: the sum of your assets and liabilities.

assets: any resources owned by a business.

liabilities: any resources owed by a business to another business or person.

down payment: the amount of money you pay when purchasing an expensive product or service if you don't pay the full amount upfront.

income statement: a statement that presents a company's revenue, expenses, net income, and earnings per share during a particular period (usually quarterly).

Chapter 13: Marketing Strategies

pay-per-click: a model of internet marketing in which advertisers pay a fee each time one of their ads is clicked.

influencer marketing: a type of marketing where you work with a well-known industry name to encourage your target audience to choose your brand.

cause marketing: a type of marketing that links the services and products of a company to a social cause or issue.

product placement: a type of marketing where companies gain exposure for their products by paying for them to be featured in the media.

word of mouth: a type of marketing dependent on personal recommendations.

Transactional marketing: a type of marketing where companies, particularly retailers, often encourage customers to buy with coupons, discounts, and huge events.

diversity marketing: a type of marketing that caters to diverse audiences by customizing and integrating different marketing strategies toward a particular group.

personalized marketing: the implementation of a strategy by which companies deliver individualized content to recipients through data collection, analysis, and the use of automation technology.

data-driven marketing: a process of creating marketing and advertising campaigns based on real consumer insight as opposed to intuition or assumptions alone.

SEO optimization: the process of improving the quality and quantity of a website's content to attract website traffic from search engines.

visitor number: total number of visitors who visit your site.

bounce rate: the percentage of visitors who leave a web page without taking an action.

content marketing: the process of generating topic ideas that appeal to your buyer persona, creating written or visual content around those ideas, and making that information accessible to your audience as a blog, video, infographic, or other format.

follower growth: a metric that refers to the total number of new followers on your social media account over a specific time period.

click rates/click-through rate: the number of clicks that your post receives divided by the number of times your post is shown.

reach: the number of people your post reaches inside and outside your network; specifically, this refers to the number of impressions on your content, *not* the number of people engaging with content through likes and comments.

referrals: the method by which users got to your content through another platform, whether within the same media service.

Chapter 14: Branding

brand: your company's identity and representation of how your consumers actually see you.

branding: the action and efforts made toward creating a brand; the marketing process by which a company creates a name and symbol that is easily identifiable as belonging to itself.

brand personality: a set of characteristics that determines we attribute to our brand as a whole.

brand voice: the way a brand personality is communicated.

brand tone: the way your brand voice translates to your audience and how they perceive it.

brand loyalty: the positive connection that consumers have with a brand, making them more likely to buy your products or service.

flywheel effect: the idea that a company's success comes from the accumulation of little wins over time/

Chapter 15: Measuring Your Success

key performance indicators: metrics used to determine and explain how a company will progress to meet its business and marketing goals.

lagging indicator: a type of KPI that measures past performance.

leading indicator: a type of KPI that measures ongoing performance.

customer lifetime value: your average net profit from your entire relationship with one customer.

objectives and key results: an effective goal-setting tool for communicating what you want to accomplish and what milestones you'll need to meet in order to accomplish it.

S.M.A.R.T. goals: a framework to guide the setting of goals and objectives for more effective results; Specific, Measurable, Achievable, Realistic/relevant, and Timely.

logic model: a framework that allows you to visually map the cause-effect relationships behind everything you do in your business.

balanced scorecard: a framework used to keep track of a business' financial goals and measures but that also reflects operational goals and measures like customer satisfaction and the organization's innovation.

Chapter 16: Bringing It All Together: Making Sense of Business Models, Executive Summaries, and Pitching

executive summary: a document that summarizes your business plan.

pitch deck: a slideshow that summarizes your business plan in PowerPoint format, often accompanied by verbal presentation, to investors and stakeholders.

business model canvas: a type of framework that visually shows the building blocks of your company's plan to deliver value and earn revenue.

Appendix

Tiffany Yau TEDx Talk: Yau, Tiffany. "Dream Big, Think Smaller." Filmed October 26, 2020, in Berwyn, PA. TED video, 12:58, October 26, 2020. https://www.ted.com/talks/tiffany_yau_dream_big_think_smaller.

Bill Gates annual reading: StackCommerce. "Whether You Love Him or Hate Him, Bill Gates Reads and Retains Roughly 50 Books per Year." Financial Post, June 17, 2021. https://financialpost.com/personal-finance/business-essentials/bill-gates-reads-roughly-50-books-per-year-and-remembers-what-he-reads#:~:text=Microsoft%20founder%2C%20Bill%20Gates%2C%20reads.

Greta Thunberg Nobel Peace Prize nomination: Buli, Nora, and Gwladys Fouche. "Nobel Peace Prize: Is This Greta Thunberg's Year?" Reuters, October 1, 2021. https://www.reuters.com/world/europe/nobel-peace-prize-is-this-greta-thunbergs-year-2021-10-01/.

If every American recycled: May, Ashley. 2017. "What Would Happen If Everyone Recycled?" USA TODAY. USA TODAY. June 22, 2017. https://www.usatoday.com/story/news/nation-now/2017/06/22/what-would-happen-if-everyone-recycled/374773001/.

Small business job creation: "Small Businesses Drive Job Growth in United States; They Account for 1.8 Million Net New Jobs, Latest Data Show." n.d. SBA's Office of Advocacy. https://advocacy.sba.gov/2019/04/24/small-businesses-drive-job-growth-in-united-states-they-account-for-1-8-million-net-new-jobs-latest-data-show/.

For every $100 spent at a small business: Wirthman, Lisa. n.d. "CenturyLink BrandVoice: 5 Benefits of Shopping Locally on Small Business Saturday." Forbes. Accessed November 29, 2022. https://www.forbes.com/sites/centurylink/2017/11/20/5-benefits-of-shopping-locally-on-small-business-saturday/?sh=4ac68a9a668b.

Globalization: Pologeorgis, Nicolas. 2019. "How Globalization Affects Developed Countries." Investopedia. May 9, 2019. https://www.investopedia.com/articles/economics/10/globalization-developed-countries.asp.

Value creation definition: F.Dieffenbacher, Stefan. 2022. "Value Creation Definition, Model, Principles, Importance & Steps." Digital Leadership. June 11, 2022. https://digitalleadership.com/blog/value-creation/#:~:text=Value%20Creation%20is%20the%20process.

Stakeholders: Chen, James. 2021. "Learn What Stakeholders Are and the Roles That They Play." Investopedia. August 19, 2021. https://www.investopedia.com/terms/s/stakeholder.asp#:~:text=A%20stakeholder%20has%20a%20vested.

Triple Bottom Line: Miller, Kelsey. 2020. "The Triple Bottom Line: What It Is & Why It's Important." Harvard Business School Online.

December 8, 2020. https://online.hbs.edu/blog/post/what-is-the-triple-bottom-line.

Rockefeller CSR: History.com Editors. 2018. "John D. Rockefeller." HISTORY. A&E Television Networks. September 20, 2018. https://www.history.com/topics/early-20th-century-us/john-d-rockefeller.

Howard Bowen CSR definition: Howard Rothmann Bowen, Peter Geoffrey Bowen, and Jean-Pascal Gond. (1953) 2013. Social Responsibilities of the Businessman. Iowa City: University Of Iowa Press.

Jeff Bezos corporate philanthropy with Dolly Parton: Chappell, Bill. 2022. "Dolly Parton Gets $100 Million from Jeff Bezos to Spend on Charity." NPR, November 14, 2022, sec. National. https://www.npr.org/2022/11/14/1136454716/dolly-parton-jeff-bezos-imagination-library.

Spotify diversity, equity, and inclusion efforts: Spotify. "Social Impact | Life at Spotify." n.d. www.lifeatspotify.com. https://www.lifeatspotify.com/diversity-equity-impact/social-impact.

Spotify Play Your Part campaign: Spotify. "Spotify Encourages Eligible U.S. Voters to 'Play Your Part' by Registering for and Voting in the 2020 Election." 2020. Spotify. September 9, 2020. https://newsroom.spotify.com/2020-09-09/spotify-encourages-eligible-u-s-voters-to-play-your-part-by-registering-for-and-voting-in-the-2020-election/.

S&P 500 CSR: "15 CSR Facts You Need to Know." n.d. Learn - GlobalGiving. https://www.globalgiving.org/learn/listicle/csr-facts-you-need-to-know.

TOM's Buy-One-Give One Model: Peters, Adele. 2019. "Toms Made Buy-One, Give-One Famous. Now It's Updating the Model." Fast Company. May 7, 2019. https://www.fastcompany.com/90344987/toms-made-buy-one-give-one-famous-now-its-updating-the-model.

Market economy definition: Chappelow, Jim. 2019. "Market Economy Definition." Investopedia. 2019. https://www.investopedia.com/terms/m/marketeconomy.asp.

Four types of social entrepreneurs: Group, Welfont. 2018. "Types of Social Entrepreneurs." Medium. April 11, 2018. https://medium.com/@groupwelfont/types-of-social-entrepreneurs-a7dc8ac57e34.

Prosperity Paradox: Christensen, Clayton M, Efosa Ojomo, and Karen Dillon. 2019. The Prosperity Paradox : How Innovation Can Lift Nations out of Poverty. New York, Ny: Harperbusiness.

Homeboy Industries: "Our Mission | Homeboy Industries." 2019. Homeboy Industries. 2019. https://homeboyindustries.org/our-story/our-mission/.

African donated clothing in landfill: Besser, Linton. 2021. "'It's an Insult': In an African Clothing Market, a Bale of Used Clothes Donated by Australians Is Opened." ABC News. August 11, 2021. https://www.abc.net.au/news/2021-08-12/fast-fashion-turning-parts-ghana-into-toxic-landfill/100358702.

African leaders pushing regulations against clothing industry: The Washington Post. 2018. "African Nations Are Fed up with the West's Hand-Me-Downs. But It's Tough to Keep Them Out.," May 29, 2018. https://www.washingtonpost.com/world/africa/african-nations-are-fed-up-with-the-wests-hand-me-downs-but-its-tough-to-keep-them-out/2018/05/28/c4041c8c-5478-11e8-a6d4-ca1d035642ce_story.html.

Zaaf: Zaaf. "A Little Bit about ZAAF…." n.d. ZAAFCollection.com. Accessed January 9, 2023. https://zaafcollection.com/pages/our-story.

Abai Schulze, founder of Zaaf: "Abai Schulze, the Founder of ZAAF on CNN African Voices." YouTube video, November 7, 2018. https://www.youtube.com/watch?v=Wr9bRBNQxfs.

Abai Schulze TEDx Talk: Schulze, Abai. "'Made in Africa' - the Power of Shifting Perceptions | Abai Schulze | TEDxNashville." n.d. www.youtube.com. https://www.youtube.com/watch?v=s7KvKqsYCZE.

Social entrepreneurship's promise for empathy: Greater Good Magazine. 2009. "Empathy Definition | What Is Empathy." Greater Good. 2009. https://greatergood.berkeley.edu/topic/empathy/definition.

Global citizenship definition: United Nations. 2022. "Global Citizenship." United Nations. 2022. https://www.un.org/en/academic-impact/global-citizenship.

Ron Israel with the Global Citizenship Initiative quote: Israel, Ronald. 2014. "What Does It Mean to Be a Global Citizen? - Kosmos Journal." Kosmosjournal.org. April 2014.

UNESCO ranking of global citizenship: Unesco. 2018. "Global Citizenship Education." UNESCO. July 25, 2018. https://en.unesco.org/themes/gced.

HBR potential of local collaboration: Kramer, Mark R., Marc W. Pfitzer, and Helge Mahne. 2020. "How Global Leaders Should Think about Solving Our Biggest Problems." *Harvard Business Review*, January 16, 2020. https://hbr.org/2020/01/how-global-leaders-should-think-about-solving-our-biggest-problems.

UN Sustainable Development Goals (SDGs): United Nations. 2015. "The 17 Sustainable Development Goals." United Nations. United nations. 2015. https://sdgs.un.org/goals.

UNSDG Goal 1: United Nations. 2020. "Goal 1 | Department of Economic and Social Affairs." Sdgs.un.org. United Nations. 2020. https://sdgs.un.org/goals/goal1.

UNSDG Goal 2: United Nations. 2022. "Goal 2 | Department of Economic and Social Affairs." Sdgs.un.org. 2022. https://sdgs.un.org/goals/goal2.

UNSDG Goal 3: United Nations. 2021. "Goal 3: Ensure Healthy Lives and Promote Well-Being for All at All Ages." Sdgs.un.org. United Nations. 2021. https://sdgs.un.org/goals/goal3.

UNSDG Goal 4: United Nations. "Goal 4 | Department of Economic and Social Affairs." 2021. Sdgs.un.org. United Nations. 2021. https://sdgs.un.org/goals/goal4.

UNSDG Goal 5: United Nations. 2022. "Goal 5 | Department of Economic and Social Affairs." Sdgs.un.org. United Nations. 2022. https://sdgs.un.org/goals/goal5.

UNSDG Goal 6: United Nations. 2015. "Goal 6 | Department of Economic and Social Affairs." Sdgs.un.org. 2015. https://sdgs.un.org/goals/goal6.

UNSDG Goal 7: United Nations. 2022. "Goal 7 | Department of Economic and Social Affairs." Sdgs.un.org. United Nations. 2022. https://sdgs.un.org/goals/goal7.

UNSDG Goal 8: United Nations. 2021. "Goal 8 | Department of Economic and Social Affairs." United Nations. United Nations. 2021. https://sdgs.un.org/goals/goal8.

UNSDG Goal 9: United Nations. 2021. "Goal 9 | Department of Economic and Social Affairs." Sdgs.un.org. 2021. https://sdgs.un.org/goals/goal9.

UNSDG Goal 10: United Nations. 2021. "Goal 10 | Department of Economic and Social Affairs." Sdgs.un.org. 2021. https://sdgs.un.org/goals/goal10.

UNSDG Goal 11: United Nations. 2021. "Goal 11 | Department of Economic and Social Affairs." United Nations. 2021. https://sdgs.un.org/goals/goal11.

UNSDG Goal 12: United Nations. 2022. "Goal 12 | Department of Economic and Social Affairs." Sdgs.un.org. United Nations. 2022. https://sdgs.un.org/goals/goal12.

UNSDG Goal 13: United Nations. 2022. "Goal 13 | Department of Economic and Social Affairs." Sdgs.un.org. United Nations. 2022. https://sdgs.un.org/goals/goal13.

UNSDG Goal 14: United Nations. 2021. "Goal 14 | Department of Economic and Social Affairs." Sdgs.un.org. United Nations. 2021. https://sdgs.un.org/goals/goal14.

UNSDG Goal 15: United Nations. 2020. "Goal 15 | Department of Economic and Social Affairs." United Nations. 2020. https://sdgs.un.org/goals/goal15.

UNSDG Goal 16: United Nations. 2021. "Goal 16 | Department of Economic and Social Affairs." Sdgs.un.org. United Nations. 2021. https://sdgs.un.org/goals/goal16.

UNSDG Goal 17: United Nations. 2021. "Goal 17 | Department of Economic and Social Affairs." Sdgs.un.org. 2021. https://sdgs.un.org/goals/goal17.

Longermism: Macaskill, William. 2022. What We Owe the Future. New York, Ny: Hachette Book Group, Inc.

Hamilton musical quote: Lin-Manuel Miranda, "Hamilton: An American Musical," In *Hamilton: The Revolution*, ed. Jeremy McCarter (New York: Grand Central Publishing, 2016).

Designing Your Life **North Star:** Burnett, William, and David J Evans. 2018. Designing Your Life : Build a Life That Works for You. London: Vintage Books.

Interaction Design Foundation design thinking definition: "What Is Design Thinking?" n.d. The Interaction Design Foundation. https://www.interaction-design.org/literature/topics/design-thinking?page=2#:~:text=Design%20thinking%20is%20a%20non.

Lean startup method: Blank, Steve. 2013. "Why the Lean Start-up Changes Everything." *Harvard Business Review*, May 2013, https://hbr.org/2013/05/why-the-lean-start-up-changes-everything.

PepsioCo design quote: Vries, James de. 2015. "PepsiCo's Chief Design Officer on Creating an Organization Where Design Can Thrive." *Harvard Business Review*, August 11, 2015, https://hbr.org/2015/08/pepsicos-chief-design-officer-on-creating-an-organization-where-design-can-thrive.

Inequitable education opportunities: The White House. "FACT SHEET: Let Girls Learn – A Comprehensive Investment in Adolescent Girls Education." October 11, 2016. https://obamawhitehouse.archives.gov/the-press-office/2016/10/11/fact-sheet-let-girls-learn-comprehensive-investment-adolescent-girls.

Simon Sinek TED Talk: Sinek, Simon. 2009. "How Great Leaders Inspire Action." Ted.com. TED Talks. September 2009. https://www.ted.com/talks/simon_sinek_how_great_leaders_inspire_action?language=en.

Hunger in Nicaragua case study: Timmer, Andria. 2005. "Competing Discourses on the Political Economy of Hunger." Nutritional Anthropology 27-28 (1-2): 1–13. https://doi.org/10.1111/j.1548-7172.2005.tb00086.x.

Prototype definition: Meriam Webster, "Definition of PROTOTYPE." n.d. www.merriam-Webster.com. https://www.merriam-webster.com/dictionary/prototype#:~:text=The%20prefix%20prot%2D%2C%20or%20proto.

Divergent and convergent thinking: Brown, Tim, *Change by Design: How Design Thinking Transforms Organizations and Inspires Innovation* (New York: Harper Business, 2009) ##.

SCAMPER:, Olivier Serrat, *The SCAMPER Technique* (Manila, Philippines: Asian Development Bank, 2009), https://hdl.handle.net/1813/87753.

Instagram case study: Blystone, Dan. 2022. "The Story of Instagram: The Rise of the # 1 Photo-Sharing App (FB)," *Investopedia*, March 29, 2022, https://www.investopedia.com/articles/investing/102615/story-instagram-rise-1-photo0sharing-app.asp.

U.S. retail coffee market size: "The Retail Market for Coffee in the US - Market Size 2005-2027," IBIS World, updated April 26, 2021, https://www.ibisworld.com/industry-statistics/market-size/the-retail-market-for-coffee-united-states/.

California GDP: "List of US States by GDP, 2010-2021," Knoema, updated November 3, 2022, https://knoema.com/rhjjehg/list-of-us-states-by-gdp-2010-2021.

U.S. population by sex and age: Erin Duffin, "Resident population of the United States by sex and age as of July 1, 2021 (in millions)," Statista. September 30, 2022, https://www.statista.com/statistics/241488/population-of-the-us-by-sex-and-age/.

California demographics: "CA Demographic Statistics," Infoplease, accessed February 14, 2023, https://www.infoplease.com/us/census/california/demographic-statistics.

Netflix subscribers: Maglio, Tony. "Disney+ Soars, Netflix Sinks: Here's How Many Subscribers 10 Key Streamers Have Now," *IndieWire*, August 11, 2022, https://www.indiewire.com/2022/08/how-many-subscribers-netflix-hbo-max-disney-plus-1234744445/.

Netflix disruption: McAlone, Nathan. "The Father of 'Disruption' Theory Explains Why Netflix Is the Perfect Example – and Uber Isn't," *Business Insider*, November 18, 2015, https://www.businessinsider.com/the-father-of-disruption-theory-explains-why-netflix-is-the-perfect-example-and-uber-isnt-2015-11.

Amazon 1-click ordering: "Why Amazon's '1-Click' Ordering Was a Game Changer," September 14, 2017, in *Knowledge at Wharton podcast*, podcast, 26:06, https://knowledge.wharton.upenn.edu/article/amazons-1-click-goes-off-patent/.

Starbucks everything but the coffee: Simon, Bryant. *Everything but the Coffee: Learning about America from Starbucks*. Berkeley: University of California Press, 2011.

Apple premium prices: Nielson, Samantha. "Apple's Premium Pricing Strategy and Product Differentiation," *Yahoo! Finance*,

February 6, 2014, https://finance.yahoo.com/news/s/apple-premium-pricing-strategy-product-191247308.html.

Porter's five forces: "Porter's 5 Forces Explained and How to Use the Model," *Investopedia*, updated August 1, 2022, https://www.investopedia.com/terms/p/porter.asp.

Taylor Swift re-recording songs: Tsioulcas, Anastasia. "Look What They Made Her Do: Taylor Swift to Re-Record Her Catalog," *NPR*, August 22, 2019, https://www.npr.org/2019/08/22/753393630/look-what-they-made-her-do-taylor-swift-to-re-record-her-catalog.

Taylor Swift power of buyers: "Taylor Swift's Fans Demanded a 10 Minute Version of 'All Too Well'," in *The Graham Norton Show*, accessed January 10, 2023, https://www.youtube.com/watch?v=MwNdxjnwr1A.

Taylor Swift vs. Katy Perry feud: Kinane, Ruth. "Taylor Swift and Katy Perry: A Timeline of Their Feud." *Entertainment Weekly*, updated August 4, 2022, https://ew.com/music/taylor-swift-katy-perry-timeline/.

Bohemian Rhapsody: Lee, Nathaniel. "'Bohemian Rhapsody': The 6-Minute Rock Single That Changed the Face of Music." *Business Insider*, November 8, 2018, https://www.businessinsider.com/bohemian-rhapsody-queen-greatest-song-written-freddie-mercury-2018-10.

Billie Eilish Calvin Klein video: Calvin Klein, "Billie Eilish #MYTRUTH #MYCALVINS," Facebook, May 10, 2019, https://

www.facebook.com/CalvinKlein/videos/billie-eilish-mytruth-mycalvins/288431508712825/.

Jack Dorsey Instagram early adopter: Kelly, Brandon, and Heather Kelly. "23 Key Moments from Twitter History." *CNN Business*, updated September 16, 2013, https://www.cnn.com/2013/09/13/tech/social-media/twitter-key-moments.

Justin Bieber Instagram early adopter: Gayomali, Chris. "Justin Bieber Joins Instagram, World Explodes." *Time*, July 22, 2011, https://techland.time.com/2011/07/22/justin-bieber-joins-instagram-world-explodes/.

Airbnb's Craigslist email campaign: Gobry, Pascal-Emmanuel. "Airbnb Admits It Farmed Craigslist, Blames Outside Salespeople." *Business Insider*, June 2, 2011, https://www.businessinsider.com/airbnb-craigslist-blame-2011-6.

Marketing definition: Barone, Adam. "Marketing Strategy: What it is, How it Works, How to Create One." *Investopedia*, updated June 13, 2022, https://www.investopedia.com/terms/m/marketing-strategy.asp.

Pricing for book covers: Lavanya. "Book Pricing: How the Cover Price of a Book Is Set." *Booksoarus* (blog), February 28, 2014, https://www.booksoarus.com/book-pricing-how-cover-price-is-set/.

Harry Potter first edition sales: "'Harry Potter' First Edition Sells for Smashing $471,000," *Reuters*, December 9, 2021, https://www.reuters.com/lifestyle/harry-potter-first-edition-sells-smashing-471000-2021-12-09/.

Harry Potter and the Deathly Hallows sales: "Scholastic Announces Record Breaking Sales of 11.5 Million Copies of Harry Potter and the Deathly Hallows in First Ten Days," Scholastic Media Room, August 2, 2007, http://mediaroom.scholastic.com/press-release/scholastic-announces-record-breaking-sales-115-million-copies-harry-potter-and-deathly.

Pampers marketing: "Pampers '1 Pack = 1 Vaccine' Campaign: 'Happy Birthday' Ad." YouTube video, October 30, 2016, https://www.youtube.com/watch?v=Ca3gOvpoJHU.

Tesla least ad spending: Loveday, Steven, "Tesla Spends Least on Ads, Most on R&D: Report," *InsideEVs*, March 25, 2022, https://insideevs.com/news/575848/tesla-highest-research-development-no-ads/.

Stranger Things and Eggo product placement: Beer, Jeff, "Netflix's 'Stranger Things' Is Dangerously close to Becoming 'Sponsored Things'," *Fast Company*, July 1, 2019, https://www.fastcompany.com/90370526/netflixs-stranger-things-is-dangerously-close-to-becoming-sponsored-things.

Stranger Things and Eggo placement: Wittmer, Carrie. n.d. "Netflix's 'Stranger Things' Boosted Eggo Waffle Sales Because One of the Main Characters Is Obsessed with Them." Business Insider. https://www.businessinsider.com/netflixs-stranger-things-boosted-eggo-waffle-sales-2018-2.

Pear company product placement: "Pear Company," ICarly Wiki, accessed November 29, 2022, https://icarly.fandom.com/wiki/

Pear_Company#:~:text=Pear%20Company%20is%20an%20obvious.

Coca-Cola ads: Tan, Jon, "9 Brilliant Coca Cola Advertising Examples of Referral Marketing," *ReferralCandy* (blog), April 29, 2022, https://www.referralcandy.com/blog/coke-word-of-mouth-marketing-strategy.

Dropbox referral: "How to Refer Friends to Dropbox and Get More Storage Space," Dropbox, accessed February 14, 2023, https://help.dropbox.com/storage-space/earn-space-referring-friends.

Coca-Cola America is Beautiful: Cause Marketing. "Coca-Cola #AmericaIsBeautiful 2014 Super Bowl Commercial." YouTube video, January 1, 2017. https://www.youtube.com/watch?v=4-KxPRptu_Y.

Harley Davidson market expansion: Barrett, Rick, "In Quest to Expand Market, Harley-Davidson Reaches out to Women," *Milwaukee Journal Sentinel,* August 28, 2013, https://archive.jsonline.com/business/in-quest-to-expand-market-harley-davidson-reaches-out-to-women-b9984573z1-221524671.html/.

Cheerios interracial family ad: Elliott, Stuart, "Vitriol Online for Cheerios Ad With Interracial Family," *The New York Times,* May 31, 2013, https://www.nytimes.com/2013/06/01/business/media/cheerios-ad-with-interracial-family-brings-out-internet-hate.html.

McDonald's Think Global, Act Local ad: Vignali, Claudio. "McDonald's: 'Think Global, Act Local' – the Marketing Mix." *British Food Journal* 103, no. 2 (March 2001): 97–111, https://doi.org/10.1108/00070700110383154.

Average daily screen time: Georgiev, Deyan. "How Much Time Do Americans Spend on Their Phones in 2020?" *TechJury* (blog), April 21, 2020. https://techjury.net/blog/how-much-time-does-the-average-american-spend-on-their-phone/#gref.

Steps to customizing marketing: Peppers, Don, Martha Rogers, and Bob Dorf. "Is Your Company Ready for One-To-One Marketing?" *Harvard Business Review*, January–February 1999, https://hbr.org/1999/01/is-your-company-ready-for-one-to-one-marketing.

Adobe 15 minutes consuming content: "The State of Content: Expectations on the Rise." Slideshow. Adobe, 2015. https://blogs.adobe.com/creative/files/2015/12/Adobe-State-of-Content-Report.pdf.

Spotify's control of the global streaming industry: Schnoor, Aaron. "Understanding Spotify's Marketing Mastery," *Medium*, May 12, 2020, https://bettermarketing.pub/understanding-spotifys-marketing-mastery-4531ad5cd890.

Spotify millennial listeners: Cummings, Carrie. "Infographic: 72% of Spotify Listeners Are Millennials. Here's How They Use the Service." *Adweek*. April 17, 2016, https://www.adweek.com/brand-marketing/infographic-what-marketers-need-know-about-millennials-music-habits-170869/.

Spotify millennial listeners: Götting, Marie Charlotte. "Spotify Users in the U.S. 2018, by age." *Statista*. January 18, 2022, https://www.statista.com/statistics/475821/spotify-users-age-usa/.

Spotify millennial marketing guide: "Marketing to Millennials on Spotify: Key Streaming Moments," Spotify Advertising, accessed

February 14, 2023, https://ads.spotify.com/en-US/millennials-on-spotify/.

Spotify's "Thanks 2016, It's been weird" campaign: Roberts, Hannah. "Spotify Says: 'Thanks 2016, It's Been Weird,' in Its Largest Ad Campaign Yet." *Business Insider*. November 29, 2016, https://www.businessinsider.com/spotify-global-ad-campaign-signing-off-2016-2016-11.

Spotify sharing data: Fidaul, Izza. "Data-Driven Marketing Campaigns: How Spotify #2020Wrapped Nailed the Human Desire for Reflection," *Wavemakers* (blog), January 5, 2021, https://wavemakers.co/data-driven-marketing-campaigns-how-spotify-2020wrapped-nailed-the-human-desire-for-reflection/.

Spotify 2021 shareholder letter: "Spotify: Shareholder Letter Q4 2021." Spotify. February 2, 2022, https://s29.q4cdn.com/175625835/files/doc_financials/2021/q4/Shareholder-Letter-Q4-2021_FINAL.pdf.

Instagram age distribution: Dixon, S. "Instagram: Age Distribution of Global Audiences 2018," Statista. May 12, 2022. https://www.statista.com/statistics/325587/instagram-global-age-group/.

TikTok active users: Geyser, Werner. "50 TikTok Stats That Will Blow Your Mind in 2020," Influencer Marketing Hub. March 31, 2022, https://influencermarketinghub.com/tiktok-stats/.

Facebook users: "Facebook Users Worldwide 2020." Statista. February 14, 2022. https://www.statista.com/statistics/264810/number-of-monthly-active-facebook-users-worldwide/.

Pinterest users: Sehl, Katie. "23 Pinterest Statistics That Matter to Marketers in 2019." Hootsuite Social Media Management. February

27, 2019. https://blog.hootsuite.com/pinterest-statistics-for-business/.

Traction: Weinberg, Gabriel, and Justin Mares. *Traction: How Any Startup Can Achieve Explosive Customer Growth* (New York, New York: Portfolio/Penguin, 2015).

Starbucks background: "Timeline." Starbucks, accessed February 14, 2023, https://stories.starbucks.com/uploads/2019/01/AboutUs-Company-Timeline-1.6.21-FINAL.pdf.

Starbucks background: "Our Mission." Starbucks archive, accessed February 14, 2023, https://archive.starbucks.com/record/our-mission.

Brand voice: Tinoco, Antonio. "Discover the Brand Voice Examples that Bring Success to Businesses." *Rock Content* (blog), February 5, 2022, https://rockcontent.com/blog/brand-voice-examples/.

Pepsi slogan changes: "Pepsi Slogans and Logos throughout the Years." G&M Distributors, December 11, 2012, https://gmdist.com/blog/pepsi-slogans-and-logos-throughout-the-years.

Pepsi slogan changes: Sarosh, Sehrish. "How Pepsi Slogans Connect with Generations over the Years." *Advergize*. March 28, 2017. https://www.advergize.com/marketing/history-of-pepsi-slogans-connect-generations-years/#The_History_of_Pepsi_and_the_First_Pepsi_Slogan_Ever.

KFC slogan: Kentucky Fried Chicken. "And the Winner of the Award for the Most Inappropriate Slogan for 2020 Goes to...KFC," press release, August 24, 2020, https://global.kfc.com/press-releases/

and-the-winner-of-the-award-for-the-most-inappropriate-slogan-for-2020-goes-to-kfc/.

***Shoe Dog*:** Knight, Phil. *Shoe Dog: A Memoir by the Creator of Nike.* London: Simon & Schuster, 2016.

Nike's name: Levinson, Philip. "How Nike Almost Ended up with a Very Different Name." *Business Insider*, January 19, 2016, https://www.businessinsider.com/how-nike-got-its-name-2016-1.

Nike's name after Goddess of Victory: The Editors of Encyclopedia Britannica. 2014. "Nike | Greek Goddess." In Encyclopædia Britannica. https://www.britannica.com/topic/Nike-Greek-goddess.

Nike "Dream Crazy" commercial: "Colin Kaepernick Nike Commercial FULL VIDEO," posted by ND J, September 7, 2018, YouTube video, 2:05. https://www.youtube.com/watch?v=lomlpJREDzw.

Nike "Play New" commercial: "Play New | Nike," posted by Surtido Pe, May 7, 2021, YouTube video, 0:30, https://www.youtube.com/watch?v=BUvEEVq4woU.

Nike "For Once, Don't Do It" commercial: Cohen, Seth. "'For Once, Don't Do It': The Powerful Idea behind Nike's New Anti-Racism Ad." *Forbes*, May 30, 2020, https://www.forbes.com/sites/sethcohen/2020/05/30/for-once-dont-do-it---the-powerful-idea-behind-nikes-new-anti-racism-ad/?sh=5dca6a1e2fdb.

Nike's Monk Yukai Shimizu feature: Nike (@nike), "A spiritual practice and running routine in perfect balance," Instagram photo, June 8, 2021, https://www.instagram.com/p/CP3JysmBAkW/?hl=en.

Nike's Monk Yukai Shimizu feature: Sugai, Nickolaus. "On the Mountain Trails of Japan, a Buddhist Monk Runs Toward Clarity," *Nike* (blog), updated February 28, 2022, https://www.nike.com/a/yukai-shimizu-runs-toward-clarity.

Uber's company timeline: "The History of Uber," Uber Newsroom, accessed February 14, 2023, https://www.uber.com/newsroom/history/.

UberKITTENS: Lindsey, "The Cat's Out of the Bag, UberKITTENS is Here!" Uber Newsroom, October 28, 2015, https://www.uber.com/newsroom/uberkittens/.

Uber and Goodwill collaboration: "Uber and Goodwill® Make Spring Cleaning Easy," Goodwill Industries International, accessed February 14, 2023, https://www.goodwill.org/blog/news-updates/uber-and-goodwill-make-spring-cleaning-easy/.

Airbnb slogan: "A Message from Co-Founder and CEO Brian Chesky," Airbnb Newsroom, May 5, 2020, https://news.airbnb.com/a-message-from-co-founder-and-ceo-brian-chesky/.

Airbnb logo: "What Airbnb Teaches Us about Having a Strong Brand Identity," *SOCi* (blog), accessed February 14, 2023, https://www.meetsoci.com/blog/what-airbnb-teaches-us-about-having-a-strong-brand-identity/.

Balanced Scorecard: Kaplan, Robert S., and David P. Norton. "The Balanced Scorecard—Measures That Drive Performance." *Harvard*

Business Review, February 1992, https://hbr.org/1992/01/the-balanced-scorecard-measures-that-drive-performance-2.

Presentation quote: Anderson, Chris. "How to Give a Killer Presentation," *Harvard Business Review*, June 2013, https://hbr.org/2013/06/how-to-give-a-killer-presentation.

How to Get On Shark Tank: Crouse, Lois, "How to Get on Shark Tank," Shark Tank Products, accessed February 14, 2023, https://allsharktankproducts.com/how-to-get-on-shark-tank/.

Business Model Canvas: Osterwalder, Alexander, and Yves Pigneur. *Business Model Generation: A Handbook for Visionaries, Game Changers, and Challengers* Hoboken, New Jersey: Wiley, 2010.

Guy Kawasaki 10 slides: Kawasaki, Guy. "The Only 10 Slides You Need in a Pitch," Guy Kawasaki, March 5, 2015, https://guykawasaki.com/the-only-10-slides-you-need-in-your-pitch/.

Fear of Public Speaking: Heeren, Alexandre, Grazia Ceschi, David P. Valentiner, Vincent Dethier, and Pierre Philippot. "Assessing Public Speaking Fear with the Short Form of the Personal Report of Confidence as a Speaker Scale: Confirmatory Factor Analyses among a French-Speaking Community Sample," *Neuropsychiatric Disease and Treatment* 2013, no. 9 (May 2013): 609–618, https://doi.org/10.2147/ndt.s43097.

Prehistoric fear of being watched: Gershman, Sarah. "To Overcome Your Fear of Public Speaking, Stop Thinking about Yourself," *Harvard Business Review*, September 17, 2019, https://hbr.org/2019/09/to-overcome-your-fear-of-public-speaking-stop-thinking-about-yourself.

Bibliography

"15 CSR Facts You Need to Know." n.d. Learn - GlobalGiving. https://www.globalgiving.org/learn/listicle/csr-facts-you-need-to-know.

"Abai Schulze, the Founder of ZAAF on CNN African Voices," posted by ZAAF Collection, November 7, 2018, YouTube video, 7:15. https://www.youtube.com/watch?v=Wr9bRBNQxfs.

Anderson, Chris. "How to Give a Killer Presentation." *Harvard Business Review*, June 2013, https://hbr.org/2013/06/how-to-give-a-killer-presentation.

Barone, Adam. "Marketing Strategy: What it is, How it Works, How to Create One." Investopedia. Updated June 13, 2022. https://www.investopedia.com/terms/m/marketing-strategy.asp.

Barrett, Rick. "In Quest to Expand Market, Harley-Davidson Reaches out to Women." *Milwaukee Journal Sentinel*, August 28, 2013, https://archive.jsonline.com/business/in-quest-to-expand-market-harley-davidson-reaches-out-to-women-b99845731z1-221524671.html/.

Bearak, Max, and David J. Lynch. "African Nations are Fed Up with the West's Hand-Me-Downs. But It's Tough to Keep Them Out." *The Washington Post*, May 29, 2018, https://www.washingtonpost.com/world/africa/african-nations-are-fed-up-with-the-wests-hand-me-downs-but-its-tough-to-keep-them-out/2018/05/28/c4041c8c-5478-11e8-a6d4-ca1d035642ce_story.html.

Beer, Jeff. "Netflix's 'Stranger Things' Is Dangerously close to Becoming 'Sponsored Things'." Fast Company. July 1, 2019. https://www.fastcompany.com/90370526/netflixs-stranger-things-is-dangerously-close-to-becoming-sponsored-things.

Besser, Linton. "'It's an Insult': In an African Clothing Market, a Bale of Used Clothes Donated by Australians Is Opened." *ABC News*, August 11, 2021, https://www.abc.net.au/news/2021-08-12/fast-fashion-turning-parts-ghana-into-toxic-landfill/100358702.

Blank, Steve. "Why the Lean Start-up Changes Everything." *Harvard Business Review*, May 2013, https://hbr.org/2013/05/why-the-lean-start-up-changes-everything.

Blystone, Dan. "The Story of Instagram: The Rise of the # 1 Photo-Sharing App (FB)." Investopedia. March 29, 2022. https://www.investopedia.com/articles/investing/102615/story-instagram-rise-1-photo0sharing-app.asp.

Bowen, Howard Rothmann. *Social Responsibilities of the Businessman*. Iowa City: University of Iowa Press, 2013.

Brown, Tim. *Change by Design: How Design Thinking Transforms Organizations and Inspires Innovation*. New York: Harper Business, 2009.

Buli, Nora, and Gwladys Fouche. "Nobel Peace Prize: Is This Greta Thunberg's Year?" *Reuters*, October 1, 2021, https://www.reuters.com/world/europe/nobel-peace-prize-is-this-greta-thunbergs-year-2021-10-01/.

Burnett, William, and David J. Evans. *Designing Your Life: Build a Life That Works for You*. London: Vintage Books, 2018.

"CA Demographic Statistics." Infoplease. Accessed February 14, 2023. https://www.infoplease.com/us/census/california/demographic-statistics.

Calvin Klein. "Billie Eilish #MYTRUTH #MYCALVINS." Facebook post, May 10, 2019, https://www.facebook.com/CalvinKlein/videos/billie-eilish-mytruth-mycalvins/288431508712825/.

Cause Marketing. "Coca-Cola #AmericaIsBeautiful 2014 Super Bowl Commercial." YouTube video, January 1, 2017. https://www.youtube.com/watch?v=4-KxPRptu_Y.

Chappell, Bill. "Dolly Parton Gets $100 Million from Jeff Bezos to Spend on Charity." *NPR*, November 14, 2022, https://www.npr.org/2022/11/14/1136454716/dolly-parton-jeff-bezos-imagination-library.

Chappelow, Jim. "Market Economy Definition." Investopedia. 2019. https://www.investopedia.com/terms/m/marketeconomy.asp.

Chen, James. "Learn What Stakeholders Are and the Roles That They Play." Investopedia. August 19, 2021. https://www.investopedia.com/terms/s/stakeholder.asp#:~:text=A%20stakeholder%20has%20a%20vested.

Christensen, Clayton M., Efosa Ojomo, and Karen Dillon. *The Prosperity Paradox: How Innovation Can Lift Nations out of Poverty*. New York: Harper Business, 2019.

Cohen, Seth. "'For Once, Don't Do It': The Powerful Idea behind Nike's New Anti-Racism Ad." *Forbes*, May 30, 2020, https://www.forbes.com/sites/sethcohen/2020/05/30/for-once-dont-do-it---the-powerful-idea-behind-nikes-new-anti-racism-ad/?sh=5dca6a1e2fdb.

"Colin Kaepernick Nike Commercial FULL VIDEO," posted by ND J, September 7, 2018, YouTube video, 2:05. https://www.youtube.com/watch?v=lomlpJREDzw.

Crouse, Lois. "How to Get on Shark Tank." Shark Tank Products. Accessed February 14, 2023. https://allsharktankproducts.com/how-to-get-on-shark-tank/.

Cummings, Carrie. "Infographic: 72% of Spotify Listeners Are Millennials. Here's How They Use the Service." *Adweek*, April 17, 2016, https://www.adweek.com/brand-marketing/

infographic-what-marketers-need-know-about-millennials-music-habits-170869/.

de Vries, James. "PepsiCo's Chief Design Officer on Creating an Organization Where Design Can Thrive." *Harvard Business Review*, August 11, 2015, https://hbr.org/2015/08/pepsicos-chief-design-officer-on-creating-an-organization-where-design-can-thrive.

"Design Thinking." Interaction Design Foundation. Accessed February 14, 2023. https://www.interaction-design.org/literature/topics/design-thinking?page=2.

Dieffenbacher, Stefan F. "Value Creation Definition, Model, Principles, Importance & Steps." Digital Leadership. June 11, 2022. https://digitalleadership.com/blog/value-creation.

Dixon, S. "Instagram: Age Distribution of Global Audiences 2018." Statista. May 12, 2022. https://www.statista.com/statistics/325587/instagram-global-age-group/.

Duffin, Erin. "Resident Population of the United States by Sex and Age as of July 1, 2021 (in Millions)." Statista. September 30, 2022. https://www.statista.com/statistics/241488/population-of-the-us-by-sex-and-age/.

Elliott, Stuart. "Vitriol Online for Cheerios Ad with Interracial Family." *The New York Times*, May 31, 2013, https://www.nytimes.com/2013/06/01/business/media/cheerios-ad-with-interracial-family-brings-out-internet-hate.html.

"Facebook Users Worldwide 2020." Statista. Accessed February 14, 2023. https://www.statista.com/statistics/264810/number-of-monthly-active-facebook-users-worldwide/.

Fidaul, Izza. "Data-Driven Marketing Campaigns: How Spotify #2020Wrapped Nailed the Human Desire for Reflection." *Wavemakers* (blog), January 5, 2021, https://wavemakers.co/data-driven-marketing-campaigns-how-spotify-2020wrapped-nailed-the-human-desire-for-reflection/.

Gayomali, Chris. "Justin Bieber Joins Instagram, World Explodes." *Time*, July 22, 2011, https://techland.time.com/2011/07/22/justin-bieber-joins-instagram-world-explodes/.

Geyser, Werner. "50 TikTok Stats That Will Blow Your Mind in 2020." Influencer Marketing Hub. March 31, 2022. https://influencermarketinghub.com/tiktok-stats/.

"Global Citizenship." United Nations. Accessed February 14, 2023. https://www.un.org/en/academic-impact/global-citizenship.

Götting, Marie Charlotte. "Spotify Users in the U.S. 2018, by Age." Statista. January 18, 2022. https://www.statista.com/statistics/475821/spotify-users-age-usa/.

Gobry, Pascal-Emmanuel. "Airbnb Admits It Farmed Craigslist, Blames Outside Salespeople." *Business Insider*, June 2, 2011, https://www.businessinsider.com/airbnb-craigslist-blame-2011-6.

Georgiev, Deyan. "How Much Time Do Americans Spend on Their Phones in 2020?" *TechJury* (blog), April 21, 2020. https://techjury.net/blog/how-much-time-does-the-average-american-spend-on-their-phone/#gref.

Gershman, Sarah. "To Overcome Your Fear of Public Speaking, Stop Thinking about Yourself." *Harvard Business Review*, September 17, 2019, https://hbr.org/2019/09/to-overcome-your-fear-of-public-speaking-stop-thinking-about-yourself.

Group, Welfont. "Types of Social Entrepreneurs." Medium. April 11, 2018. https://medium.com/@groupwelfont/types-of-social-entrepreneurs-a7dc8ac57e34.

"'Harry Potter' First Edition Sells for Smashing $471,000," *Reuters*, December 9, 2021, https://www.reuters.com/lifestyle/harry-potter-first-edition-sells-smashing-471000-2021-12-09/.

Heeren, Alexandre, Grazia Ceschi, David P. Valentiner, Vincent Dethier, and Pierre Philippot. "Assessing Public Speaking

Fear with the Short Form of the Personal Report of Confidence as a Speaker Scale: Confirmatory Factor Analyses among a French-Speaking Community Sample." *Neuropsychiatric Disease and Treatment* 2013, no. 9 (May 2013): 609–618. https://doi.org/10.2147/ndt.s43097.

"The History of Uber." Uber Newsroom. Accessed February 14, 2023. https://www.uber.com/newsroom/history/.

"How to Refer Friends to Dropbox and Get More Storage Space." Dropbox. Accessed February 14, 2023. https://help.dropbox.com/storage-space/earn-space-referring-friends.

Israel, Ronald C. "What Does it Mean to be a Global Citizen?" *Kosmos*, 2014. https://www.kosmosjournal.org/article/what-does-it-mean-to-be-a-global-citizen/

"John D. Rockefeller." History.com, A&E Television Networks. September 20, 2018. https://www.history.com/topics/early-20th-century-us/john-d-rockefeller.

Kaplan, Robert S., and David P. Norton. "The Balanced Scorecard—Measures That Drive Performance." *Harvard Business Review*, February 1992, https://hbr.org/1992/01/the-balanced-scorecard-measures-that-drive-performance-2.

Kawasaki, Guy. "The Only 10 Slides You Need in a Pitch." Guy Kawasaki. March 5, 2015. https://guykawasaki.com/the-only-10-slides-you-need-in-your-pitch/.

Kelly, Brandon, and Heather Kelly. "23 Key Moments from Twitter History." *CNN Business*, updated September 16, 2013, https://www.cnn.com/2013/09/13/tech/social-media/twitter-key-moments.

Kentucky Fried Chicken. "And the Winner of the Award for the Most Inappropriate Slogan for 2020 Goes to...KFC," press release, August 24, 2020, https://global.kfc.com/press-releases/and-the-winner-of-the-award-for-the-most-inappropriate-slogan-for-2020-goes-to-kfc/.

Kinane, Ruth. "Taylor Swift and Katy Perry: A Timeline of Their Feud." *Entertainment Weekly*, updated August 4, 2022, https://ew.com/music/taylor-swift-katy-perry-timeline/.

Knight, Phil. *Shoe Dog: A Memoir by the Creator of Nike*. London: Simon & Schuster, 2016.

Kramer, Mark R., Marc W. Pfitzer, and Helge Mahne. "How Global Leaders Should Think About Solving Our Biggest Problems." *Harvard Business Review*, January 16, 2020, https://hbr.org/2020/01/how-global-leaders-should-think-about-solving-our-biggest-problems.

Lavanya. "Book Pricing: How the Cover Price of a Book Is Set." *Booksoarus* (blog), February 28, 2014, https://www.booksoarus.com/book-pricing-how-cover-price-is-set/.

Lee, Nathaniel. "'Bohemian Rhapsody': The 6-Minute Rock Single That Changed the Face of Music." *Business Insider*, November 8, 2018, https://www.businessinsider.com/bohemian-rhapsody-queen-greatest-song-written-freddie-mercury-2018-10.

Levinson, Philip. "How Nike Almost Ended up with a Very Different Name." *Business Insider*, January 19, 2016, https://www.businessinsider.com/how-nike-got-its-name-2016-1.

Lindsey. "The Cat's Out of the Bag, UberKITTENS is Here!" Uber Newsroom. October 28, 2015. https://www.uber.com/newsroom/uberkittens/.

"List of US States by GDP, 2010-2021." Knoema. Updated November 3, 2022. https://knoema.com/rhjjehg/list-of-us-states-by-gdp-2010-2021.

"A Little Bit about ZAAF...." ZAAF. Accessed January 9, 2023. https://zaafcollection.com/pages/our-story.

Loveday, Steven. "Tesla Spends Least on Ads, Most on R&D: Report." *InsideEVs*, March 25, 2022, https://insideevs.com/news/575848/tesla-highest-research-development-no-ads/.

Macaskill, William. *What We Owe the Future*. New York: Hachette Book Group, Inc, 2022.

Maglio, Tony. "Disney+ Soars, Netflix Sinks: Here's How Many Subscribers 10 Key Streamers Have Now." *IndieWire*, August 11, 2022, https://www.indiewire.com/2022/08/how-many-subscribers-netflix-hbo-max-disney-plus-1234744445/.

"Marketing to Millennials on Spotify: Key Streaming Moments." Spotify Advertising. Accessed February 14, 2023. https://ads.spotify.com/en-US/millennials-on-spotify/.

May, Ashley. "What Would Happen If Everyone Recycled?" *USA Today*, updated June 23, 2017, https://www.usatoday.com/story/news/nation-now/2017/06/22/what-would-happen-if-everyone-recycled/374773001/.

McAlone, Nathan. "The Father of 'Disruption' Theory Explains Why Netflix Is the Perfect Example — and Uber Isn't." *Business Insider*, November 18, 2015, https://www.businessinsider.com/the-father-of-disruption-theory-explains-why-netflix-is-the-perfect-example-and-uber-isnt-2015-11.

"A Message from Co-Founder and CEO Brian Chesky." Airbnb Newsroom. May 5, 2020. https://news.airbnb.com/a-message-from-co-founder-and-ceo-brian-chesky/.

Miller, Kelsey. "The Triple Bottom Line: What It Is & Why It's Important." *Harvard Business School Online*, December 8, 2020, https://online.hbs.edu/blog/post/what-is-the-triple-bottom-line.

Nielson, Samantha. "Apple's Premium Pricing Strategy and Product Differentiation." *Yahoo! Finance*, February 6, 2014, https://finance.yahoo.com/news/s/apple-premium-pricing-strategy-product-191247308.html.

Nike (@nike), "A spiritual practice and running routine in perfect balance," Instagram photo, June 8, 2021, https://www.instagram.com/p/CP3JysmBAkW/?hl=en.

Osterwalder, Alexander, and Yves Pigneur. *Business Model Generation: A Handbook for Visionaries, Game Changers, and Challengers*. Hoboken, New Jersey: Wiley, 2010.

"Our Mission." Homeboy Industries. Accessed February 14, 2023. https://homeboyindustries.org/our-story/our-mission/.

"Our Mission." Starbucks archive. Accessed February 14, 2023. https://archive.starbucks.com/record/our-mission.

"Pampers '1 Pack = 1 Vaccine' Campaign: 'Happy Birthday' Ad," posted by Cause Marketing, October 30, 2016, YouTube video, 0:46. https://www.youtube.com/watch?v=Ca3gOvpoJHU.

"Pear Company." iCarly Wiki. Accessed November 29, 2022. https://icarly.fandom.com/wiki/Pear_Company#:~:text=Pear%20Company%20is%20an%20obvious.

Peppers, Don, Martha Rogers, and Bob Dorf. "Is Your Company Ready for One-To-One Marketing?" *Harvard Business Review*, January–February 1999, https://hbr.org/1999/01/is-your-company-ready-for-one-to-one-marketing.

"Pepsi Slogans and Logos throughout the Years." G&M Distributors. December 11, 2012. https://gmdist.com/blog/pepsi-slogans-and-logos-throughout-the-years.

Peters, Adele. "Toms Made Buy-One, Give-One Famous. Now It's Updating the Model." Fast Company. May 7, 2019. https://www.fastcompany.com/90344987/toms-made-buy-one-give-one-famous-now-its-updating-the-model.

"Play New | Nike," posted by Surtido Pe, May 7, 2021, YouTube video, 0:30. https://www.youtube.com/watch?v=BUvEEVq4woU.

Pollack, Jeffrey M., Matthew W. Rutherford, Brian G. Nagy. "Preparedness and Cognitive Legitimacy as Antecedents of New Venture Funding in Televised Business Pitches." *Entrepreneurship Theory and Practice* 36, no. 5 (September 2012): 915–939. https://doi.org/ 0.1111/j.1540-6520.2012.00531.x.

Pologeorgis, Nicolas. "How Globalization Affects Developed Countries." Investopedia. May 9, 2019. https://www.investopedia.com/articles/economics/10/globalization-developed-countries.asp.

"Porter's 5 Forces Explained and How to Use the Model," Investopedia. Updated August 1, 2022. https://www.investopedia.com/terms/p/porter.asp.

"The Retail Market for Coffee in the US – Market Size 2005-2027." IBIS World. updated April 26, 2021. https://www.ibisworld.com/industry-statistics/market-size/the-retail-market-for-coffee-united-states/.

Roberts, Hannah. "Spotify Says: 'Thanks 2016, It's Been Weird,' in Its Largest Ad Campaign Yet." *Business Insider*, November 29, 2016, https://www.businessinsider.com/spotify-global-ad-campaign-signing-off-2016-2016-11.

Sarosh, Sehrish. "How Pepsi Slogans Connect with Generations over the Years." Advergize. March 28, 2017. https://www.advergize.com/marketing/history-of-pepsi-slogans-connect-generations-years/#The_History_of_Pepsi_and_the_First_Pepsi_Slogan_Ever.

"Scholastic Announces Record Breaking Sales of 11.5 Million Copies of Harry Potter and the Deathly Hallows in First Ten Days." Scholastic Media Room. August 2, 2007. http://mediaroom.scholastic.com/press-release/scholastic-announces-record-breaking-sales-115-million-copies-harry-potter-and-deathly.

Schulze, Abai. "'Made in Africa' – The Power of Shifting Perceptions." Filmed March 2, 2019, in Nashville, TN. TEDx video, 13:36, https://www.ted.com/talks/abai_schulze_made_in_africa_the_power_of_shifting_perceptions.

Schnoor, Aaron. "Understanding Spotify's Marketing Mastery." *Medium*. May 12, 2020. https://bettermarketing.pub/understanding-spotifys-marketing-mastery-4531ad5cd890.

Sehl, Katie. "23 Pinterest Statistics That Matter to Marketers in 2019." Hootsuite Social Media Management. February 27, 2019. https://blog.hootsuite.com/pinterest-statistics-for-business/.

Serrat, Olivier. *The SCAMPER Technique*. Manila, Philippines: Asian Development Bank, 2009. https://hdl.handle.net/1813/87753.

Simon, Bryant. *Everything but the Coffee: Learning about America from Starbucks*. Berkeley: University of California Press, 2011.

Sinek, Simon. "How Great Leaders Inspire Action." Filmed September 2009 in Puget Sound. TED Talks video, 17:48, https://www.ted.com/talks/simon_sinek_how_great_leaders_inspire_action?language=en.

"Social Impact." Spotify. Accessed February 14, 2023, https://www.lifeatspotify.com/diversity-equity-impact/social-impact.

"Spotify Encourages Eligible U.S. Voters to 'Play Your Part' by Registering for and Voting in the 2020 Election." Spotify Newsroom. September 9, 2020. https://newsroom.spotify.com/2020-09-09/spotify-encourages-eligible-u-s-voters-to-play-your-part-by-registering-for-and-voting-in-the-2020-election/.

"Spotify: Shareholder Letter Q4 2021." Spotify. February 2, 2022. https://s29.q4cdn.com/175625835/files/doc_financials/2021/q4/Shareholder-Letter-Q4-2021_FINAL.pdf.

StackCommerce. "Whether You Love Him or Hate Him, Bill Gates Reads and Retains Roughly 50 Books per Year." *Financial Post*, June 17, 2021, https://financialpost.com/personal-finance/business-essentials/bill-gates-reads-roughly-50-books-per-year-and-remembers-what-he-reads#:~:text=Microsoft%20founder%2C%20Bill%20Gates%2C%20reads.

"The State of Content: Expectations on the Rise." Slideshow. Adobe, 2015. https://blogs.adobe.com/creative/files/2015/12/Adobe-State-of-Content-Report.pdf.

Sugai, Nickolaus. "On the Mountain Trails of Japan, a Buddhist Monk Runs Toward Clarity." *Nike* (blog), updated February 28, 2022, https://www.nike.com/a/yukai-shimizu-runs-toward-clarity.

Tan, Jon. "9 Brilliant Coca Cola Advertising Examples of Referral Marketing." *ReferralCandy* (blog), April 29, 2022, https://www.referralcandy.com/blog/coke-word-of-mouth-marketing-strategy.

"Taylor Swift's Fans Demanded a 10 Minute Version of 'All Too Well'," in *The Graham Norton Show*, accessed January 10, 2023, https://www.youtube.com/watch?v=MwNdxjnwr1A.

"Timeline." Starbucks. Accessed February 14, 2023. https://stories.starbucks.com/uploads/2019/01/AboutUs-Company-Timeline-1.6.21-FINAL.pdf.

Timmer, Andria. "Competing Discourses on the Political Economy of Hunger." *Nutritional Anthropology* 27-28 nos. 1-2 (Spring 2005–2006): 1–13. https://doi.org/10.1111/j.1548-7172.2005.tb00086.x.

Tinoco, Antonio. "Discover the Brand Voice Examples that Bring Success to Businesses." *Rock Content* (blog), February 5, 2022, https://rockcontent.com/blog/brand-voice-examples/.

Tsioulcas, Anastasia. "Look What They Made Her Do: Taylor Swift to Re-Record Her Catalog." *NPR*, August 22, 2019, https://www.npr.org/2019/08/22/753393630/look-what-they-made-her-do-taylor-swift-to-re-record-her-catalog.

"Uber and Goodwill® Make Spring Cleaning Easy." Goodwill Industries International. Accessed February 14, 2023. https://www.goodwill.org/blog/news-updates/uber-and-goodwill-make-spring-cleaning-easy/.

United Nations. "The 17 Goals." Accessed February 14, 2023. https://sdgs.un.org/goals.

———. "Goal 1 | Department of Economic and Social Affairs." Accessed February 14, 2023. https://sdgs.un.org/goals/goal1.

———. "Goal 2 | Department of Economic and Social Affairs." Accessed February 14, 2023. https://sdgs.un.org/goals/goal2.

———. "Goal 3: Ensure Healthy Lives and Promote Well-Being for All at All Ages." Accessed February 14, 2023. https://sdgs.un.org/goals/goal3.

———. "Goal 4 | Department of Economic and Social Affairs." Accessed February 14, 2023. https://sdgs.un.org/goals/goal4.

———. "Goal 5 | Department of Economic and Social Affairs." Accessed February 14, 2023. https://sdgs.un.org/goals/goal5.

———. "Goal 6 | Department of Economic and Social Affairs." Accessed February 14, 2023. https://sdgs.un.org/goals/goal6.

———. "Goal 7 | Department of Economic and Social Affairs." Accessed February 14, 2023. https://sdgs.un.org/goals/goal7.

———. "Goal 8 | Department of Economic and Social Affairs." Accessed February 14, 2023. https://sdgs.un.org/goals/goal8.

———. "Goal 9 | Department of Economic and Social Affairs." Accessed February 14, 2023. https://sdgs.un.org/goals/goal9.

———. "Goal 10 | Department of Economic and Social Affairs." Accessed February 14, 2023. https://sdgs.un.org/goals/goal10.

———. "Goal 11 | Department of Economic and Social Affairs." Accessed February 14, 2023. https://sdgs.un.org/goals/goal11.

———. "Goal 12 | Department of Economic and Social Affairs." Accessed February 14, 2023. https://sdgs.un.org/goals/goal12.

———. "Goal 13 | Department of Economic and Social Affairs." Accessed February 14, 2023. https://sdgs.un.org/goals/goal13.

———. "Goal 14 | Department of Economic and Social Affairs." Accessed February 14, 2023. https://sdgs.un.org/goals/goal14.

———. "Goal 15 | Department of Economic and Social Affairs." Accessed February 14, 2023. https://sdgs.un.org/goals/goal15.

———. "Goal 16 | Department of Economic and Social Affairs." Accessed February 14, 2023. https://sdgs.un.org/goals/goal16.

———. "Goal 17 | Department of Economic and Social Affairs." Accessed February 14, 2023. https://sdgs.un.org/goals/goal17.

USAID. "#LetGirlsLearn Factsheet." Accessed February 14, 2023. https://www.usaid.gov/sites/default/files/documents/1869/USAID_LGL_FactSheet.pdf.

U.S. Small Business Administration. "Small Businesses Drive Job Growth in United States; They Account for 1.8 Million Net New Jobs, Latest Data Show." News release no. 19-4 ADV. April 24, 2019. https://advocacy.sba.gov/2019/04/24/small-businesses-drive-job-growth-in-united-states-they-account-for-1-8-million-net-new-jobs-latest-data-show/.

Van Edwards, Vanessa. "5 Secrets of a Successful TED Talk." Science of People. Accessed February 15, 2023. https://www.scienceofpeople.com/secrets-of-a-successful-ted-talk/.

Vignali, Claudio. "McDonald's: 'Think Global, Act Local' – the Marketing Mix." *British Food Journal* 103, no. 2 (March 2001): 97–111. https://doi.org/10.1108/00070700110383154.

Weinberg, Gabriel, and Justin Mares. *Traction: How Any Startup Can Achieve Explosive Customer Growth.* New York: Portfolio/Penguin, 2015.

"What Airbnb Teaches Us about Having a Strong Brand Identity." *SOCi* (blog), accessed February 14, 2023, https://www.meetsoci.com/blog/what-airbnb-teaches-us-about-having-a-strong-brand-identity/.

"What Is Empathy?" *Greater Good Magazine*, accessed February 14, 2023, https://greatergood.berkeley.edu/topic/empathy/definition

The White House. "FACT SHEET: Let Girls Learn – A Comprehensive Investment in Adolescent Girls Education." 2016. Accessed February 14, 2023. https://obamawhitehouse.archives.gov/the-press-office/2016/10/11/fact-sheet-let-girls-learn-comprehensive-investmentadolescent-girls.

"Why Amazon's '1-Click' Ordering Was a Game Changer," September 14, 2017, in *Knowledge at Wharton podcast*, podcast, 26:06, https://knowledge.wharton.upenn.edu/article/amazons-1-click-goes-off-patent/.

Wirthman, Lisa. "5 Benefits of Shopping Locally on Small Business Saturday." *Forbes*, November 20, 2017, https://www.forbes.com/sites/centurylink/2017/11/20/5-benefits-of-shopping-locally-on-small-business-saturday/?sh=4ac68a9a668b.

Wittmer, Carrie. "Netflix's 'Stranger Things' Boosted Eggo Waffle Sales Because One of the Main Characters Is Obsessed with Them." *Business Insider*, February 21, 2018, https://www.businessinsider.com/netflixs-stranger-things-boosted-eggo-waffle-sales-2018-2.

Yau, Tiffany. "Dream Big, Think Smaller." Filmed October 26, 2020, in Berwyn, PA. TED video, 12:58. https://www.ted.com/talks/tiffany_yau_dream_big_think_smaller.

Printed in the USA
CPSIA information can be obtained
at www.ICGtesting.com
CBHW030308160724
11656CB00007B/225

9 798987 741108